CW00952918

JEFF TURNER

COCKNEY REJECT

JB

JOHN BLAKE

Published by John Blake Publishing Ltd,
3, Bramber Court, 2 Bramber Road,
London W14 9PB, England

www.blake.co.uk

First published in hardback in 2005

ISBN 1 84454 054 5

British Library Cataloguing-in-Publication Data:

A catalogue record for this book is available from the British Library.

Design by www.envydesign.co.uk

Printed in Great Britain by Creative Print and Design (Wales),
Ebbow Vale, Gwent

1 3 5 7 9 10 8 6 4 2

Papers used by John Blake Publishing Ltd are natural, recyclable products made from wood grown in sustainable forests. The manufacturing processes conform to the environmental regulations of the country of origin.

Every attempt has been made to contact the relevant copyright-holders, but some were unobtainable. We would be grateful if the appropriate people could contact us.

For dad

When I first heard Jeff Turner sing, it brought to mind a street trader of the *old* East End – or else a kid in Canning Town swimming baths gulping too much chlorinated water. An interesting yelp – hard and indifferent with a condescending roll, yet also a bit sentimental. I imagined someone who had willingly bypassed standardised education in place of enjoyment and the self and walking directly into trouble – all very envious occupations, I thought. Jeff Turner was obviously singing in order to avoid murdering someone – which was, *I suppose*, diplomatic.

The sound of the Rejects was, *then*, a ringing hum of human energy – stories of disorder, and how this country was generally done for. I say *was* because I am trying to explain how I felt about the sound when I first heard it – I don't mean to imply that the Rejects no longer exist. 'Subculture', I think, is lost greatness. I don't exactly understand the words – but the voice, I thought, was fantastic – even when slightly off-key (which wasn't *extremely rare...*). It's a very King Of The Swill voice, and the songs were the escape from his social position – otherwise Jeff Turner would probably have ended up stacking deckchairs in Malaga... as *we all* would.

I couldn't detect any S.E.X. in the voice. I imagined he treated all women like buses... or he'd never met one (a woman, not a bus).

The best *pop groups* give off a natural air of being a clan in the right – and the Rejects had that, certainly in skinnier times. And it was often very funny. With Jeff Turner, I think it's a combination of the truth in his heart and the full of his lungs – which is good enough for me.

Morrissey

Acknowledgements

Jeff Turner would like to thank:

Karon Saunders, for her total support and love throughout.

Garry Bushell, for believing in this book and seeing it through.

Mum, for always being there for me.

Mick Geggus, for co-operation beyond the call of duty.

John Blake, for giving me the chance to tell my story.

Morrissey, for getting behind us.

Shelly Lindsay, for transcribing the interviews.

Also many thanks to the Geggus clan: Steve, Linda, Janet, Trevor and Clare, Chantelle, Jeff and Jay. Tony Frater, Les Cobb Junior, Cass Pennant, Steve Stone, John Oakman, Andy 'Skully' Russell, Bernie Houlihan, Hoxton Tom McCourt, Robert and Linda Arthey, Lee Dury, Tania Bushell, Clyde Ward, Alan Osbourne,

Neil Bowers, Stuart Black, Kieran Lipper, Martin King, Darren Chatty, Pete Way, Lars Frederiksen, Kate Moore, Jesus, Patsy Duggan, Squibbs, Paul Rossi, Steve Birkett Junior (for giving me the idea), and last but not least all the Rejects fans throughout the world who have stood by us through thick and thin. I salute you all. NOW GO FOR IT!

Contents

A lot of nonsense has been written about The Cockney Rejects. This book sets out to tell the truth about them. In their time, the Rejects were the wildest, most exciting rock band to emerge from the London punk scene. They were also frustrating, funny, self-destructive, uncompromising, pig-headed, provocative… and bloody marvellous. I was their manager briefly, so I inadvertently helped to light the touch-paper for the mayhem that subsequently unfolded. But it also means I can testify to the honesty of Jeff Turner's account of his life and the band's explosive career.

Many people hated the Rejects, and it's easy to see why. At a time when it was fashionable to fake proletarian credentials, this band was the real thing: working-class yobs from the heart of London's East End who wore their roots, like their love of West Ham United, on their sleeves. They caused chaos wherever they went. They bit the hand that fed them and they suffered no fools.

They liked a fight and hated fakes, posers and anyone unfortunate enough to have been born upper-class.

They rucked at *Sounds*, the rock paper which first wrote about them, and both inside and outside the offices of their record company, EMI. They upset bosses at *Top Of The Pops*, and crossed swords with everyone from Billy Idol to neo-Nazis, via muggers, the police and Cambridge University Hooray Henrys.

Their concert at the Birmingham Cedar club in 1980 remains the most shocking example of gig violence ever seen in Britain. Yet the band was also the vanguard for the rebirth of punk in the late 1970s; a defiant V-sign to every *NME* pseud who wanted rock to disappear up its own artistry again.

The late, great John Peel once told me that The Cockney Rejects reminded him of The Faces. They were hooligans who could rock with the best, but who treated rock with the irreverence it deserved. Peely pointed out that The Beatles had started out in a similar way. Sadly there was no Brian Epstein on hand to harness the Rejects' energy more productively, just a procession of parasites and con men. So, they never built on their initial chart successes.

But the band's best songs stand the test of time. Listen to beefy, abrasive anthems like 'Bad Man', 'I'm Not A Fool' and 'The Power & The Glory' and you can understand how they inspired a street-punk movement that is still going strong twenty-six years later.

That's why Joe Strummer dubbed them 'the real deal'. And why Ozzy Osbourne called them 'men after my own heart'.

Garry Bushell

CHAPTER ONE

Roots

Tell you about the place where I've lived all my life
Tell you all the truth about the trouble and strife
All the toffs say it's a bit of a dive
It's the only place left anyone is alive.

('EAST END', THE COCKNEY REJECTS)

The first time I got my nose broken I was seven years old. The fella who hit me was thirty-six. He was my next-door neighbour! The good old East End, eh?

It all started when I had an altercation in the street with his son. We were the same age, same height, same build and we had a row. I bashed him and he went in crying. Typical silly kids' thing, nothing serious. The next thing we knew, his dad was calling my old man out over the fence. He was effing and blinding, shouting his mouth off about what he was going to do to him. I had a younger brother and sister and they were terrified.

My mum said, 'Oi, we've got kids in here,' but he wouldn't stop so my old man went out and they started fighting in the street. Now my dad was in his mid-fifties by then, so the neighbour had a good twenty years on him, but me old man was getting the better of him. I was watching from the front door and Dad started really giving it to him, so much so that all the other neighbours had to come out and pull me old man off him to break it up – but not before a woman from down the road, some old demented bat, came over screaming and kicked me old man in the eye.

The next-door neighbour was clearly embarrassed 'cos everyone had watched him being given a pasting by a much older man. He spotted me in the front door, ran at me, pulled his fist back and smashed me straight in the nose. I was seven! Me nose just went 'pop'. There was claret everywhere. He split it to bits. I think it was just out of frustration, but what sort of a man smacks a kid in the face? He was low-life.

The Old Bill were called, of course, and everyone was bound over to keep the peace, but no one was charged because no one would tell the Filth who'd done what to who. You didn't grass. It didn't happen.

I admit I panicked a bit when he hit me. Well, anyone would. But really it just felt strange. What affected me more was seeing me mum and dad in the street brawling and shouting. It was terrible with young kids in the house, but that was the kind of neighbours we had around there.

There was always a fight out in the street when I was little. We'd stand by our bedroom window and watch it. It'd be one neighbour fighting another or sometimes they'd get their boys to fight. There were mob fights. It was a rotten way to grow up. But that was what it was like in Varley Road. It was what I would call a snide street. Not nice at all.

I was born there, in Custom House, East London, on 20 April 1964, so I've got the same birthday as Hitler; although Adolf probably didn't cause half as much chaos and devastation to our neighbourhood as me and my brother Mick did. My real name is Jeff Geggus, the surname is Greek. My great-grandfather Peter was a bubble. He was banged up in Greece, but got bail, jumped on a ship in Piraeus and jumped off at Silvertown of all places. He could have made it up the river to Henley or somewhere posh, but no, he set down in the arse hole of the East End and that's where the English branch of the Geggus dynasty took root.

He married an English girl, and his son Jack, my granddad, was born and bred in Custom House. Granddad Jack played in goal for West Ham just before the First World War, when all the matches were played at the Memorial Grounds. He was a terrible man. He actually out-did Eric Cantona for fighting supporters. In one game, West Ham were 4–1 down and the fans started giving him stick. Jack ran over to the supporters, clumped a couple of them, knocked one clean out and then marched off the pitch. West Ham sacked him, of course. I've seen a few match reports and I reckon the fans were in the right. By all accounts he was a shit goalie.

After West Ham, I heard he signed for Millwall. I'd like to verify that one day. It might just be a vicious rumour.

Jack Geggus wasn't an easy man to get along with. In fact, he was a real nasty bastard. He loved a scrap. He was very off with people, very quick-tempered. He used to walk a goat around on a rope and tether it to a lamp post outside his local, the Nottingham Arms, go in, have a few beers and have a fight. This was a regular occurrence. And he was nasty with it, a bully. One of my aunts had a cat that Granddad took against because it had crapped in the house, so he hung it by the neck on the washing line and killed the poor animal. Horrible.

When he wasn't being a crap goalie, he delivered coal for a living. Coalmen were tough guys and he ruled the family with an iron fist. He was also one of those people who had stricter rules for everyone else than he had for himself. He had a gambling problem; he was always in the bookies spunking his wages away. He had a brother, my great-uncle Peter, who died of syphilis. Yeah, died of the pox. So he was probably putting it about during the war, having a bit on the black market. Apparently he was well endowed but unfortunately I never inherited any of that.

Jack's wife was Irish Catholic, her maiden name was Brewer, but I never met my nan on that side or my mum's parents either. They died before I was even thought about.

Somehow Jack managed to stop fighting, boozing and gambling long enough to father four kids – three boys and a girl called Catherine. He was really hard on her. If any boys came near her, he'd chase them up the street. He wouldn't let her go on a date, and consequently she never married. She lived alone and died a spinster in about 1999.

Granddad Jack fought in the First World War – I don't know what regiment he was in but the way he was it almost makes you feel sorry for the Germans. When Jack came back from the trenches he gave up humping coal and became a docker, and years later me dad followed in his footsteps. Working in the docks was passed down from father to son. That's how it was.

My dad, Fred, was born in 1915. His full name was Frederick James Geggus. He was a quiet man; it was always hard to get much out of him. He tended to bottle up his emotions. He wasn't like Granddad at all. He treated people decently and was more of a family man. He was tall, with a moustache. In fact, he looked like a cross between Dick Dastardly from *Wacky Races* and Bill The Butcher from *Gangs Of New York*.

Dad was twenty-four when the Second World War broke out. He enlisted in the Queen's Own Regiment and fought his way across France. He came back without a scratch. He did his bit for King and country, although at one stage he had enough of it and tried to cop out by pretending he was sick in the head. He attacked a sergeant, knocked him out, and the army stuck him in the glass house. Dad just made out he'd lost the plot and didn't know what he was doing. The army kept him banged up for a while then he was sent back out into the thick of it.

I don't know what made him do it. He was proud of fighting for his country and he kept all his army regalia, but, as I said, he was a quiet geezer and it was hard to get anything out of him.

Before the war me old man worked as a dog trainer over at Walthamstow Stadium. Both of his brothers were top trainers there and he loved everything about dog racing. But, after he was demobbed in 1946, he followed my granddad into the docks. It probably paid better. He was in East India dock first, then the Victoria and Albert.

He met and married Jean, me mum, after the war too. Her maiden name was Derby, she was Jean Doreen Derby. She was only eighteen when they got married, and me dad was about thirty-five. Her father had been a tool-maker but he and her mum had died young and she was left to bring up her three sisters on her own. She was evacuated all over the place during the war, even as far away as Middlesbrough at one stage, but she came from Varley Road in Custom House and that's where she ended back at, in the house where I was born in 1964.

I was the fifth of seven children; all nine of us in one tiny, three-bedroom house. Steve, my oldest brother, was born in March

1953, my sister Linda was next in June 1956. Mick was born in February 1961, Janet in December 1962, then it was me; me brother Trevor was born in January 1969 and Clare my sister in March 1971. My old man was forty-nine when he knocked me out and he had his last child when he was fifty-six. Let's hope I've inherited his stamina.

We were a close family but things were hard. We didn't have anything really; not a pot to piss in. There were seven kids and we had to survive on just Dad's wages. There was illness in the family, too. Mick was really badly asthmatic. He was so thin as a kid he looked two-dimensional and he had a punctured lung. I suffered from asthma too, but not as bad. When it got really foggy, I had to have a snot rag tied around my face so I could breathe properly.

We didn't have many holidays or anything like that at the start. There was one family holiday to Dymchurch when I was only a few months old. It was a palaver even getting there, taking five kids on the train with suitcases, two prams and nappies they had to wash out. We never had a car until much later. Me old man always used to go back and forth to work on his bike. It was all he needed.

Growing up, I didn't really like having a lot of brothers and sisters because all the other kids at school seemed to be decked out in immaculate gear and I knew I could never have it. For me it was always hand-me-downs and snake belts. I remember being in me first football team at school and they were wearing Adidas and I was wearing boots from Curtis – a really bottom-of-the-range shoe shop. I remember turning up to play and I had to make out they were rugby boots. The stick I got! Everyone was going, 'Look at your fucking boots.'

Rosetta Road Primary School was a haven for bullies, too. It was horrible, it really was, and if you didn't have what the others kids had you were the target. Woodside Comprehensive School wasn't much better but at least when I got there I could handle myself.

When I first went to school, I was a quiet kid. I remember the first proper fight I had. I was about nine and some Welsh boy at our school who used to bully people tried it on with me. In those days the thing to do was to go over the park and settle things. I said to me old man I know I'm going to have to have a row with this kid and he came along, too, to make sure it didn't get out of hand. Well, I gave it to him, beat him fair and square and me old man, who had just stood back and watched, come up and pulled me off the kid. The kid was crying and Dad said to him, 'Now you go home and that's it, you've had a straight-up and that's the end of it.' He would never get involved but obviously he was there to watch my back in case anybody did anything untoward. He had a strong sense of fair play, me old man. He didn't like bullies, maybe because his dad had been one.

There was never much laid on for kids when I was growing up. We used to go over to the old bomb sites and air raid shelters at Beckton dumps and have a laugh. That was a good day out for us. There was never a threat in the air, no kiddy-fiddlers or anything like that. Round our way we had souvenirs of the Blitz alongside reminders of the many failures of post-war local government. The infamous tower block Ronan Point had stood just at the end of our road. It blew up when I was four, killing five people. It was a gas explosion but it had been caused by shoddy materials and building practices; the direct result of corruption, backhanders and collusion between some contractors and some members of the local council, who were supposed to be our own people, Labour.

At least they stopped building them after that.

As I grew older, I learned to appreciate being in a big close family. We made our own fun. We used to torment my sister

Linda something chronic. She convinced herself she had a long neck for some reason, so we used to get her down in the front room, each one would hold a leg, and me being the youngest, I would pull her neck to stretch it and she used to go absolutely mad and beat the fuck out of us. Great stuff.

To tell you the truth, me old man wasn't always an honest docker. There were usually things around that were knocked off. He got nicked at one stage, but that was outrageous. He was accused of stealing beer: he and some other dockers had cracked open a crate of beer while they were working because it was so hot and the Port of London Authority actually nicked him for it. He kept his job, but it made the local paper.

Dad was Labour. Being in the docks he was a union man, but I remember him becoming very disillusioned with it all. His attitude was 'You can never trust 'em.' He said the union officials were looking after themselves and did nothing for us. When they closed down his dock, the Victoria and Albert, and bombed him out of work, he had a massive heart attack.

It was 1977 and I was about thirteen. I remember it vividly. We were in the front room, I went into the kitchen and all of a sudden he just went. He was on the sofa, he grabbed his chest and he went down. He was sixty-two then, and he was rolling around on the deck. We were kids; we ran out of the house and took off up the street. We couldn't face it. Me mum and me older brother Steve were there and they called an ambulance. I remember the ambulance turning the corner, and us walking round the block, thinking: Is he all right? Let him be all right, and when we got back the ambulance was outside and so we walked round the block again. Then I watched them bring him out. He had an oxygen mask on and they took him to St Andrew's Hospital at Bow. He was in a bad way; he was in

8

intensive care for about seven weeks and obviously me mum was going up there on the bus and the train throughout the summer. I went up there a few times but I didn't really like it. It was horrible as a kid to see your father like that. I honestly thought he was going to die, I really did, but he eventually got better.

The docks paid him about £4,000 as severance; atrocious it was, that was his cut for more than twenty years of hard graft. £4,000. That's probably about £15,000 now, nowhere near enough for the rest of your life.

That was the start of them closing down the London docks and moving them out to Tilbury in Essex. It was a common belief that the union leaders had been bought off. It was all done by 1984, and that was it; they'd ripped the heart out of East London and thrown thousands of men on the scrapheap for a pittance. And it was a Labour government that started it.

It had a devastating effect on the area. Before that, when you came down Prince Regent Lane, it was always thriving with people going to and from work all the time; all the pubs were open and there was always a throng of geezers who could have stepped straight out of the olden days with their flat caps on and their mufflers. It looked like a Chas & Dave video. Afterwards? Fuck all. They'd torn the guts out of the place.

CHAPTER TWO

Enter The Bull

I never really knew how notorious Custom House and neighbouring Canning Town were until much later on in life. It was a tough area; people used to lie about coming from there just to make themselves seem harder. They thought it gave them street-cred. You'd always hear people say, 'Keep clear of them, they're Custom House.' It was renowned for being the hardest part of East London, like the Gorbals in Glasgow, and it was full of faces. The main villains on our manor were the Dixon brothers, George and Alan who worked for the Krays. Ronnie Kray tried to shoot George once but the gun jammed. He kept the bullet as a souvenir. Another East End villain, Jack 'The Hat' McVitie, wasn't so lucky. Reggie used the same .32 when he tried to shoot him. The gun jammed again but Reg stabbed him to death with a carving knife.

Jack The Hat was our bass-player's uncle.

There were always a lot of armed robberies in the area. It wasn't unheard of for a bank to be in the process of being robbed by one firm only to have another firm turn up to do the same job. When that happened, the smaller firm would give way to the bigger one, no matter who had got there first. There was a pecking order. And that's why there are no longer any banks left in Canning Town.

I wasn't even aware of the gang culture in the area when I was a kid. Later I found out the place was full of naughty little firms, people with razors who would cut anyone who crossed them as soon as look at them. Nicky Gerrard, the gangland killer, was one of the biggest names round here. He got his head blown off outside a party in Stratford. Then there was Danny Woods, and Terry Smith – the armed robber who's been on the Channel Four TV show *The Heist*, showing people how to hold up banks. The Tibbses from Canning Town were a family to be reckoned with, too. Jimmy Tibbs is the famous boxing trainer.

Billy Murray, the actor, grew up a couple of streets away, and still works out at the Peacock gym. The Who's manager Bill Curbishley is another local boy. But when you were young you didn't know about these people.

It always struck me as ironic that, despite growing up in such a notorious area, the only harm I ever came to was accidental. As a kid I was like Wile E. Coyote in the Roadrunner cartoons, very accident prone. It started when I was two years old. I was trying to get to me mother. She had a lean-to, and it had a crack in the glass. As I put my hand on it, it went right through. It nearly cut my right hand off. They had to hold it together and get me to hospital. They thought I was going to lose it.

When I was four I was in hospital having my tonsils out and me old man and woman come in to find me with me forehead all stitched up. The blind had fallen on my head, knocked me out and I'd needed six stitches for that.

Another year, when I was nine, I came downstairs at home just as Mickey turned round with a red hot poker in his hand. He accidentally stuffed it in me right eye and they had to rush me to Moorfields Hospital to save the sight in it. It's a wonder I didn't grow up to look like Abu Hamza.

When I was six, Mick and me both got chopper bikes for Christmas – well, he had a chopper, I had the smaller version, the chipper. So naturally we went outside for a race. As I had the smaller bike, I made sure I started first; and as I looked round to see where he was, me bike went straight into a lamppost. I went over, hit the pavement and knocked me tooth clean out of my mouth.

The following Christmas I got the game Rebound. Mick beat me at it and there was a bit of a set-to, so I smashed it over his head, he nutted me and me other tooth went. So two Christmases running I lost me teeth, and I also ruined me game. It was a bad holiday all round that one. I was in and out of the dentist's for years because of that. They drilled in to the roots, they kept putting crowns in me teeth which I kept losing. I swallowed one in a jam tart. I had a night brace but nothing seemed to work. Then to cap it all they decided to give me silver teeth, one at the top and one at the bottom. I had to go to my first year of comprehensive school looking like a cut-price pirate.

It got worse though, a year or two later when *The Spy Who Loved Me* came out. That's the James Bond film with Jaws, the indestructible steel-toothed assassin. You can imagine the stick I took for that. I got absolutely ruined! But it could have been worse. The poker incident could have left me as Golden Eye.

I was never Golden Bollocks, I know that.

Boxing was very much part of the culture in East London. I started boxing in the third year of junior school, when I was about eight years old. My first proper bout was at an inter-school boxing match which was held in Curwen School. A few of us from Rosetta Road went in for it. They set up a ring in the school and I was fighting some big Asian kid. I was fucking useless, I didn't have a clue. I kept going in with me head down and all that and the ref disqualified me after the second round. I was the butt of all the jokes the next day at school but that just made me more determined to master it.

It was *Sportsnight* that really got me hooked on boxing. I used to love watching it on the BBC. There was a show on at the Albert Hall on a Tuesday every couple of months and you'd have people like Alan Minter and John H Stracey fighting. Quality boxers. We'd sit and watch it at home and I'd think, This is where I want to be. When I was ten, I took it up properly. I went round to a few clubs to find one that suited me. The first one I tried was the St George's boxing club, but they were all a bit too good there. So I tried West Ham, which was local, but there were too many people I knew there and it was too cliquey. Then Repton in Bethnal Green, but again they were too hot. Finally I found a club that suited: Barking. It was at the old Monteagle School. There was an old fella there called Terry Davis and he was just like your dad. He was a lovely character: he did all sorts of tricks for us, he was welcoming and he took you in and encouraged you. I just thought to myself, This is home, this is where I want to be. There were no superstars there.

I had to pass a medical first, of course, and then I couldn't fight until I was eleven. But I still remember my first bout. It was at Custom House Working Men's Club. I was right handed but I was boxing as a southpaw because that's how I used to shape up, leading with my right instead of my left, and I lost it on points. The second fight was at York Hall, Bethnal Green. Again I lost it on points. Terry said, 'You're going to have to change round and lead with your left.' It did the trick. I had a couple of fights and won. I started getting me confidence back.

Then Terry invited me and Mickey to the Liberal & Labour Club in Barking to watch all the old black-and-white fights on the reel-to-reel. So we got the bus up there, he got the projector out and said, 'Now this is one man I want you to watch, the greatest fighter ever – Sugar Ray Robinson.' He showed us a film of Sugar Ray beating Jake La Motta for the world championship on 14 February 1951. The Valentine's Day Massacre they called it. I'd never seen anything like it. It absolutely changed my life. The guy was poetry in motion, he could do it all. His style was breathtaking. Poor Jake La Motta was absolutely pummelled. I think they fought six times. La Motta won the first bout but Sugar Ray won the next five. It was fantastic to watch. I'd never seen anyone hit a man like he did, before or since.

After that I started taking magazines. *Boxing International* came out monthly and *Boxing News* was weekly. I knew I could never be as good as Sugar Ray but watching him turned me on to boxing so much I became obsessed with it. After that I just kept winning fight after fight.

Mickey and I used to go up to the Royal Oak, the boxing Mecca, which Terry Lawless had. All the top fighters were up there, people like Stracey, John L. Gardener, Maurice Hope, who was known as Mighty Mo, and the great Jimmy Batten. We'd go along to watch them train and try to get friendly with them. And we used to go and watch Dave 'Boy' Green fight at the Albert Hall and up at Wembley, too. There would always be a coach load of us for that. We'd meet the coach at the Londoner pub in Commercial Road and hype ourselves up for it on the journey. All the time we were getting more and more involved. We started getting all the American magazines too, and then we had the idea of making one of our own. And that's how *Slugger* was born.

It was on a par with the punk fanzines that were to come a year of two later. It was a boxing fanzine, but it was very tongue-in-cheek. It had a kind of Pythonesque humour. We'd run photos of fake fighters. Mick would put on a moustache and he'd become Carlos Rudi, the heavyweight champion. We had interviews, fight reports and totally fictitious fighters, like Badger Baldcock, the Assassin. One of our boxers used to fight in a mask and nobody knew his identity. I suppose *Viz* started the same way, but we never got round to photocopying the pages and making magazines to sell. Instead, once each new issue was finished we'd sneak it into our local sweet shop and while Mick kept the shopkeeper busy I'd slip a copy of *Slugger* into the revolving magazine rack. It would always have 'Hot off the press' written in pen on the front and 'price 5p'. Whenever we went back the next day it had always gone. I liked to think someone bought it each time, but it probably went straight in the rubbish bin.

Our first big boxing disappointment was John H Stracey. He'd just come back after losing his world title to Carlos Palomino and we blagged in to him, and got friendly with him as he started his training for his comeback fight against Dave 'Boy' Green. Now Green was the man coming up then, and Stracey always used to say to us, 'He's a wanker, that Green, I'll cane him.' So I used to tell everyone I knew that Stracey was going to kill him.

He used to take us running in Victoria Park, in Hackney. He was a tight bastard but he was a nice geezer. He gave us some of his memorabilia like his big Gola boots which he wore when he won his European title. Even though they were three sizes too big I wore them when I fought. Stracey even came down to Broad Street when I was fighting for the Essex schoolboys. He actually came to watch and I knocked the kid out in the first round – I've got the clipping. Afterwards, we walked through the bar and John H Stracey was with us. That made me feel really proud. But then he had his big fight against Green at Wembley. We went there and Green battered Stracey, ruined him, absolutely knocked ten tons of shit out of him. After that, Stracey just disappeared. He changed his phone number, I couldn't get hold of him. We never saw him again. I was a bit gutted, but then I started winning fights and doing well for myself as a boxer. That year, 1977, I won the Essex Schoolboy Championship and got to the British Schoolboy Finals.

What a nightmare that turned out to be. It was held at Pontin's holiday camp in Blackpool. Ten of us kids from the club went up in a minibus on the Friday. Inevitably, it broke down. We all had to hitch a lift to somewhere like Blackburn and get a train the rest of the way. We arrived at Pontin's at ten o'clock at night. I had a fight the next morning! And it was the biggest fight of my life. So I was stressed and I was knackered but at least I was there. The next morning I've got to the weigh-in and I was overweight. I had to run all round the camp trying to lose a few ounces. Went back to weigh in again and I was still over so I ended up back in the chalet in tracksuit bottoms covered in polyphene trying to burn it off by skipping. I finally made the weight at the last attempt. I got in the ring, to face this Welsh kid called England.

Now you get a lot of dodgy decisions in schoolboy boxing, and the fight before me had been a London boy against a Welsh lad, and everyone said the Welsh kid won it but they gave it to the Londoner. So straight away I was thinking, Fuck, if this goes tight, they'll give it to him. Well, it was tight. I put him over in the first round but it went to three rounds and they gave the decision to him. I was absolutely gutted. It kind of knocked the soul out of me. But later that day, they said I could have a return match and that I was selected for the England team; so that really softened the blow. I had just turned thirteen and I was boxing for England. I've still got the letter framed.

Well, I fought the Welsh kid a second time, and it was close, but again he won it on points. I wasn't disheartened, though. I was fighting for my country.

Back in London, Mick and me started going back to the Oak, and this time Charlie Magri had just turned pro. There were only three flyweights in the country at this time, a Scot, a northerner and Charlie, so he had no sparring partners.

So Mick's talking to Lawless, who was moaning about it, and Mick piped up and said, 'Jeff'll spar with him.' I thought, Thanks, Mick!, but I agreed to do it as long as he went easy. I was shitting myself at school the next day but I still turned up to spar. I was thirteen years old, Magri was nineteen or twenty, but he'd fought in the Olympics and he'd just turned pro. We were leagues apart.

The bell went, we came out and he was as good as his word, he went easy on me for the first round but he was on top of me all the time. I couldn't get past him. It was really frustrating. The second round was much the same. I was doing all right but he was right on top of me. In the third round, he came up and I've gone 'bap', hit with a left hand, right on the nose. Well, he backed me up against the ropes and started giving it to me. I don't blame him, it's a boxer's instinct, but I was thirteen and he hit me smack in the kidney with a left hook. I keeled over to one side and groaned. I thought, Fuck, I'm gonna go over. He took the wind right out of my sails. I heard Terry Lawless shout, 'Time, time, call time', and I just thought, Thank fuck for that. I got out and Lawless said to me, 'Have you learned anything from that?'

I said, 'Yeah probably never to get in the ring with him again.'

That dig from Magri knocked all the passion I had for boxing right out of me. I still did it for another few years but never with the same results. I'm not blaming Magri at all, but Lawless was at fault. He should never have put a thirteen-year-old boy in there with him in the first place. He could have got into trouble for that.

The next year I got through to the British Schoolboys Final but then I got chicken pox three days before the fight. I caught it from a kid at the gym who shouldn't have even been there. I left the Barking club because of that.

I joined West Ham boxing club next. Soon after, we had to go up to Washington, near Newcastle-upon-Tyne, for West Ham versus the Northern Counties Select; we all went up in a minibus and they put us up in people's houses. Everyone was friendly. It was a good atmosphere, a real community spirit on the boxing circuit.

There was a pretty northern girl with one of the families and all of us were trying to pull her. She said to me, 'Which one of you is fighting David McDermot?' I said I was. She said, 'He's the toughest kid on the estate, the hardest kid in our school.' I thought, Fuck, it would be me, then.

On the day, we got to the hall and everyone was dressed like headbangers. It was 1978 but all the northerners were decked out in denim and flares and had really long hair. It was like a Meatloaf gig, rockers everywhere. Norris, one of our boys, went in first. All the Geordies were screaming abuse at him but Norris caned their kid in the first round. I was up next, to face this so-called 'king of the estate'. Well, I'm no Rocky but I went in and absolutely pummelled the geezer. He was fucking easy. I went back in that house and said, 'He weren't so tough tonight, was he?' and there was nothing anyone could say. I never got the girl though. All in all it was a great day for West Ham. We came away ecstatic. We had such a laugh in the van on the way back, we were singing, joking, chucking things at the driver. In the end, he stopped the van and threatened to turf us out and leave us on the hard shoulder.

I carried on boxing but not with great success. My last fight was June 1979, in the Junior ABA final at Battersea Town Hall. I had so many distractions by then with the band and everything that I didn't have time to train properly and I lost my bout on a split decision. By then, boxing didn't seem so important. I'd started getting in trouble at school and then with the Old Bill, getting nicked. Music was also a big deal for me now. Just four days before the junior ABA finals I was with the band recording our first demos; instead of training, I'd come up to Covent Garden to talk music with Garry Bushell at the *Sounds* office. It was absolutely ridiculous, but I didn't give a fuck. *Sounds* and punk and the band seemed so much more exciting.

That said, even if the band hadn't come along, I don't think I'd have carried on. Mick would have done better than I would ever have done. He never lost a fight. He could have turned pro. He had a knock-out punch. I saw him fight a geezer called David Noel at Broad Street once and the whole place was on its feet. It was a humdinger. Mick was thin but he could really bang 'em over. He could have gone a lot further than me. I was mediocre compared to Mick, I never applied myself.

Boxing was my first passion as a kid, then football. I was never interested in politics or politicians; in fact, I was actively hostile to them. Nothing they said seemed relevant to our lives. At school we had a maths teacher called Goodwin who always used to stand up Stratford Market every Saturday selling the *Socialist Worker* newspaper. He had hair like Ian Hunter out of Mott The Hoople. But listen to him and his mates from the local college talk and it

20

was more a case of All The Young Pseuds. He started trying to brainwash us with politics when I was twelve. I remember staying behind after school when we were in the first year for maths arguing the toss with him. Young as I was, I could see the difference between facts and theories. To be honest, I was more interested in reading Marvel comics. They were a real big thing for me. I'd go down to East Ham market with me pocket money and snap up all the latest ones: Spider Man, Fantastic Four, the mighty Thor. Iron Man was my hero. Me and Mick always tried to act out our own comic-book adventures. Mick was Disc-Man, he'd throw a magical disc and it'd go over next door's fence. But he got me to believe that I could be a hero called The Bull.

I had to have a super-hero costume: tracksuit bottoms, an old pair of boxing boots, a mauve crash helmet and a T-shirt with the sleeves cut so they stood out like Iron Man's costume did. The Bull was extremely tough; there was nothing he couldn't do. So the big idea was to get in the garden, and build up a huge construction out of anything we could get our hands on – a stall, an old pram, an old record player that had been chucked out. We'd build it as high as possible because my super power was to run into the thing head first and knock it down.

I started doing that when I was nine or ten – old enough to know better – but I really believed in it. I remember once when we were going to get our comics I decided we had to make the trip wearing our costumes for authenticity. I was totally involved in this make-believe world. I used to look at New York as it was in the Spider Man comics when he's swinging from skyscraper to skyscraper, and think it looked a bit like Ilford in Essex. I'd go to Ilford and believe I was a hero walking the streets of Manhattan. There were times when we got changed in the local toilet. We'd put on our costumes and bowl through Ilford/New York looking for adventures – or in my case things to knock over. I had to stop eventually 'cos I was getting too many fucking headaches.

CHAPTER THREE

Police Car

They're gonna put me away
On a rap that I ain't done
Well I only really did it
'Cos I wanted some fun.

('THEY'RE GONNA PUT ME AWAY', THE COCKNEY REJECTS)

The first time I got nicked I was fourteen years old, a late starter in Custom House. It was in October 1978. I was in a little gang who used to hang about at the local club. It was called the Shipman Youth Club, as in Dr Harold. I was younger than the others, and when we came out we'd always go and look for mischief. There was an Asian geezer who lived nearby who kept having his windows put through. Not by us, but it was common knowledge that it was happening. One night we knocked on his door and said we knew who was doing it and that we could stop them but he'd have to pay us. We told him that it would cost him £200,000. We said we had links to Interpol. It was utter bollocks, of course. We didn't even know what Interpol meant. We were kids.

The bloke's race wasn't a factor to us; one of us was black, a kid called Andrew Crawford. We were just having a laugh. Every other night when we had nothing to do we'd go round there. And to make the whole thing even more ludicrous, we'd had pictures done in a photo booth of us wearing dark glasses and trying to look mean and mysterious. We showed them to the fella and said they were government snap-shots of secret agents who were working for us and that, if he coughed up the £200,000 the next night, our agents would reveal who had been breaking his windows. It was absolute cobblers. No one could take that seriously, could they?

The following night we went round there and knocked on his door. We weren't actually expecting him to give us any cash; I'd have been surprised if he'd had a tenner to spare. It was just a wind-up. We were killing time, sodding about 'cos there was fuck all else to do. But, as he came out of his house, his garage doors flew open and a load of Old Bill piled out. We took off and got away. An hour or so later, though, sitting at the top of me own street, a Black Maria pulled up and they nicked three of us, me, Andrew Crawford and a kid called Tony Ling. Even then we didn't think much would come of it, but they really gave us a bad time. They chucked us in the back of the van and they were shouting and swearing at us, shoving us about like we'd got away with the crown jewels. This one cop had his face right in mine and he was hollering, 'You fucking bastards! I'm going to fucking kick your fucking heads in.' And I just kept saying, 'What have I done?'

They got us in separate cells, we weren't allowed a solicitor or a phone call, and then they started all the psychological bullshit. All of us got told that we were going to get done for blackmail, conspiracy and all sorts of things. It frightened the life out of us. They wanted other names but I kept saying I didn't know what they were talking about. Deny, deny, deny.

I was banged up for about eight hours before they brought me mum and dad up there. I made a statement, with no solicitor present; and they could pretty much do what they wanted with it. I had to go back a week later. They brought this DI down who was saying to me mum and dad, don't worry, he's a nice boy, we know that this has all been blown up and I'll put in a good word for him. Then they charged me with demanding money with menaces. OK, what we'd done was wrong but it was also farcical. It was just silly. We hadn't meant any harm. It hadn't been us smashing the guy's windows. But suddenly a daft kids' game had turned serious. I could have been looking at twelve months inside for my first offence. I thought, I can't handle this. And it soon got a lot worse.

> Freedom? There ain't no fucking freedom
> I like punk and I like Sham
> I got nicked over West Ham
> I'm a fool, I guess it's true
> Before I knew I was in the back with you
> In a police car.
>
> ('POLICE CAR', THE COCKNEY REJECTS)

About three weeks later I went over to West Ham for Billy Bond's testimonial match against Tottenham. I was in the South Bank and when West Ham scored naturally everyone jumped up and down, cheering. Out of the blue this copper came over and grabbed me. 'That's it,' he said, 'you're nicked.' I said, 'Nicked for what?' But he wouldn't answer. He took me down to East Ham station, and banged me up in a cell. It was like the black hole of Calcutta in there. They'd crammed fifteen of us into it but there was only one bed, so you had to fight to get on it. I remember this big fat skinhead who kept farting. The stench was disgusting. It was like a rat had died up his arse. And of course the rest of us kept going up to the bars and trying to get gulps of oxygen from the air-vent outside. Naturally the smelly cunt got the bed.

The cops called me old man up there, and he was disgusted with me, the boxing club was disgusted. I think they wanted me to leave. I got charged with threatening behaviour and yet I'd done absolutely nothing. It wasn't a case of innocent until proven guilty; I was guilty just by being me.

Of the two charges, the more serious one of demanding money with menaces came to court first. All three of us were accused of it, and the police case was utter bollocks. They told the court that we'd been running down the road singing 'National Front, National Front.' It never happened. Why would us and our black mate Andrew Crawford be chanting that? It didn't make any sense but they were really putting it on us. The case was going badly, and then the DI who'd promised me mum that he'd put in a good word for us got up. I thought, At last some good news. Well, he got on the witness stand and he absolutely ruined me. He said that I'd shown no remorse, he tried to say that we were after £50 a week off the Asian fella. Load of old bollocks. I wouldn't have had a clue how to do it. It was lie after lie.

In the circumstances, I was lucky I only got a suspended sentence and a £100 fine. But that wasn't the end of the worry, though, because a suspended meant that if I did anything wrong in the next two years I'd go to jail. As far as I was concerned that meant I was definitely going down because I knew I still had the threatening behaviour charge hanging over my head.

It took ten long months for that one to come to trial. You can image what was going through my mind week in week out. It was eventually heard in a magistrates court. Me and a fella called Stephen Nash were tried together. The trial had already been adjourned once because the copper forgot his notes, but this time there were no hitches. We didn't have solicitors 'cos the ones I'd hired for the demanding money with menaces case weren't worth a light. I might as well have had my milkman defending me. So, I decided to represent myself. I got up and gave my own evidence. It was a very simple argument: why would I be shouting, punching and kicking in an end full of my own supporters? I said that it beggared belief. Nash said the same. The magistrates obviously agreed because they gave the copper a grilling. Then they summed up the case in no time and said that the two of us were not guilty and we were free to go.

The police case had been a fabrication from start to finish, but that's what they used to do at the time at West Ham. They pretty much nicked anyone just to get the number of arrests up. You could drop your hot dog and they'd nick you. But, in our case, justice was done and as a bonus I got a song out of it. That was the incident that inspired our song 'Police Car'.

That was the first and only time I ever got nicked at football. I started going to matches when I was eight. Me old man took me at first, and so did my brother Stevie. He'd been involved in football hooliganism when it first started making the headlines. In his time, Joey Williams and the Mile End mob were really the boys. And Steve got nicked in Sheffield in 1970 and ended up on an ID parade after a Sheffield United supporter got stabbed. He didn't do it but he did like a fight.

Although the Rejects became renowned for their football hooligan following and although it ran in the family, I never got heavily involved in rucking at games until after the band took off. I was aware of the ICF from a fairly early age, though. When I started at secondary school, we used to bunk off and go and walk round Upton Park a lot. The letters 'ICF' were sprayed up all over the place. At first we were baffled. What the fuck's all this ICF about? Then you started getting wise. Your older brothers told you. ICF: Inter-City Firm, the most notorious gang of football hooligans ever.

There were other gangs of course, but the ICF were the ones who became world famous. They'd been in existence for years, but you can trace their rebirth in the late 1970s to the intense rivalry between West Ham and Millwall. That was the catalyst that changed them from a gang into something more like a small army: organised, dedicated and resourceful.

Every army needs an enemy and ours was Millwall. It was October 1978 when I first really became aware of it. Then, the rivalry between the two firms of supporters was reaching its height. When we got relegated that year, there was a silver lining in the cloud: we knew we'd get to play Millwall. The build-up to that match was phenomenal. Feelings were running high. There had been an incident at New Cross station in South London when a geezer had got pushed under a train. West Ham had a song about it: 'We're all mad, we're insane, we push Millwall under trains.' Sick, but that's how it was. So obviously the blood was boiling; and Millwall had some serious firms of their own.

They had The Treatment, F-Troop, the Bushwhackers and the Half Way Line geezers who wore hoods. West Ham were expecting them to go all out for revenge. There was talk all round East London that Millwall were going to come over the night before the match; and loads of us turned up and walked around the ground that night but no one came. The next day the expectations were even higher. I had never seen so many West Ham supporters. There were thousands all lined up from Upton Park station on both sides, waiting for the big Millwall invasion. People of all ages were there, ready for them, ready to ruck.

Then, all of a sudden we saw the Old Bill emerge with the away supporters and they got pushed straight back into the station. Bless 'em, there could only have been about 200 Millwall fans. They got escorted to the away enclosure in the South Bank, and the push that day to get in amongst 'em was incredible. That's where the pictures came from for our 'War On the Terraces' single.

In the end it didn't matter that Millwall's mob hadn't even shown up. The anticipation of their invasion had an electrifying effect on the hooligan element of West Ham. That day was responsible for the rebirth of the ICF.

Even at fourteen, I'd heard of people like Cass Pennant, Bill Gardener and Bunter, but I didn't know who they were until we started the group and we picked up an ICF following. Round our way you had other little firms like the Canning Town Snipers – kids like Johnny Smith and Danny Brown who were a bit older than us. You had the Prince Regent Lane firm too. But I hit on the great idea of forming the Rubber Glove Firm, it was like an alternative mob for us fourteen-year-olds. It was a piss-take really; a weedy firm, absolutely pathetic. Some of the boys involved could have a row. There was Joey Millington, Stevie Stone, who was the lieutenant – he was probably the top boy in our year – Terry King, Johnny Matthews, David Clark, Johnny Oakman. But we took all the wallies under our wing, too. We weren't bullies, we were just after a good time.

Our rival schools were our chief targets. We used to march over to Brampton for a good hit and run raid. I remember going in three-handed into the playground at Trinity School, sorting out their top boys and having everyone chase us back. It was great, a real buzz. But it was always tongue-in-cheek. To be in the Rubber Glove Firm, you had to wear one Marigold: we changed the colour every month – first yellow, then red, then back to yellow again. We had a chant: 'We Are the RGF!' If we were bunking school, we used to have this game called Jury. We'd sit at the back of a bus and decree a sentence on one of us and then kick the fuck out of them. There was one geezer called Hogey who had a massive great big cock and his sentence, 'cos we heard he could do it, was to bend over and suck it on the back of the 278 bus. And he did it too. If I could have done that, I would have never left home…

Our biggest raid was at the Imperial War Museum. We knew, if we went there, there'd be bundles of other schools about on educational trips, and for us that was a field day. We used to bowl through there, sometimes just six-handed, get the rubber gloves on and start laying in to them by the Crimean War display. Everyone would scatter, and run for the doors. But in the end the other schools all teamed up and hunted us. There were about sixty of them, all in their blazers and we had to get out. Retreat was the better part of valour.

It sounds violent but it wasn't. It was a good-natured thing. You went to other schools and they'd be so bored in there an RGF raid would brighten up their day. We were different from other gangs. You used to get the bully element in our school who reckoned themselves. But we always tried to have a laugh with it, make it funny. There was a geezer who sold ice-creams and hot-dogs from a caravan in the high street out the back of the school and one of the things we used to like doing was to come out of school about fifteen-handed, get round his van singing 'We Will, We Will Rock You' and start rocking his caravan so his hot-dogs, onions, sauces and his 99 flakes would go everywhere. He would come out of there furious and chase down the road after us. We'd laugh for hours. That's what we'd do. It was about having a crack, not cracking people's heads.

The Rubber Glove Firm were the first Cockney Rejects fans. They were even pictured in *Sounds*, which was hilarious. It was all a big piss-take. But, as we started to make an impact, we started to get introduced to people who were obviously the real thing, like Tony Barker and Andy Swallow, and that's when I thought it was time to ditch the whole RGF caper, y'know, put away childish things. By the time I was fifteen, through punk and through the band, I was mixing with a lot of older people and I knew the RGF had to be outed. The difference between a fifteen-year-old and an eighteen-year-old is a huge gulf, as big as the difference between the RGF and the ICF.

It also turned out to be the difference between having a laugh and fighting for your life.

CHAPTER FOUR

Playground Punk – Lairy Of The Fourth Form

'Here's a chord, here's another chord –
now form a band.' *(SNIFFIN' GLUE)*

My first day at senior school was a bit traumatic. I remember me mum sending me in wearing shorts and sandals, and what with me silver teeth and me long hair it caused a few eyebrows to raise. My teacher took me to one side and she said, 'I'm not being funny but are you a girl or a boy?' I went beetroot red. I said to me mum, 'You can't send me to school like this, I'm gonna get killed.'

I was a bit of a late starter when it came to girls. I don't think I had a girlfriend at school, not one. It wasn't that I wasn't interested in them but I just didn't have it, couldn't do it. Girls were like an alien race. I couldn't communicate with 'em. I didn't get a girlfriend till much later. To be honest I was quite a quiet kid. I didn't really start to get lairy and wanting to come out of myself until a couple of years later when punk happened and then I wanted to be at the front of it all.

I was twelve when I first saw the name the Sex Pistols and, naturally, being a kid it made me laugh 'cos it sounded rude, a bit saucy. We were down in Hastings on one of our traditional five-day family holidays – we'd all go down in the car, a clapped-out old Ford Zephyr, and the car always broke down. It was the same every year. But in 1976, I spotted this Sex Pistols poster at the Pier and it intrigued me. Later that year, Janet Street-Porter did a show about punk for LWT and she put me off it. I mean, who'd want to get involved with that?

I've loved music since I was five. I saw the Rolling Stones on TV doing 'Gimme Shelter' and I thought it was fucking brilliant. My brother Mick would come home with records by Nazareth, Purple, Sabbath, Zeppelin, Queen, Aerosmith. I used to pilfer them and rock on me bed as I played them, imagining I was the singer or the drummer. Then in 1977 Mick brought a tape home and said, 'Listen to this.' It was 'God save the Queen', and I thought, What the fuck is this? This is different, this is great. He went, 'That's punk rock, that's the Sex Pistols,' and that was it, I was hooked. I was converted on the spot.

I started buying all the records I could get my hands on: The Buzzcocks, The Clash, The Damned. The first punk single I bought was 'Get A Grip On Yerself' by the Stranglers, with 'London Lady' on the B-side. It was fucking great. I couldn't stand bands like X-Ray Spex or Eater. I liked the ones with tunes. I thought The Clash were superb. Even when they changed direction with 'London Calling', I still thought they were a great band. Of course, I found out later that a lot of the early punk bands were plastic, and faking their accents and backgrounds, but at the time I loved it. Punk brought the rock scene back down to our level. Suddenly you didn't need to have long hair down your back singing songs that sounded like Einstein's theory of relativity set to music. That Clash first album had numbers like 'Cheat', 'Garageland' and '48 Hours'. They were singing about different things, reality. It wasn't David Coverdale banging on about having his heart broken again. I mean, I didn't know what it was like to have my heart broken anyway. It meant nothing to me. Punk was more about everyday life. I thought it was blinding, anyone could start a band now; anyone could do it. It was fresh and exciting, and obviously the next step was me wanting to go to punk gigs.

I started going to the Bridge House in Canning Town to suffer our local punk band, The Tickets. Then I ventured further afield to see bands like 999, The Rezillos and The Ramones. One night a gig we were going to got cancelled and we got tickets to see The Boomtown Rats at Hammersmith instead. There was a film crew outside and a geezer came up and asked me if I knew the moves to 'Do The Rat'. It was the B-side of their crap single 'Mary Of The Fourth Form' and it had this stupid dance that went with it. Of course, I went 'yeah!' 'cos I wanted to get myself up front by the stage. I was fourteen! I'd forgotten all about that recording until Jonathan Ross showed it on his BBC1 show in 2003. I thought it was dead and buried, I never thought it would come back to haunt me. That film footage is my secret shame.

Even though I was going to punk gigs, I never really got into drinking. I never sniffed glue or any of that shit either. Girls were still an unknown territory for me, too. My main vice at the time was fireworks, which were recklessly disposed of. There was violence associated with punk right from the beginning; there was that famous picture of that wanker Sid

Vicious with blood trickling down his face and that was how it was. I remember going to see the Lurkers at Woolwich Poly in 1978 and being surprised at how much trouble there was at the gig. There's a geezer on stage trying to look like Brian May and all these skinheads in the audience bashing the granny out of one another.

Oddly enough, I was never really into Sham 69, even though Jimmy Pursey ended up working with us so closely. I liked the UK Subs, the Skids, the Ruts and the Angelic Upstarts when they came out, but there was something about Sham I didn't take to. 'Borstal Breakout' was a good song, but after that Pursey was tying himself up in knots trying to get his daft messages across. Later on he completely lost the plot and went as mad as a March hare.

I still liked rock as well at this time. I was still buying Queen albums even though I wasn't supposed to. I always knew my own mind.

After I got the punk bug, I desperately wanted to form a band. In October 1978 the family went on another five-day holiday to Hastings. We stayed at Coombe Haven caravan park which always had entertainers. I was desperate to get on the stage. On the Saturday night they had a competition. There was a regular drummer and a piano player, and people would get up and murder 'Strangers In The Night' and all that shit. I asked the pianist if he knew 'Holidays In The Sun' by the Sex Pistols. To my amazement both him and the drummer did, so he started banging it out on the joanna and we got up there and went absolutely barmy. All these old dears sitting there doing their knitting were looking up with their jaws hitting the floor but we won the competition. It was the worst-singer contest and we pissed it. I thought, There's nothing to this getting on stage lark, I'm going to take this further.

The first thing I needed was a suitably spiky name. All the big punk stars used aliases: Johnny Rotten, Sid Vicious, Joe Strummer, Billy Idol and the rest. Who could I be? My dad had gone to St Joachim's primary school in Custom House with a kid called Turner whose nickname was 'Stinky' because of his unstable bowels. The name had always made me smile, and it seemed to capture the punk ethic to a tee. 'I'll be Stinky Turner,' I said. And from that day I was.

By this time my brother Mick had got his first guitar, an old SG copy, and he was teaching himself to play. I didn't know anything about music at all, but that didn't stop me forming me own band with three of me mates from school. There was me, Terry King, Stevie Stone and Johnny Matthews. Obviously none of us could play a note. We had an acoustic guitar, a shitty Bontempi organ and a couple of upturned buckets that we used for drums. I called us the Cockney Rejects. I dunno where the name came from exactly. I'd seen the word Reject in a magazine and liked the sound of it. I toyed with the East London Rejects, but thought it'd be better to use the word Cockney. There had already been Steve Harley's mob Cockney Rebel, who'd been having hits for a few years, and Cock Sparrer, who were also from East London. The Cockney Rejects just seemed to fit. We were rejects – we were never gonna be part of respectable society – and of course we were Cockneys. It was a perfect name, it summed us up. It was what we were and it stuck out.

Unfortunately, Mick thought so too. He nicked the name for his band, even though he didn't really have one at this stage; he was just jamming about with more accomplished people, mates of his own age who had guitars and proper drums. But he took our name for himself and my band got saddled with the less impressive moniker of The Postmen. Why? I'd like to say it was because we always delivered, or 'cos we always knocked you out, or up, twice, but the truth is a bit less thought out. I was just bunking school one day with a geezer called Paul Smith and talking about possible names for punk bands when we noticed this old postie going from house to house delivering letters. I thought, Yeah, that's a good name for a band: the postmen are there but you don't really notice them, people take them for granted, they're a bit mysterious in their own way, and quite powerful too while seeming insignificant. The name seemed suggestive at the same time as being everyday and banal.

The Postmen were always quite a hazy project. We got ourselves something that resembled a drum kit, no one could play to save our lives, but we decided who'd do what and that I was going to sing and that we wanted keyboards involved. There was a big music shop up near the Abbey Arms, called Hutchins Music Shop, which was run by this huge, fat hippy. Every time you went in you could always tell he didn't want you there. One day we spotted he had a new Wasp synthesiser in; it cost about £300. We couldn't afford it but I decided it had to go. So I went down there with me mates; I'd never thieved anything in me life but I wanted this band to work so we went in there and I said to one of me mates, as soon as I've got his attention, just go, whip it and go. So I went in and struck up a conversation with him about a Ludwig drum kit, and, while he's showing me the kit, two of me mates came in, one of them picked up the synth and walked straight out the shop with it. The hippy geezer didn't know a thing about it, didn't see a thing. I said, 'This is the kit I want but I've got to see me mum and see if she'll put up the money for it.' Of course, I never went back. I left the shop and they're waiting round the corner for me with £300 worth of synthesiser. What a touch!

My brother Steve had a flat in Elkington Road. We decided to dub it Elkington Studios and that was our base for the band. It was our rehearsal studio, we recorded there, we even played gigs there. But now we had the synth, The Postmen went on the back-burner. I really wanted to get a band going with me brother and now I had the synthesiser we formed The Shitters, with Mick on guitar and me on vocals and synth. We designed our own logo for our label, which was called Rude Records. The logo was very tasteful; it was a geezer's arse hanging out of a khazi seat.

Then we set about writing songs for our first album. There was 'I Am The Wasp', a song called 'Gola Bag', 'cos I always had a Gola bag with me, and another one called 'Old Boy At The Pictures'. That was inspired by the time we went to see *Up Pompeii* with Frankie Howerd. There was an old fella at the front eating toffees who kept laughing really loud so everyone was gobbing over his back. When he left, there were loads of greenies hanging off the back of his coat. The chorus went: 'He's an old boy at the pictures/He's sucking toffees/Old boy at the pictures/Got rheumatism in his knees…' Absolute crap.

We had a football-related number called 'TBF', Teddy Bunter Firm. Another song called 'Dennis Lillee'. I don't know what that was doing in there. It was about that time when he attacked a cricketer with an aluminium bat. But we had a whole set and it felt like it was all coming together. We'd do gigs in our back garden and rehearse in the shed. It seemed great to us. Then we did our first demo recording with the synth; we did 'I Am The Wasp', and when we listened back we realised it was absolutely fucking terrible. That's when we knew we had to change direction. So The Shitters were binned and we re-formed as The Cockney Rejects.

Back then we didn't know what we were doing or what we were

writing. It was all hit and miss, and much more miss than hit. But we always had the gift of the gab. Around this time, the White Cats, who were Rat Scabies's break-away band from The Damned, were playing at the Bridge House. Mick went down there and next thing I know he's on the phone. He'd blagged Rat Scabies into giving me drum lessons. So I went down there and met Rat, lovely geezer, and he agreed to give me lessons free of charge. Nothing ever came of it but it gave us the impetus to recruit a line-up. We were determined to make The Cockney Rejects happen. My ex-brother-in-law Chrissie Murrell, who was engaged to my sister Janet at the time, was given the bass guitar and told to learn to play it. He was dark and quite Italian looking. A bit too pretty, maybe, but he spiked his hair up and wore a leather jacket and I suppose that counted more than his bass-playing. He looked the part and that was about it. We still didn't have a drummer, though – but that was never going to stop Mick. We might not have had a full band but we had the idea and back then, in the anything-can-happen 1970s with Mick's gift of the gab, that was enough.

I'll never forget what happened next. I was at school, in a technical-drawing class and as usual it was an absolute riot in there. We did whatever we wanted, things were thrown about. It was terrible. But the teacher, a Greek fella called Mr Manucos, didn't seem to care. All of a sudden, Mick appeared in the class. Mr Manucos asked him what he wanted.

Mick said, 'Never mind that. Jeff, you're coming with me.'

I said, 'Where are we going?'

Mick replied, 'I've been in contact with Garry Bushell at *Sounds*. He wants to meet us.'

So I just fucked off out the class.

It turned out that Mick had somehow contacted the *Sounds*

journalist Garry Bushell. He loved the name of the band, so he said he would contact Jimmy Pursey for us and see if he could fix us up with a demo at Polydor.

When Mick told me I said, 'Shit, Mick, we ain't even got a drummer.' We didn't have a full band, we'd never played a gig, and the bassist could play three notes. Mick never mentioned any of that to Bushell, though.

So we went all the way up to the Spotlight building in Long Acre, Covent Garden, where the *Sounds* offices were, just over the tube station. To us it was a big deal meeting Bushell because he was the top punk writer at that time.

We got to the reception and, it being between the hours of midday and 3.00 pm, they immediately redirected us to the White Lion pub round the corner. Bushell was in there with fellow journalist Robbi Millar. It was a small place but it was quite a big rock boozer in its day. Loads of famous faces drank in there with the *Sounds* mob: John Peel, Chrissie Hynde, The Jam, Bon Scott, Lemmy, Bad Manners, UFO, U2, the Angelic Upstarts, Secret Affair, Paul Di'Anno, Phil Lynott, Max Splodge. You'd see 'em all in there at different times. We bowled in with our West Ham scarves on and introduced ourselves. I was relieved that Bushell was down-to-earth like Rat Scabies had been. Mick had a pint, I sat there with a coke and Bushell told us about Pursey's new venture, JP Productions. Bushell said he could get us in to do a demo. We came away walking on air. This was when I was still boxing. I was supposed to be in training for the ABAs.

Garry Bushell got back in contact with us in no time and said he'd spoken to Jimmy Pursey, who also liked the sound of the band and the name and wanted us to go along to Polydor Studios and make a demo. We had to record four songs. Pursey wouldn't be there, but his engineer Pete Wilson, the hippy, would be.

Great. We needed four songs so we wrote them immediately. 'Police Car', 'Flares 'N' Slippers', 'Fight Song' and 'I Wanna Be A Star' which ended with me ad-libbing about wanting 'twenty new Gibsons, playing Hammersmith at £10 a ticket with Iggy Pop supporting'.

Mick also thought of a way around the problem of the drummer; he decided to tell Pete Wilson that our drummer had just had a car crash and to ask Wilson if he could find a session drummer for us on the day.

The next thing I know we've met Pete and we're recording in a twenty-four-track studio at Polydor! I'd never made a proper recording in my life. I'd sung a few things into a little cassette player, but now we were in a big fuck-off studio and we ain't even got a drummer. So Mick told Pete Wilson the terrible story of our non-existent drummer's car accident. Pete just shrugged and said, 'Never mind, I'll play for you!' What a touch.

And that was how and why our first four songs were written and recorded. 'Flares 'N' Slippers', which was our first-ever song, was written about a kid called Gary Rollinson in our school who thought he was trendy. Trainers then were known as slippers, and this Rollinson always had flares and slippers on. I'd see him walking down the street like that and I thought, He'll do for the first song. That's the truth.

We'd had the idea for a couple of the other songs from the days of The Shitters. 'Police Car' was about me being nicked and falsely accused of threatening behaviour at West Ham. It was Mickey who suggested that I start it by shouting, 'Freedom, there ain't no fucking freedom.' It captured how we felt because in those days the Old Bill really did persecute us. I know, because Bushell told us at the time that 'Police Car' was the song that won over the *Sounds* office. Both Bushell and Dave McCullough had it on their play-lists. I think a couple of the others did as well, including Robbi Millar and Eric Fuller, who was the top reggae writer at the time. Even though we'd gone into that studio half-cocked, we knew what we recorded had to be good. There would have been no point in us talking our way into *Sounds* and Polydor if what we'd done in the studio was crap.

Now the dream of The Cockney Rejects was becoming a reality. We'd got this far on the old barrow-boy charm, but it wouldn't take us much further. From here on in, the band's future success would take commitment, determination and sheer hard graft.

CHAPTER FIVE

Meeting The Faces

I wanna go back to where it all began
I wanna do a gig in my back garden
I wanna have a laugh before the press get it
'Cos if you give half a chance they'll destroy
the fuckin' thing.

('JOIN THE REJECTS', THE COCKNEY REJECTS)

The high of making the demo tape soon evaporated. It had gone down well with Pete Wilson and with *Sounds* but we didn't hear back from Jimmy Pursey for months; not until the October, in fact. And, at our age, that felt like a lifetime. It was only because Pursey was busy with Sham 69. They'd brought out the 'Hersham Boys' single in August which went Top Ten; plus they had a new album out and were off promoting it on a UK tour. But we weren't content to sit around waiting. There was always the possibility that Pursey wasn't interested so we started making our own arrangements to keep the momentum going. We had the demo and we figured that was enough to get us at least a deal for a single. There was an indie label called Small Wonder down the road from us in Walthamstow. They'd put out records by Menace and Crass, but what mattered more was that they were only one bus ride from the top of our road on a 262. So Mick rang up Pete Stennett who ran the label and told him about the band. Stennett wasn't off-hand but he wasn't that excited either. He obviously heard the same thing every day of his life. He told Mick to post him the demo tape. Mick said no, we were in the vicinity and we'd bring it up.

So we got the bus to Walthamstow. We walked in and there was a little scruffy hippy geezer with long hair and a tea cosy on his head. He looked like he lived under a carpet. This turned out to be Pete Stennett. We introduced ourselves and he told us to leave the tape on a pile with hundreds of others. Mick said, 'Well, make sure you listen to it, here's our phone number,' and he wrote down me mum's number. It wasn't a promising start but by the time we'd got home Stennett had rung up raving about the tape. He wanted to sign us and make a record. He'd even already booked a studio for us in Leytonstone.

Which was all well and good, except we *still* didn't have a drummer.

Luckily, me brother in-law knew one, a fella called Paul Harvey, who worked on the fruit-and-veg stall in Stratford Market and had suffered a lifetime of jokes about his plums. He turned out to be a piss-poor drummer but at the time he was better than nothing. He'd do.

Pete Stennett booked us in to Alan Gordon's studios and, as a foretaste of things to come, Les McKeown from the Bay City Rollers turned out to be recording in the next studio. The Rollers had been huge teeny-bop pop stars of course, so, as soon as we knew he was in there, we started fucking about. We were kicking his door and, when he came out shouting, there'd be nobody there. It was driving him mad. Eventually he came in to us and growled something at me and Stevie Stone who had come along for the crack and who just happened to be holding a broom. Stevie just snapped at him. 'Fuck off, you daft Scottish cunt,' he said, and he shoved the broom at him. Wallop. Done him right in the chin with it. We were only kids, we couldn't give a fuck. 'You Jock cunt,' Steve said. 'Have that, fucking Bay Shitty Roller.' McKeown went straight back to his studio and got us kicked out. So we were out of there and booked ourselves into an eight-track studio in Islington.

Pete Stennett got in Bob Sergeant to produce us; he went on to produce The Beat. And this was where we did the 'Flares 'N' Slippers' Ep; three songs: 'I Wanna Be A Star', 'Police Car' and 'Flares 'N' Slippers'.

It was a miracle we got them done at all. We had murders in there. For a start, Paul Harvey could hardly play. Bob had to sit in there with him 'cos he couldn't keep time. He had to get the engineer to record the bass drum on a separate track 'cos Harvey couldn't manage to play that, the high-hat, the snare and the toms all together. It was disgraceful. We knew he'd have to go.

And, to make matters worse, our mum had become dead-set against us going into the music game. The night before we were due to record the single, there had been an *Arena* programme on BBC2 about Sham 69 and the violence they were experiencing at their gigs. Pursey was there crying his eyes out on stage; and Mum was horrified. She was in tears saying, 'I don't want yous to get involved in that. That's a shit scene, I can't stand it.'

We convinced her that this was what we wanted to do, and that we wouldn't make the same mistakes as Jimmy Pursey. She agreed to let us go ahead and make the single on condition that she could hear it. And she was adamant that she didn't want there to be any swearing on it. But, of course, we knew how well the 'Freedom, there ain't no fuckin' freedom' line had gone down with Bushell and *Sounds* and everyone else who heard it and so it had to be on there. So we got two acetates cut by Pete Stennett, one for Mum to hear without the swearing and the proper one.

Around this time we'd met up with Garrie Lammin, formerly of Cock Sparrer, who had a new R'n'B band called the Little Roosters, with Alison Moyet on backing vocals. And, on the strength of the single, he offered us a support gig at our local rock venue the Bridge House, run by ex-boxer Terry Murphy, up by Canning Town fly-over. This may not sound a lot to anyone else, but to us it was a real big thing. At home, we used to make joke posters up in felt-tip pen: 'Terry Murphy presents "Police Car" – The Cockney Rejects live at the Bridge House.' Now it was coming true. The dream was happening, I'm putting out a single, I'm playing me first gig…

We knocked up a few more songs and we had about a twenty-minute set. The gig itself was a bit of a let-down, though. There were only thirty people there. A year later we'd be getting 700 in, hundreds over what the fire regulations allowed. But this night you could have comfortably swung a cow round in there. We played the set anyway, we lost our cherry. Garrie Lammin, bless him, thought he was Ronnie Wood. This was his big moment, but twenty of the people in there were with us. Only ten had turned out for the Roosters. He was playing the blues and old-style R'n'B, a far cry from Sparrer. But give him his due, he was good.

I didn't really care that no one had turned up; all that mattered was that we'd played. Things were happening for us but the gig made us realise that we had to give Chrissie and Paul Harvey the tin-tack. Neither could really play, and Chrissie for one was never going to learn because he was courting me sister Janet and it was taking up far too much of his time.

We tried out another bassist, a fella called Blake Deayton, but he was an absolute snide. Nearly got us killed, too. He joined at a time when we'd been trying to drum up awareness of the band for months. We went round spraying 'Cockney Rejects' everywhere we could. We did it round Canning Town Market, on every brick wall and every garage. One Sunday night we were out spraying and two Mercs full of yuppie types pulled up at a junction. Deayton took it upon himself to spray their cars with white paint. We didn't know he'd done it; we were over doing a wall. There were ten of them, City geezers, big-built, five in each motor. They jumped out, understandably pissed off. Deayton just legged it, so they came at me and Mick. We were trying to fight the lot of them. Obviously we really copped it, with those odds we had no chance, but we had a go. A couple of them got whacked in the process. But Deayton caused it all and when it came on top he ran away. He was a fucking bottler, so he had to go. That was the birth of a song called 'Shitter', which was on the first album:

> Shitter, look what you've done to me
> Shitter, just can't you see
> You left me when you sprayed that car
> Couldn't find you, you ran so far
> Geezer gave me a good slap
> Now I wanna get you back.

So, we needed a bassist fast. Around this time, I'd joined a football team called Tarana in Custom House. I was only fourteen and

49

they were all men, twenty-six, twenty-seven, but I didn't want to play in the school team, I had to be with a man's team. It was more me. The team was full of characters, Custom House boys like Jimmy Maher and Barry Sudell who were a great laugh but were a bit handy with their fists. One time this guy who was with the other team kept heckling us from the side-line. Maher and Sudell walked off the pitch, bashed him and walked him over to a bus stop saying, 'Come back and we'll kill ya.' Every time we played there was trouble. There were countless incidents with rival teams, especially the lot from the Raffles pub who were our big local rivals. The very first time I played for Tarana, I came on as a sub in the second half and Sudell nutted a bloke on the other team because he'd called one of our players a cunt. He got sent off. But when it kicked off en masse everyone used to get stuck in. One game we had four players sent off in the first half-hour. We were losing 10–2, then another one of us got the red card and they had to abandon the game. There weren't enough of us left to play. Eventually Tarana got slung out of the league.

The weekend after we'd sacked Deayton from the band there was a five-a-side football tournament in Sheerness in Kent. The Army & Navy pub in Plaistow had a team playing there which turned out to include Vince Riordan, the Sham 69 roadie. Everyone had heard of Vince. He was about twenty, twenty-one, which to us seemed much older, and he had a reputation both from football and from being part of the punk rock scene. He played rhythm guitar in a local band called the Dead Flowers, who were Darren Murphy's band with Kenny Scott before he formed Wasted Youth. They were fucking awful, a real racket, the worst band I'd ever seen. They used to walk off stage to the sound of their own footsteps. Vince would put his guitar down, order a pint and light up a fag as casually as if he'd just walked into the pub. But at least he knew a few chords. After the match, Mick got speaking to him over a few beers and decided Vince was the man for the band. He had the right profile. He had the look; he was into the music and was part of the scene. So Mick just came out and asked him if he fancied learning the bass and joining the band.

Two days later they had a meet in the Army. Vince said he was on board and they went and bought a bass guitar. We recruited Andy Scott on drums, who was Kenny's brother. Andy didn't have the look for the band, because he was a Goth, but he was a shit-hot drummer. We started doing rehearsals and the band really began to click. There was chemistry there.

In the meantime, we'd had a photo session for the single. We invited Garry Bushell and Jimmy Pursey along to be on the cover with me and Mickey because in fairness the record would never have happened without the two of them. The photos were shot in Polydor Studios. Mick designed the back using old photos of us as kids. And that was it: we had our first single out. Now we needed to play more gigs to spread the word.

The first one with the new line-up was a half-hour slot supporting The Tickets at the good old Bridge House. Bushell came down with Robbi Millar to review it – we never told them it was only our second-ever gig in front of a paying audience. We were a bit rough on the night, but it went well. What I noticed immediately was that another, older crowd had turned up to see us. It wasn't just family and the Rubber Glove Firm any more. Because of the Vince connection, all these people I'd never met came along. A lot of them turned out to be ICF. There was Gary Hodges, Johnny Butler, Gary Dickle, Carlton Leach, who were all notorious in their own right as the Britannia Disco Groovers. Grant Fleming was there, too, through the Sham connection, along with some of the Glory Boys who'd followed Secret Affair, like Hoxton Tom McCourt. Tom was Spurs; he was a legendary character in youth cult circles and went on to form the 4-Skins with Hodges. Other West Ham faces included Wellsy, Binnsy and Steve 'H' Harmer, who were all to become our road crew. Then there was Barney Rubble, who was the poet laureate of West Ham, Bernie Hoolihan, Ken and Frank, Doug with his perm, Danny Harrison, Mad Dickie and Mark Nelson, formerly of the Beacontree skins. John O'Connor, who was Arsenal and a Menace fan, was there, Danny Thompson the boxer. I think Mutt and Jeff, the Dim brothers from Leytonstone were there too. Plus some of the other Brit Disco Groovers like Ted Lack. There was a real range of youth cult styles in that audience as well, from soul-boys to suedeheads, as well as terrace geezers. If you'd looked closely you'd have seen ex-skinheads, Mods and Glory Boys with grown-out crops, tonic jackets, Sta-Prest, Levis and Harringtons. A real amalgamation. They were boys from North London, South London, Essex and Kent. They were mostly smart and as hard as fuck. It was the most awesome collection of street-fighters and headcases that I'd ever seen gathered in any one place that wasn't a football ground. They all seemed to be under one roof that night and for some reason or other it all just clicked. We went down really well, which was even more surprising. They called us back on for an encore. I remember shrugging and saying, 'OK, punish y'selves.' There was a real buzz about the group all over London from that night on. The review in *Sounds* called us 'the real Sham'.

After the gig I remember sitting talking to this big geezer who turned out to be Hoxton Tom, and I thought, What a nice fella. Tom and the other older blokes were telling us all about the Sham days. They seemed to take to us because we were the real thing, East End boys. We weren't playing at it and dropping aitches for effect.

It was quite amazing. This was only our second gig and all these faces had turned up and it felt so right. We had met the people who were to become the hardcore Cockney Rejects firm. Later, their ranks would be swelled by other notorious characters such as Andy Swallow, Scully, Tony Barker and the Meakin brothers, Danny and Ricky.

I suppose I was in awe of them in a way. I knew they were big players. I was aware of the ICF and curious about them. But the funny thing was, although they were older, none of them ever took liberties with me and Mick. I think that was because a lot of them were from Stratford or further out in Essex and we had that bit of Custom House mystique about us. That stood us in good stead because we were an unknown quantity.

The gig also got us our first review in *Sounds*. The single was out. The first pressing of 5,000 sold out in a fortnight, and it went on to sell 30,000 copies. It was an alternative-chart Number One.

Suddenly, it felt like we were truly on our way.

CHAPTER SIX

We Are The Firm

There ain't gonna be no argument
There ain't gonna be no sentiment
I don't like what you just said
Now I'm gonna smash your head
R-R-R-R-R are you ready to ruck?

('ARE YOU READY TO RUCK?', THE COCKNEY REJECTS)

The Bridge House was our generation's equivalent of the Roxy. I've lost count of how many times we played there. It was our base, the best gig in East London. It was known primarily as a rock venue. Stevie Marriott often played there. Iron Maiden did a few gigs there too, but mostly it was twelve-bar blues bands like Remus Down Boulevard, Filthy McNaughty, Zaine Griff and Jackie Lynton. I think Terry Murphy the guv'nor would have been content if it had stayed a pub-rock venue, but he was always shrewd around a pound note and he had an open booking policy.

Somehow, without Terry ever being fully aware of what was happening, the Bridge House became a legendary youth cult venue. All the new generation Mod groups played there, bands like The Chords, Purple Hearts and Secret Affair. Everyone from Sham to Madness, Judge Dread to the Selecter played the Bridge. The London Oi scene incubated there. But goth bands and groups like Depeche Mode played it too, with their synthesisers set up on beer crates.

There was never any trouble. They didn't need bouncers at the Bridge. They had the Murphys. Terry had boxed for England, and his sons Lloyd, young Terry and Glen could all handle themselves. I once saw Terry Murphy knock six sailors out in one night. Glen, who went on to star in *London's Burning*, was a middleweight to light-heavyweight who had been in the ring against five world champions. You didn't mess with the Murphys. Everyone in the area had a lot of respect for them. They were a hard family with links to some serious people. Terry had known the Krays and had run with the hounds. His brother John, who had the Royal Oak, was tragically stabbed to death in a gangland killing a couple of years later.

The Bridge House was our home turf, but we knew we had to get gigs outside of East London if we were ever going to get any further. We had our entourage, but not many places were willing to put us on. That's where Garry Bushell came in again. I knew that he knew Mensi from the Angelic Upstarts and in July 1979 they were playing up at the Nashville. Bushell introduced me to Mensi, but because of his strong South Shields accent I couldn't understand a word he was saying. I thought he was asking who our drummer was and kept telling him 'Andy Scott'. He was actually asking who our distributor was for the 'Flares 'N' Slippers' Ep. I thought he was pissed. But God bless him, he told me he was playing the Electric Ballroom in Camden the following week and said we could come on the bill and play twenty minutes. He said, 'I canna pay ya.' We didn't care. We wanted the gig.

The Ballroom turned out to be another taste of things to come.

The next week we made our way down there, and we had the firm with us. There was Dickle, Carlton, Johnny Butler, Hoxton Tom, Hodges, H, Binnsy, and more. There was a mass of us. We were about thirty-handed that day.

It was a disappointing turn-out for the Upstarts. The Ballroom must have held 1,800 people but there were only 600 or so in, probably because it was a weekday. We went on stage and played. We had about seven songs. I remember there was a punk at the front who looked like Ronald McDonald with spiky hair. He tried to chuck something at us so Vince just went crash and booted him in the mouth, took a few teeth out. There was blood everywhere. I thought, This ain't like the Bridge House, know what I mean? I wasn't used to this.

After that, it started to go off in the audience. We looked down and saw Hoxton Tom upping some boneheads, so we all piled down off the stage and sorted it out, all except for Andy Scott who just held the punk up. He was a bit of a jacket holder. Later we found out it was Tom's suit that started it. Tom was wearing a grey/green mohair whistle (£150 from Levene's in Shoreditch High Street), a light-blue Fred Perry and Hush Puppies: it was the height of suedehead fashion, very dapper. A mob of about forty or so skinheads had gathered around Tom while he was having a beer and watching us play with Doug, Woolwich, Ken, Frank and Barney Rubble. One of them called him a 'fucking soul-boy'. He grinned which wound them up even more. What these idiots didn't know was that Tom was one of the first punks in London: he's pictured on the 'Clash City Rockers' Ep; him and John O'Connor from the days of fighting the Teds up the Kings Road in 1977. Tom was one of the first skins and first Glory Boys too. Think of a youth cult and Tom was in the vanguard of it.

'We're fucking skins,' says one of these spotty muppets.

'No you're not,' replied Tom, who was completely unfazed by the number of them. 'You're just a glue sniffer with a crop.'

And that was it. It kicked off. That's when us and the road-crew steamed off the stage and got stuck in. We were outnumbered but we pummelled them with ease. It ended up with the so-called 'skins' taking refuge behind the bouncers on the stairs up to the fire exit. Tom pulled one over the top of the bouncers and gave him a dig. The bouncers didn't do a thing. They backed off and that was it. We got back on stage and finished the set.

Afterwards, all of us went on to what was laughably called the VIP bar upstairs. It was nothing special, just an empty bar with a bird's-eye view of the main Ballroom dance-floor. We got some beers in and settled down to watch the Upstarts. There was a little fat middle-aged bald geezer up there who looked like Danny DeVito and who turned out to be their manager Tony Gordon, our future manager.

The band came on and we noticed that the lowlife 'skins' had now grown to a mob of about ninety strong. Thinking we'd gone, they started picking on these three punks in the audience for no reason. Turned out the boneheads were Chelsea, and mostly British Movement. The punks weren't hurting anyone. The skins were attacking them just because they were punks. They got hold of one young kid and started playing football with him, kicking him around the floor, bashing the shit out of him. There was a lot of silly '*sieg heil*-ing' going on.

Mensi was getting all concerned on stage but he didn't *do* anything. We just looked at each other, and Vince said, 'Fuck it, this ain't right.'

We put our beers down, took our coats off and H said, 'Come on then, we know what we've gotta do.'

We piled down both sets of stairs in a pincer movement and absolutely mullered those boneheads. We were outnumbered three-to-one by the glue-sniffing scum but we caned 'em all over the hall. As Tom said later, it felt like a spaghetti western.

Barney picked up the young punk off the floor and made sure he was OK. On stage Mensi had started crying. He walked off, the gig was cut short and we were asked to leave by the security, very politely. We felt elated. We'd won the day. We'd beaten the granny out of the lowlife.

On the way out I caught sight of Tony Gordon shaking his head. Afterwards he said to Mensi, 'Don't you ever, ever, ever come into contact with that scum again.' Meaning us! Although, of course, when there was a pound note in it for him, he was round us like a fly round shit.

We never found out what the boneheads didn't like about Tom's suit, whether it was the colour or the stitching.

I think we did the right thing that night, we stopped these punks getting victimised; but at the same time we'd ruined the gig for Mensi, so I had mixed feelings about it. From a purely selfish point of view, I was worried that we'd never get booked for another gig outside East London again. But I felt sorry for Mensi too. I didn't know him well enough then to contact him and apologise. I don't think I could have stopped it if I'd wanted too. It wasn't in my hands; if everyone is piling in, you're obliged to stand by your mates. That's how they operate. They'd done it to keep the peace at Sham gigs; they did it all the time at West Ham.

That's how it was. You were either in with it or you weren't and, unfortunately, from that day on I was in.

CHAPTER SEVEN

The Greatest Cockney Rip Off

A couple of weeks later we got a phone call from Rat Scabies. The Damned were playing the Bridge House and they wanted us to support them. We leaped at the chance. This was an opportunity for us to prove ourselves as a band opening up for punk icons on our home turf. Maybe we'd even blow them off the stage.

The gig happened shortly after the IRA had blown up Lord Mountbatten. The Damned were on stage sound checking when we arrived. There were a lot of people in the place already and the atmosphere was unusually hostile. A few bods were really screwing out Captain Sensible. I have no idea why; he didn't deserve it. But give him his due, the Captain kept his nerve. Scabies was shitting himself. He said to us, 'Are we going to be all right?'

I said, 'Course you are, you're with us.' And they would have been too, if only they'd thought about where they were and what they were saying.

By the time we went on stage, the place was heaving. There was a small pocket of older British Movement there. The BM was a small, violent neo-Nazi sect. We called them the German Movement. This particular little firm was the mob which used to follow Sham and had caused Pursey so much grief. They were the reason Sham could no longer play London. They were older than our firm and had a reputation. There were people like 'Mad' Matty Morgan, his brother Steve, Dick Barton, Glenn Bennett and their hangers-on. We didn't want anything to do with them. We hated their politics as much as we hated the hippy Left. We were anti-politics, we fucking hated all politicians with a vengeance, but we were prepared to tolerate them in the audience as long as they didn't cause us any grief. As soon as we came on stage, they started a bit of silly *sieg heil*-ing and immediately I said, 'Fucking cut that out for starters, we don't want none of that.' And they did, which was just as well. I could see our boys getting the hump with them. It was very rare to see any of that shit at the Bridge House anyway. No one wanted it. I know for sure that we could have battered them if it had come to it. Our firm was heavier than they were, but, because they were a bit older than us, we were a little bit wary of them. It wasn't until a bit later that we sorted them out properly – and for good.

We went down well, and there was no trouble... until The Damned came on stage and that idiot Sensible said, 'This is a song for Lord Mountbatten, it's called "Stretcher Case"...' Well, Hoxton Tom was absolutely livid – and he wasn't the only one. A large section of the crowd now wanted to kill Sensible. If there hadn't been such widespread respect for the Murphys, the band would have been lynched there and then on the stage. As it was they played a short set to a hostile audience. In every respect we'd blown them away. The stage had been invaded by our fans, we did encores. The Damned went down like a sack of shit. They got nothing from the crowd except disdain. Afterwards, they locked themselves away upstairs with their little mob of supporters, called the Croydon gang. Tom wanted to steam up there and decimate them, but in the end Lloyd Murphy and one mate went in there and absolutely sorted them out. They upped a couple of the mouthier ones, told them their fortune, paid them and chucked them out. They left very quietly. The Damned were doomed in East London after that night. I felt for Rat Scabies because he was a nice, genuine geezer, he'd do anything to help you. But for once the trouble wasn't down to us.

We decided to get our heads down and work. We'd asked Garry Bushell to be our manager and he agreed, even though it meant he wouldn't be able to write about us in *Sounds* any more. The first thing we had to do was write new songs. We got into a rehearsal studio in Poplar and wrote numbers like 'I Ain't Got Nothing'. Vince and his driving bass lines had changed our musical direction. We were developing a heavier sound and leaving the poppier, Skids-y, Lurkers-style feel of early songs like 'Flares 'N' Slippers' behind us. We were finding our own niche.

Bushell chased up Pursey, and booked us to go and see him at Polydor and play him some of our new songs. He liked 'I Ain't Got Nothing', but he wanted to change the lyrics. He wanted to call it 'I'm Not A Fool'. He'd written these words which even when I sing them now strike me as doggerel. His lyrics went: 'I'm not so ignorant/I'm not a fool/So keep your intelligence/I am not a fool.' I was dead against this because his words were meaningless shit. I said, 'I can't sing these.' But Pursey was adamant. What could we do? He was the established star, we were in his studio, on his time, we had to give in to him or walk out. We gave in. We figured maybe he knew what he was doing. Pursey was very charismatic, full of gusto. He had clout and he was very persuasive. Also he was very in with Bushell, even though I know at the time Bushell wasn't seeing eye to eye with the direction Sham were taking. He was going a bit loopy with soppy songs like 'Mister You're A Better Man Than I'. Musically, Sham were on a slippery slope, but Pursey saw in us that raw energy that Sham had at the beginning – and which would eventually make his band seem redundant. So we set up the guitars and the sound was awesome. We knocked that one out and we did 'East End' too, both recorded and mixed in the same night. They were great tracks, despite the ropey words.

The next day Bushell and Pursey got stuck in to the next big obstacle: getting us a deal. It was manic. We had offers in from Decca, Polydor and Warner Brothers. We were close to signing with Polydor, and then out of the blue EMI wanted to see us. And what made us laugh was we'd only played a handful of gigs. Probably no more than the Sex Pistols had. This was our version of the Great Rock 'n' Roll Swindle or, as we called it later, the Greatest Cockney Rip Off.

Bushell and Pursey took us up to this big meeting with Chris Briggs at EMI's offices in Manchester Square – there was me, Mick and Vince; we didn't bother taking Andy Scott because we knew we were going to replace him pretty soon. He was drumming with his brother's band Wasted Youth who were signing to Terry Murphy's Bridge House label anyway, and obviously he couldn't stay in two bands. We sat there and Pursey played the new stuff on a big reel-to-reel. Briggs listened quietly, tapping his foot and said, 'Yeah, I love it; we'll have to do something.' Then Bushell and Pursey negotiated a deal, I think it was a £25,000 advance for the first album and a few other odds

and sods. In fact, the deal they hammered out for us was for
£130,000 because we were signed for four albums, with the
advance going up £5K per album; with options on both sides after
the four contracted albums. After the deal was done, Bushell told
us he couldn't carry on managing us any more. Now that we were
signed, he couldn't combine being our manager and writing for
Sounds. He had to choose, and he decided to carry on writing. It
was heart-breaking. He'd done so much for us. He advised us to
sign with a proper management company who could deal with
EMI and the publishers and all the other suits. Jimmy Pursey said
he knew just the man – our old mate Tony Gordon, who was his
manager and Mensi's manager, too. The man who had called us
scum now wanted to represent us. But Pursey was very insistent.
He said we could trust Gordon, that he'd be the right man for us
and that we could achieve great things with him at the helm. And
we listened. The outcome was fairly predictable: signing with
Tony Gordon turned out to be one of the biggest professional
mistakes we were ever going to make.

It was up there with signing with Wilf Wright, the manager
who eventually replaced him.

CHAPTER EIGHT

Flash Gordon

Tony Gordon's company, Wedge Music, had a basement office in the West End; in Grosvenor Street, just off Bond Street. It was quite impressive, with plush carpets and Lulu gold discs on the wall – he'd managed her before he took on Sham 69. When we signed up with him, my dad had to come along with me because I was only fifteen and I needed an adult to sign on my behalf. My dad took the guilt of signing me up with that man to the grave. Things never worked out as we expected them to. Gordon sat me and me dad down in big leather chairs in his office and outlined all these great plans he had for our future. He said in three years I would own my own detached house. He asked me what car I wanted. I was fifteen. The only car I'd ever had came with a remote control. He said to my dad, 'We'll get him a Mercedes', and when he saw Dad wasn't impressed with that he changed tack and said he was going to put all our earnings in trust until I was eighteen, and take care of the pension and National

Insurance side of things. I'd never have to worry about money again. It was a lovely idea. To be honest, I never liked the bloke, but he had a way with words. I'll give him that.

It all seemed fantastic but we didn't sign there and then; we took the contracts away and showed them to a lawyer. It wasn't until years later that we found out that this bloke was bent. The contract he advised us it was OK to sign was one he'd drawn up. He said it was all standard. I mean, we needed someone to decipher it. The contract seemed as big as the *Yellow Pages* and full of clauses and sub-clauses. I didn't know what a clause was, and I don't think me dad had much of a clue either. He'd worked in the docks all his life.

The lawyers set a signing date to complete the deal at EMI; and Gordon took us in his chauffeur-driven limo back to the record company. Inevitably, we fell out with him on the journey. One of the little things we did to pass the time back then was to go 'sticking'. If we were ever going anywhere by car, we'd have a stick and eggs with us for the express purpose of egging and sticking cyclists. The idea was to stick eggs in their spokes if they were at traffic lights or to chuck them at them if they were in motion. The stick was to whack 'em across the arse as we passed. We were sitting in the back of Gordon's limo on the way to EMI and Vince spotted a target. I hit the electronic button, the window came down and I whacked a cyclist right across the harris with this big stick. It was a classic. Tony Gordon went nuts. He was spluttering with rage. 'What the hell are you doing?' he went. 'What the hell have you done to that cyclist?'

Suddenly the limo driver is threatening to stop the car if we don't behave. In the meantime, we'd stopped at some lights and the irate cyclist caught up with us. He was ranting and raving. 'Come back here,' he yelled. 'You bunch of cunts; you think you're fucking hard.'

Well, that's when the eggs came into play. Down came the window and we gave him a proper pelting. It was fucking hilarious...

Gordon was fuming. He ordered us never to do it again. I said, 'All right, we were only having a bit of fun, that's what we do.' He never said another word to us for the rest of the journey.

We had the big meeting with EMI – and left the eggs and the stick in the limo for that. Chris Briggs came down with his corporate lawyers, we signed and he handed Tony Gordon a cheque for £25,000. Out of that, Gordon gave us all a cheque for a monkey apiece, £500. We came out of the meeting and he wouldn't let us back in the limo. I don't know why. He told us to get the underground home. Instead, we all went straight to a bank and opened accounts with our £500. I withdrew all of mine in pound notes. I thought I'd cracked it. I was bunking school for the meeting, but now, with my leather jacket stuffed with cash, I thought I'd go back and hit the tuck shop. By the time I got there it was lunchtime. I bowled up in me jacket and Doctor Martens, pulled out a big wad of notes and said, 'Right, who wants what?'

The others probably hit the pub. Not me. I just bought Kit-Kats, Bounty Bars and teas all round for me mates. It only cost me three quid! To me, it was blinding. I felt like I was as rich as Croesus. I didn't know what the fuck to spend it on. I didn't do drugs, didn't really drink. I'd had my first four pints at Custom House Working Men's Club in January 1979 when I was fourteen and I'd spewed up all the way home. My main vice was pyrotechnics. So, now I had all this wedge, I was looking for things to spend it on. The first thing I bought was a pair of steel-cap DMs and then I hit the local shops for fireworks. Me and my younger brother cleaned them out. We made three journeys up there and loaded everything into an old doll's pram which me mum had kept for sentimental reasons. With the couple of hundred quid I had left I bought an Atari Space Invaders machine. Cost me £180, I think. So it wasn't any rock 'n' roll lifestyle for me. I didn't blow my advance on birds and nightclubs. It all went on roman candles and Space Invaders. It never occurred to me to save any. I spunked the lot in two weeks.

After that, we were each on £25-a-week band wages. We weren't entirely sensible with the advance, because we needed to buy a backline. We got amps, and Thunderbird guitars. Vince and Mickey were fans of Van Halen and Sabbath and they were studying their backlines. Vince got a Peavey bass amp; Mick had big Marshall stacks, and all these different guitars. I got a Shure microphone which must have cost about fifteen quid.

I always had misgivings about signing with Tony Gordon. I knew he hated us from day one. What we needed was a manager like Terry Lawless or Frank Warren, someone who could tell us what to do and we'd respect them. With Gordon, it was a marriage of convenience. We were a source of income to him, and we saw him as the voice of music-biz experience. But even there I felt Gordon had no feel for our music at all. He made it plain from the start. When he heard the playback of the first album, he tutted. 'Why are your songs so violent?' he said. 'And why is there so much about football? Why can't you sing something more jolly?' And he gave us his suggestion, which was a silly little singsong ditty of 'We are The Cockney Rejects, we are The Cockney Rejects, we are The Cockney Rejects...' It sounded like a nursery rhyme.

We all sat there speechless and looked at Vince who just went, 'Bollocks to this,' and walked out. How this man had gone from Lulu to punk rock is anyone's guess. He was getting twenty-five per cent of our earnings on paper and he hadn't even negotiated our deal for us.

It didn't take long for our relationship to sour. We had a lot of big rows over the years, mostly about money. I remember seeing Mensi in his office near to tears because he couldn't get any float out of him. And Mensi would be demanding to see Gordon, saying, 'I need me money,' and he would never be in for him. He had a go at me once for wearing a Sex Pistols T-shirt because it had a swastika on it. He called me in to his office and started lecturing me about Auschwitz. It wasn't political at all, it was punk. It was like he was completely unaware of how the Pistols had subverted the swastika years before.

I never let him boss me around, even though I was a kid. The rows got worse as time went on because at the start he'd give you half-an-hour for a meeting but later you'd be lucky to see him at all. He had his million-pound home in Holland Park and his West End office with his receptionist and his PA and his talent scout. He was worth a mint. After us, he managed Culture Club – talk about going from one extreme to the other.

I grew to really dislike him. One time we went to his office and I felt he could've given us a bit more time than he did. He was scooting off to some meeting. I had a packet of stink bombs on me and he had a new grey hand-made suit. As he walked past us up the stairs, I broke open the stink bomb and splashed it right up the back of his jacket. He didn't notice. He just carried on walking up and out the door to get into his limo, with a big stain on his whistle and a rapidly spreading odour around him. I just thought, Have that, you fat bastard, yeah.

Just after we signed with EMI we did a gig that we never should have done. Chris Briggs asked us to play unadvertised as part of

71

Jimmy Pursey's 'Pursey's Package' night at the Moonlight club in West Hampstead. It was an odd request. The rest of the bands on the bill were Mods. It felt wrong and we weren't at all keen. But we were persuaded that it was a good idea and that it would keep the record label sweet. The EMI marketing and publicity people wanted to see us, and maybe the poor dears wouldn't feel safe in the East End. So reluctantly we agreed. There would be no advance ads in the music press or on the radio, though. It was just word of mouth. The Moonlight was only a small venue, and it held two hundred at most. It was a Monday night and there weren't that many there. All our usual entourage came along, though, along with a fella called Dicky Galvin; an absolute lunatic who spoke with a lisp. His claim to fame was that Matt Monro, the 1960s crooner, had accidentally run his brother over and killed him. Dicky Galvin hated Matt Monro with a vengeance. He wanted to do him. He once rang up Garry Bushell at *Sounds* and asked him for Matt Monro's home number. I think Bushell gave him Max Splodge's number instead. On one occasion, during a big row with Sunderland at West Ham, Dicky was found in the middle of a load of the away fans with a tape recorder. When Tom asked him what he was doing, he said, 'Taping the aggro!' He was never the full ticket. I'm not too sure where we'd picked him up but he was part of the firm for a while. And this particular night he was absolutely mashed, pilled out of his head.

So we're playing a gig without much of a crowd, there's no real atmosphere, all these bods from EMI have come along to see us live for the first time and, to complicate matters, there were rumblings that the German Movement were after us over things we'd said about them in the press. We weren't bothered, but we were on our guard a bit, just in case Dick Barton and his merry men tried to crash the gig.

We went on stage and start playing. It was a shit night. We couldn't get the crowd going and we wanted to get off stage as quickly as possible. We'd just got into the third number and all of a sudden I heard a huge crash behind me. The whole stack of amps had fallen over. I thought we were being invaded by the BM. But it wasn't that. Dicky Galvin had walked across the stage, totally out of it, tripped over all the leads from the guitars and the amps, and everything just came crashing down. The next minute, H, Binnsy and Kevin Wells were at the side of the stage absolutely kicking the fuck out of him. All I could think of was the EMI people. Briggsy was there, the A&R men, the marketing bods, the PR department. They'd just signed us and this is what they got to see. It was like unwrapping a Christmas present and finding a big fat steaming turd inside.

I don't blame the road crew for attacking Dicky Galvin. I felt like kicking the fuck out of him myself.

The only good thing about the evening was the picture of Tom, Carlton, Dickle, Vince and Johnny Butler that was taken there and which we put on the back of the first album with Mickey's boot kicking into shot.

After the amps came down that was it, show over. We'd gone down like the *Belgrano*. It was a poxy night. To make it worse, a film crew were there making a punk documentary, *Rough Cut & Ready Dubbed*. Luckily, they never filmed Dicky Galvin when he got flung down a flight of stairs later on by Wellsy. Nor when H and Binnsy steamed him. We left him out for the count in a heap. No one seemed too bothered about that.

I was absolutely gutted about the whole experience; it was a disaster of a night. I was due to go to school the next day but I couldn't face it. I was only going in now and then to keep the school board of my parents' backs, but this day I just bunked off.

I spent the day in the khazi with me head in me hands. I thought it was the end of the world. It was the first time a gig had made me depressed. It wasn't the last time.

CHAPTER NINE

Greatest Hits Volume One

The Geggus family silver is hanging on our wall. Our first album, which was modestly titled *Greatest Hits Volume One*, went silver in the UK with over 60,000 sales. It's still selling to this day on CD.

Our first job after signing with EMI and buying some decent equipment was to get into Polydor's studios, just off Bond Street, with Jimmy Pursey and Pete Wilson to record the album. We got started on it just three days after we signed the contract. Of all our early albums it's the one I'm most proud of. I can still listen to *Volume One* 'cos we put everything into it. All the classics are there. We'd already recorded 'East End' and 'I'm Not A Fool', but all the other numbers on it had that same feel. They were about who we were and what we were – songs like 'Fighting In The Streets'. They came straight from the heart.

There were fourteen songs in all and they pretty much defined the band. 'Someone Like You' was about people who were forced into nine-to-five jobs. That was the norm for people who'd gone to Woodside. You'd leave school and go to work in the Tate & Lyle factory. The choices round our way were: doss around in bed all day and be called a lazy bastard; or work in the factory for shit wages. The song wasn't a dig at people who had to work for a living. I just didn't want to be on that particular treadmill going nowhere and getting nothing but older.

The first song we recorded was 'Ready To Ruck'. To give it an authentic feel we created a bar-room brawl effect in the middle of the track by smashing bottles and glasses. Then we did the other classics: 'Bad Man', 'Shitter', 'Police Car'. We were singing about things we'd experienced. '(They're Gonna) Put Me Away' was about my wrongful arrest: 'They put me in a cell/With a bunch of drunks as well/And I can still remember/That horrible pissy smell'. 'Bad Man' was about one of my in-laws who paid off his gambling debts from the gas money.

'Where The Hell Is Babylon?' was aimed at the hippies in the music press who used to bang on about reggae all the time. It started with a kind of homage to 'Fire Corner' by Clancy Eccles then went on to take the piss out of all the sad white *NME* knobs who hated their own culture and put Rastafarianism on a pedestal. The lyrics went: 'Where the hell is Babylon/I heard it's lot of fun/Can I get there on my bike/Or straight up the M1?'

Then there was 'Fighting In The Streets'. It was about our way of life and it was the only bit of politics on the album – or anti-politics, if you like: 'You all look for solutions/But you can rack your brains/No matter what the government's do/It's never ever gonna change/Wankers hand out leaflets/They'll never ever let it be/I don't care what they do/But they better not come near me'.

Our time in the studio recording those tracks was great. It all went really well. Too well, 'cos one night temptation finally got the better of us. Trouble was, the studios were a bit of a gold mine. At that time Sony Walkmans had just come out. They were all the rage and there were loads of them in the studios, just lying about. So, five of them had to go for a start. As if that wasn't enough, another night we got really pissed and decided to smash the place up. We got into the executive offices and turned them over. There was graffiti involved – in one room there was a gold disc on the wall for Ike & Tina Turner. That soon became Ike & Stinky Turner.

It was senseless but it was a laugh. I can't blame anybody; it was a band decision, although it's fair to say that Vince was the main mover when it came to anything disappearing. He was a career thief. His uncle was Jack 'The Hat' McVitie, the hood that Reggie Kray killed. If Vince hadn't been in the band he'd have been a burglar. Thieving was his bag. People said we were a band from the wrong side of the tracks, but in Vince's case he'd have been *on* the tracks holding up the train.

Jimmy Pursey wasn't involved in any of this chaos. He'd made the mistake of going early and leaving us to our own devices. We were supposed to be doing over-dubs with poor old Pete Wilson, but he couldn't control us at all. While Mickey was in doing a guitar over-dub, or I was doing some vocals, the rest were getting up to terrible mischief. Not just nicking beer and fucking about, either. People were shitting in desks, pissing in filing cabinets, things like that. Talk about biting the hand that feeds you. Why it was done I don't know. We were fucking animals.

Not too surprisingly, when we turned up for work the next morning this huge lump of a security guard refused to let us in. The Cockney Rejects were banned from the premises. Rejected.

We played innocent, of course, but there was no way they were letting us back into the studios. We walked back to Tony Gordon's office, where he read us the riot act. Polydor Studio claimed we had caused nearly £2,000 worth of damage, he said. We basically said 'Bollocks, we don't know what you're talking about', because that's the unwritten law. Never hold your hands up to anything. But Gordon wasn't having any of that. The studio had said either we pay the two grand or we didn't get the master tapes. We were fucked. We'd done over half the album by then. To start again would have been a financial disaster. We had no choice: we had to face the music with EMI, who were not best pleased. We tried to farm out the blame a bit, saying it hadn't been us who'd caused the worst damage. It was outsiders, we said, some people we'd picked up in the pub and didn't really know. They were drinking in the studios while we were in recording, and it all got a bit out of hand. They kind of believed us and it ended up that we'd pay back the two grand out of our advance and we'd get the tapes. We were still barred from Polydor Studios, though. That was a bummer, but it was our fault.

So there we were. We'd pissed two grand down the drain and now had to trek out to Shepperton Studios in Middlesex to piece together the rest of the album. But it could have been worse; EMI could have sacked us. They would have been well within their rights. They were absolutely disgusted by us.

But looking back, it doesn't seem so terrible. To be honest, we missed a trick by not leaking the story to the tabloids. It would have been a brilliant coup. You could imagine the *Daily Mail* frothing at the mouth about these terrible foul-mouthed yobs causing anarchy: they should be given jail sentences, not recording contracts. If that happened today, with a band like Oasis or the Libertines, their management would play it for all it's worth to get a load of free publicity. After all, everyone loves a bad boy, don't they? I'm amazed no one had the sense to do it, but I think the whole industry had been badly freaked out by the Sex Pistols a couple of years before. The Pistols had really pushed boundaries and the feeling now was that a band couldn't be seen to be out of order. It's only with hindsight that the Pistols' antics have been accepted as loveable and eccentric. Even Ozzy Osborne had to endure years of hatred and contempt for his exploits before he became the patron saint of rock rebellion. I wouldn't be surprised if he ends up with a knighthood.

Do I regret what happened at Polydor? No. I'm glad we smashed it up. I couldn't stand the fucking place.

That was the first time I thought we were going to get sacked. It wasn't the last. There were at least nine other occasions when they could have given us the bullet. We never learnt our lesson. We were running wild through the industry and loving every minute. There were incidents outside EMI, goings-on inside the EMI building. Nowhere was safe.

We really got hauled over the carpet because of what we did at Capital Records, which was right next to EMI's studios. We used to do a lot of night recording sessions at EMI and we discovered that it was really easy to break into Capital. There was a window out back and we just hauled it open and let ourselves in. We had t-shirts, records, the lot. We were the only band in rock history whose road crew included a look-out.

We used to slip whole boxes of tour jackets out of that back window. We got really blatant with it, too. Once, Mickey had so much stuff shoved up inside his Harrington that as he walked past security one of the guards said, 'What's up mate, are you expecting?' He pulled open Mickey's jacket and all these records cascaded onto the floor. Mick just shrugged and said he was taking them outside for a photo session. It might have made sense if they'd been Cockney Rejects records.

It was wholesale larceny. Of course, it didn't take the record company long to work out who was responsible. They called us in. 'Capital Records has just been ransacked', they said. 'everything's been thieved, every drop of drink has gone, every t-shirt's vanished, the entire stock of albums, the singles, everything'. We denied all knowledge but it was blatantly obvious we'd done it. When you looked at the window ledge you could see the Doc Marten's footprints where we'd stood there, passing the stolen goods out.

They could have sacked us, but it probably would have cost them a few quid to do that. Plus, as usual, we didn't admit to anything. It was up to them to prove that we'd done it and they didn't have anything concrete. If they'd offered to pay us off to make us go away I probably wouldn't have been too sad. But they didn't get rid of us.

I suppose after sacking the Pistols a few years before – and seeing them go on to sell so many records for someone else –EMI were reluctant to sack anybody. Even us.

CHAPTER TEN

The Best Of Times

How we weren't banned from *Top Of The Pops* after our first appearance I have no idea. It's always amazed me. Every time we went on the show there was agg. There were punch-ups, a row with Steve Wright, we upset Legs & Co – twice. One time Vince kept collapsing on stage while we were recording. Another time we smashed up a dressing room out of sheer frustration. Then there was the time one of the Rejects pulled a blade on another band's manager in the studio as the show was being recorded. Talk about threats and rucks and rock'n'roll. And yet they had us on there three times in two months! They must have been gluttons for punishment.

This period between March and May 1980 was the best it ever got for me. I spent the whole time walking on air. Our first album charted, West Ham were having a great Cup run, and the coverage the band was getting in *Sounds* was really building up. We had those three *Top Of The Pops* appearances in six weeks with two different singles, despite all the chaos we caused up there. Could life get any better? I was absolutely riding high. Then West Ham won the FA Cup and that was it. Life was as good as it was ever going to get. Suddenly we were the biggest name on our manor. We felt like we'd made it.

I was fifteen when I did *Top Of The Pops* for the first time. It was three days before my sixteenth birthday, what a present that was! *Top Of The Pops* meant something back then. It had been my ambition to do that show ever since I was a little kid watching bands like Slade and Sweet. The show was a big event in our house. It was an appointment to view every Thursday night. We used to write down what sweets we wanted before it came on, it was always toffee treats for me. I remember eating me sweets and then Sweet would come on and set me old man off. He'd go, 'Look at them bloody poofs, with all that make-up,' and I'd be going, 'Yeah, but think of the money they're making, Dad.' That's always where I wanted to be.

We'd had a near miss in February with 'Bad Man', our second single on EMI. Back then the new chart positions used to be announced on a Tuesday afternoon and on the Monday EMI called us up to their offices for a big meeting. Going by the sales, they were expecting 'Bad Man' to go Top Fifty that week and that meant we'd get the show. We were all fired up, talking about how we were going to look, how we'd perform. A good *Top Of The Pops* appearance could make the difference between a single stagnating at thirty-something in the charts or shooting up into the Top Twenty. I went home that night so full of it I could hardly sleep. I was a kid! The next morning they phoned us up and said we'd only gone in at sixty-five. EMI were as frustrated as we were because the record had shifted enough copies to chart by normal expectations but not in the right shops. I was devastated.

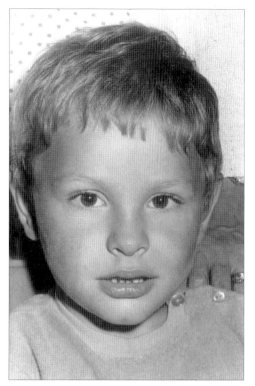

Top left: Me aged four. A couple of years on I was already rocking the mic (*top right*), though 'Stinky' Turner was yet to be born.

Bottom: Me and Mick, not half as innocent as we looked!

Jeff's show!

JEFF Geggus won an Essex boxing title on Saturday — and maintained a unique tradition for his road.

He follows in a long line of champions who have all been born and bred in Varley Road, Custom House.

Varley Road has produced Olympic representative Bobby Kelsey and former Southern Area heavyweight champion Roy Enifer.

It also produced double national schoolboy champion Kevin Bowers, who lives just next door to Geggus. And it produced men like one-time Army middleweight champion Fred Jackson, last year's National Association of Boys Clubs champion Martin Jasper, former Essex schoolboy champion, Mark Thompson, and another former Army champion Tommy Lawrence.

At East India Hall, Poplar, on Saturday Geggus took his unbeaten run to 12 contests and assured Varley Road of staying on the boxing map. Geggus who boxes for the Barking club, outpointed Tony Byrne of the Repton club.

I was well into boxing from the start. Here I am posing with my trophies and my younger brother, Trev(*top right*), holding the 1977 Barking ABC Boxer of the Year trophy, and making the papers.

Below: My dear mum and dad.

Some of our first promo shots. Up top is one from October 1979. From left there's Mickey, Me, Vince and Andy Scott who played on our first album, but left after four months in the band. (*Bottom left*) Mickey holds his Gibson, and (*bottom right*) at Polydor studios with a young Garry Bushell (next to me) and Sham 69's Jimmy Pursey, who produced *Greatest Hits Volume 1* album for us.

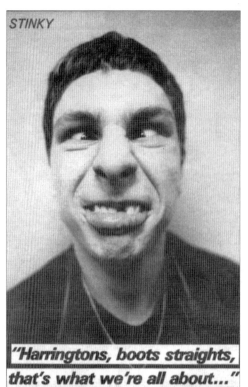

STINKY

"Harringtons, boots straights, that's what we're all about..."

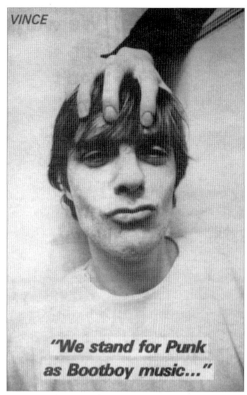

VINCE

"We stand for Punk as Bootboy music..."

NIGEL

"But we don't wanna be known as fighters..."

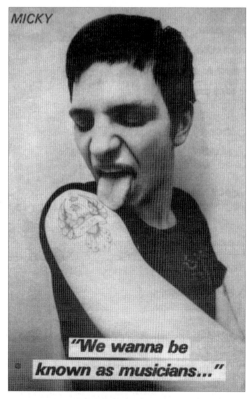

MICKY

"We wanna be known as musicians..."

The Rejects spell out our philosophy on the front page of *Sounds* in 1980.

At the Nuneaton 77 Club on our first tour in 1980. No frills, no bullshit, we gave the crowd just what they wanted – punk.

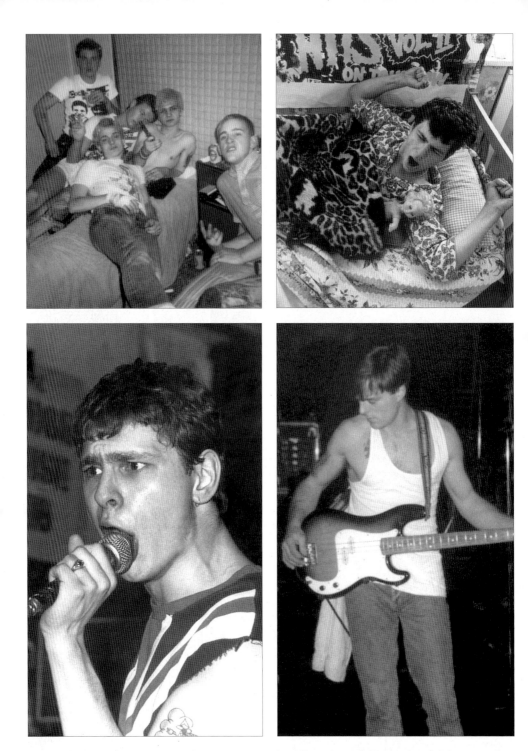

Top right: I don't know why they got me to do this promo shot, but it somehow made sense at the time!

Top left: The boys on tour. Getting wrecked back at the hotel in Northampton. (*From left to right*) Andy Swallow, Grant Fleming, John Bong, Mickey and Nigel.

Bottom: Me singing in Hackney – or 'acne'! – and Vince Riordan on bass.

Judas Priest had Harleys, I had a chopper with a flat tyre.

Top: Us at West Ham, home of the ICF and some of our most loyal fans.

Bottom: Vince, Mick and Me on 29th July 1981, Charles and Diana's wedding day, in a shoot for *Melody Maker*.

The good news came soon after though, in March. Our first album, *Greatest Hits Vol 1*, charted. Garry Bushell called us and said the album was going to go Top Thirty. And it did. It went in at number twenty-two and that was like a fantastic omen. We went on to record the new single, 'The Greatest Cockney Rip Off' and I knew in my heart of hearts that 'Rip Off' would be the song to get us on *Top Of The Pops*. When it came out, the sales for the first week were looking good. On the Tuesday morning, Mum took a call at home. Mick was in bed as usual and I heard her shout up that Rob Warr was on the phone from EMI. I ran down the stairs, leaped down the last five and picked up the phone. He went, 'All right, Stinky, I've got some really good news for you. Are you ready for this?' He was stringing it out deliberately, he was a right tart. And then he told us we were in the charts at forty-seven, we'd got the show and we had to get up to EMI as soon as possible.

I went 'YEEEESSSSS!' I slammed the phone down and pulled Mick out of bed. I had to, he was still half a-kip. I was shaking him saying, 'Come on, *Top Of The Pops* is happening. We're gonna be on fucking *Top Of The Pops*.'

Course, there were no mobile phones then, so we couldn't ring Vince. We had to run up to his house in Gardener Road near the Abbey Arms pub and hammer on his door to get him up. It was about 11.00 am. The feeling running the three-quarters of a mile up that road to his house was just euphoria. I was still at school, even though I was bunking it. It was such a buzz.

We got the tube up to EMI, and they treated us like lords and took us down to some BBC studio in Maida Vale, West London, and said we had to re-record the backing track for the show. It was nothing like the original record. It's very had to recapture the feel of a song when you first record it, and when we heard it go out on the show it wasn't the same at all. To be honest it was crap. But that's what we had to do; then we had to wait until Wednesday, because that's when *Top Of The Pops* was recorded. In the meantime, I got a message to everyone at school to let them know I'd be on the TV on Thursday night. I wanted them all to watch it and see me up there.

Of course, our first trip to the BBC didn't pass without incident. We took the underground to the studio, arriving at about 10.30 am for the sound tests. The assistant producer showed us the stage and he told us Steve Wright was going to be the presenter. Then they told us we had to be made up. No way! I had a few zits but I didn't want no fucking make-up. They said I had to have it to stop the shine on the cameras. If we refused, we couldn't do the show. That's all I heard all day, 'Do this, do that, or you won't do the show.'

They stuck us in make-up and we're sitting there, not too happy about it, when some bod came walking past with these cracking birds. I said, 'Is that Legs & Co?' and he turned round and went, 'No, it's the fucking Stranglers.'

I thought, You cheeky bastard! He was a big lump with swept-back hair, a lot bigger than me and obviously twice my age, but none of that registered. I just thought, He ain't talking to us like that. I leaped out of the chair and tried to grab him by the throat. He was going, 'Get him off of me,' squealing like a pig. It annoyed me because I was just being nice and he was sarky back. I remember he was wearing a black leather jacket and was very well spoken but I don't know who he was; he might have been a choreographer or their manager. It didn't really matter. To my mind he was just a rude arrogant pig and I went at him like a fucking tiger. The bloke shit his pants. Legs & Co were screaming, the BBC people all went into a flap. They were trying to drag me off him and there was make-up flying everywhere. Looking back, it was hilarious.

Luckily for old wobbly gob, the assistant producer knew exactly what to say to make me back off: let him go or you won't do the show. I took a bit of persuading but I eventually let him go. After that, we retired to the bar where we killed time drawing crossed hammers on the back of Mick's Harrington jacket. My choice of outfit was far more glamorous. I had a pair of braces and a Tufty Club badge, just for a piss-take. Very rock star.

We managed to stay out of trouble until the show started filming at 7.00 pm. By then we had our entourage there – Wellsy, H, Danny Harrison and Grant Fleming – and they went up to Steve Wright and asked if they could stand with him when he introduced the band. Steve Wright said, 'No problem,' but, when he came to do it, he changed his mind. He just waved at them and said, 'I don't want you here.' Very off-hand he was.

Well, that was like a red rag to a bull. Never mind 'hang the DJ', H wanted to kill him. He went into one. 'The fucking cunt,' he said. 'I'll rip his fucking head off, telling me to fuck off and that he don't want me to stand with him, I'll fucking kill him...'

Steve Wright, who heard every word of it, looked like he'd seen a ghost. The colour drained from his face. We got H into the corner and told him to calm down, but he'd caused so much commotion they'd had to stop filming the show.

The producer came downstairs and went into one, saying that if H didn't go we'd be off the show. Now what the fuck do you do? This is our big moment but H is our mate. If I tell him to go, he'll think I'm sniding him. I couldn't do it. So we let him have the choice. I said, 'If you have to walk, we'll all walk with you. Fuck the show and fuck the BBC.' That was the sort of camaraderie we had then. We'd waited so long for this but we were loyal and we stuck together through thick and thin.

Luckily, H said, 'I won't ruin it for you; I can't let you chuck away your big chance over me. I'll go.' And off he went.

You could still sense the tension in the studio but they put us on to the stage and that was it. Our big moment… which turned out to be a bit of a let-down. For starters, it wasn't a punk crowd at all, just a load of gormless-looking soul boys. To make it worse, I had to mime into a microphone. There was more atmosphere on the moon. The floor manager kept telling us to do the song again and again. When it eventually went out on TV, they cut the song back to about ninety seconds, probably to punish us for the H incident. Ninety seconds. I've had pisses that lasted longer than that.

But, despite all that, the single went up to twenty-three the next week. When it went up to twenty-one the following week we went back on *Top Of The Pops* and this time they showed the whole song. They also took us into a proper photographic studio to have a picture done for the Top Thirty countdown. So there'd be Johnny Logan, David Essex, Shalamar and then The Cockney Rejects. Priceless.

We'd arrived! Naturally we had our photo done with a West Ham scarf, just to fly the flag. It went down really well with the kids at school but not the teachers. A couple of them said they were ashamed of me and that the band looked like hooligans. But we weren't hooligans. That's just how it was and who we were.

I remember the feeling waiting to see ourselves on TV that first Thursday night. It was just fantastic. All the family sat together to watch it. The wait was agonising, and when we did come on it seemed to be over just like that. The family all loved it, but for me it felt like a bit of an anti-climax. I said to Mick, 'Was that it?' It wasn't how I'd dreamed it would be when I used to watch T. Rex and Slade on there. I mean, how can you compare what we did to someone like Noddy Holder? We belted out one minute and thirty seconds of rabble-rousing punk, he was a rock god! But then again, you can't have everything. I'd done the show and that was one ambition ticked off the list.

All I was worried about that night was my old man. He was in bad health at the time. He'd had a second heart-attack and a big operation. Someone made the mistake of showing him a *Sounds* front cover with us on it. It was a picture by Ross Halfin with me pulling the ugliest face imaginable. The shock of seeing it nearly sent dad back to casualty.

The feedback from 'Rip Off' was fantastic and a month later we were back in the charts with 'I'm Forever Blowing Bubbles'. Everything was going well for us. Looking back, that really was the high point of our career as a punk band.

'Bubbles' didn't do quite as well. I think it peaked at about thirty-five. I'd hoped it would have done better, but then again if you were a Rejects fan but you followed Arsenal or Manchester United you weren't going to buy a record about West Ham, were you? Little did we know that associating ourselves so closely with the team, and especially the ICF, was like pushing a self-destruct button.

It was EMI who asked us to do 'Bubbles'. They wanted to cash in on West Ham having an FA Cup run that year. Originally, it was going to be us or Iron Maiden who recorded it, because Maiden were from the East End and they were big Hammers fans too. When Iron Maiden pulled out, it fell to us to do it. I wish they had recorded it instead of us, 'cos they certainly wouldn't have ended up playing the places we were booked into and they wouldn't have had shit thrown at them on stage. And to be fair, their attitude was different. They'd go out wearing claret and blue sweat bands and say, 'We're West Ham, you're Leeds, let's party.' We'd go out with crossed-hammers tattoos and our attitude was more 'We're West Ham, who wants it?'

Ultimately it was EMI's decision. Maybe they thought it was more appropriate for us to do it. Maiden were very metal, it was all fucking spandex and long hair with them. I don't know if that would have gone down so well. This was before they really broke big. They'd had the same amount of press coverage as us and the same number of singles. 'Running Free' had come out that February and peaked at thirty-four. 'Sanctuary' had just got to twenty-nine. They didn't go Top Ten until 'Run To The Hills' in 1982. Before then they could have done 'Bubbles'. Paul Di'Anno was singing with them then and he could have got away with it. No disrespect to Bruce Dickinson but could you imagine him singing 'I'm forever blowing bubbles'? It would never happen, not in a million years.

But, of course, we compounded the error. We recorded 'West Side Boys' on the B-side, which was pretty suicidal. The lyrics are all about taking the Shed and the Kop! It goes, 'We meet in the Boleyn every Saturday, talk about the team that we're gonna do today, steel-capped Doctor Marten's and iron bars, smash the coaches and do 'em in the cars.' There's no mistaking what that was about. Hilariously, we had all these 'wow, hey, hi guys' types from EMI round the mic doing the backing vocals for it. Yuppie marketing men singing, 'We're not the North bank, we're not South bank, we're the West Side Upton Park,' and I'm thinking, You have not got a clue! They just jumped on the bandwagon.

Their strategy was to release 'Bubbles' if West Ham got through to the final. We went up to Elland Road for the semi-final replay on a Wednesday night. It was one-all after ninety minutes, then Frank Lampard fell over and stuck the ball in the net in extra time. Yes! That was it. West Ham was in the final and that meant EMI would rush out the single.

We got booked on *Top Of The Pops* again. We went up on the tube, yet again. No limos for us. It was the District Line from Plaistow, then the Central Line to Shepherd's Bush. We got to the BBC at ten in the morning. The bar was open, and the UK Subs were there, Charlie Harper and his boys – as good as gold. Mike Read was the DJ that day, a nice geezer. We started drinking straight away, knocking back beer like it was going out of fashion; and someone had a bag of grass. It was real heavy stuff. I didn't have any but everyone else did. Eventually, they stuck us into a changing room next to Legs & Co. Poor Legs & Co. We were all getting mangled so Mick decided to start kicking their door, trying to get them to come out and party. And they say romance is dead!

The boys were just having a laugh but Legs & Co weren't happy. They got themselves moved to another room. You can't really blame 'em.

We were waiting for our great manager Tony Gordon to come down with the float and the West Ham Shirts for us to wear. He turned up, dropped off the shirts but – typically – didn't leave us a penny. All we had was our drinking money, which was rapidly running out, and we were getting more and more steamed.

The Lambrettas, a Mod band, were on the show that day. They'd had a hit single with 'Poison Ivy' in March and had come back with the follow-up 'D-A-A-ANCE', which didn't do as well. Anyway, we're mooching about backstage and they come walking along with their manager who was only about five foot four, a proper little Hobbit. For a laugh, we started singing 'Poison Ivy' to them. They were all right about it, but the little short-arse manager was bang out of order. He said, 'If you could ever be as big as these boys, you wouldn't be taking the piss.' Here we go!

I said, 'Who are you fucking talking to, you ignorant cunt?'

His bottle went and he kept walking, but because we were really lagging we couldn't let it go. To our minds, he was taking a fucking liberty so we followed them into the studio. By now, the band was up on the stage and the cameras were rolling. We were so pissed we didn't care. We bowled over with the intention of doing 'em. Mick went up to the manager and jerked him by the shirt. This fella was screaming, 'Fuck off, get away from me, get away from me.'

One of us, I won't say who, stuck a cut-throat up to his neck and said, 'You dirty little cunt, you fucking mess with us and I'm going to put this right into your jugular.'

Well, the geezer started crying. He was quaking. There was no one to help him. I decided it was time to calm things down. I said, 'Leave it, he'll have us fucking nicked! We've made our point. We're not bullies...'

And our fella let him go. He just ran. The geezer absolutely wet himself. He'd brought it on himself by being rude in the first place, not that it merited the cut-throat. It got out of hand.

The UK Subs were up next with 'Teenage', so we went down to the side of the stage to watch. We went absolutely mad as they were playing. We were jumping up and down, pogoing, kicking and punching one another, rolling round the floor and giving it to each other. Charlie Harper was pissing himself laughing. You could hear the production team asking, 'Who the hell are these geezers with the UK Subs?' And someone turned round and said, 'It's one of the bands!' You could almost hear their jaws hitting the floor.

When it was our turn, they wanted us to go on with this bubble machine – because the song was 'Bubbles'. How corny was that? I said, 'Fuck off, we're the Rejects, you can't do that!'

But they insisted. Those magic words again, 'Do it or you don't do the show.' If we'd had a manager with us, it might have been different.

But by this time we had a bigger problem: Vince was as drunk as a sack. He couldn't even stand up. The whole thing was turning into a disaster. We shook him and slapped him into some kind of consciousness and started playing. Then I became aware of another problem – the obvious hostility of everyone else in the studio. It was packed with bods who were all trying to screw us out. The soul-boys, the crew, everyone. If looks could kill, we'd have been leaving that studio in wooden boxes. I had a terrible feeling that it was all going to go off. It might have done, too. We were all hammered and definitely in the mood for it. But, before it could kick off, disaster struck. We'd just started playing when Vince hit the floor. He went down like a pole-axed ox. He was comatose. If it had been live TV, it would have been one of those things they show endlessly on those *100 Greatest Outrageous TV Moments* programmes. As soon as the floor manager spotted Vince, it was 'Stop, stop, stop…'

I went over to Vince and slapped his face, saying, 'Get up, you daft cunt, or they're gonna throw us off.'

Somehow, he got back on his feet – but then the bubble machine broke down so there was a delay while they fixed it. We were getting more and more agitated. The third take was stopped because Mick was giving a V-sign during the lead break. We ended up doing seven takes. The producer was pulling his hair out. Vince kept falling over and getting back up. On the last take, he managed to stay upright for the first two minutes, then keeled over again. You saw it all on screen, even though they edited out what they could.

Finally we were dragged off. We went back to the changing room and wrecked it. I don't know why we did it, we just did. We just thought, Fuck it, smash it up. The furniture, the light bulbs, all the fixtures and fittings got trashed. It cheered us up a bit. Then we trooped out of the place. And that's when we realised we were pot-less. We didn't even have our tube fare home. The BBC people locked up our gear for us and we had no choice but to get the underground and bunk over the barriers at Plaistow. We'd just done *Top Of The Pops* and now we're climbing over the fucking barriers with some poor old Jamaican fella shaking his fists at us going, 'Where's your ticket money?' The glamour of pop stardom, eh?

CHAPTER ELEVEN

Nicked Again

1980 was shaping up to be our year, but inevitably there was a
down side. I came back home from school one dinnertime
and found Mick in the front room with Mum and Dad. Mum
was shaking. There was no colour in her cheeks, she looked
terrible, and Dad was furious. It turned out that they'd been
buying some groceries at the parade of shops by the Abbey Arms
when two young geezers had tried to mug them.

*To us, anyone who preyed on the old and defenceless was the
lowest of the low.* These bastards had bumped into Mum and
Dad in the street, jostled them and demanded money. They
were about seventeen, eighteen. Me old man was in his sixties
but he wouldn't take shit from anybody. He'd looked them
straight in the eye and said, 'I ain't giving you nothing.' So they
started pushing them about again. Mum had been really
frightened but she would never show it. Like Dad, she stood up
to them. She said, 'You ain't getting nothing, come near me

again and see what you get.' They gave her a load of abuse but mercifully it didn't get physical. The lowlifes had moved on to find easier pickings.

As this had only just happened, and the Abbey Arms was a five-minute ride away, I said to Mick, 'Let's get 'em.' We jumped into Dad's car, it was a big yellow estate at the time, and he took us back up there on the look-out for the two muggers. After a few minutes' driving around, my old man clocked them. He pulled over by a bus stop, me and Mick got out and walked over to the two cunts as normal as you like. 'You have one,' I said. 'I'll take the other.' They were coming towards us, full of it, like. They were bigger built than us, but we were roughly the same age. Mick was eighteen and I would have been fifteen. As they got to us, I grabbed one and Mick got hold of the other. He dragged him in to the middle of the road and started upping him. My one got away. He was screaming. I chased him across the road and he ran into an estate agents called McDowell & Francis. Like half the houses they had on their books, he was only fit to be condemned.

There was an Old Bill shop just along the road, so I knew I had to be quick. I ran after him into the office. The staff were all in a flap, but I got the geezer in the corner and absolutely kicked the shit out of him. I was hitting, kicking, head-butting, the lot. It was two up, two down and no mortgage relief. He was screaming, begging for mercy. I heard the office bods get on the phone to the police so I left him there in a pile on the floor. I'd completed.

Back in the road, Mick was still rolling about with the other geezer, pummelling him. He was screaming, everybody at the bus stop was looking on in horror and me old man was still parked up over the road, savouring the sweet revenge.

I grabbed Mick, told him that Dibble was on the way, and said it was time to call it a day. We piled back into the car and, as Dad doubled round, some big, fat white bird poked her head in the window and started calling us 'fucking bastards' as if we'd done something wrong for sorting out some dirty scum who were preying on old people. Mick just went 'wallop' and caught her one right in the eye. 'Fuck off, you fat slag,' he said, and that was that. We got back home, Mick's gone off and I went back to school for a divinity lesson or whatever.

Unfortunately, one of the people at the bus stop got our number plate. The Old Bill came round while I was at school and we were nicked again. Me old man told them that the pair of them had tried to mug him and me mum, but we both had to report to the station where we ended up in the cells. Give the cops their due for once, though, they were really good about it. It transpired that these two bastards had mugged about twenty people over the space of the previous two weeks and the Old Bill had been after them. Now one of them had a broken jaw and their old man wanted the police to press charges. He wanted us done for GBH, ABH, assault and battery. You name it. He was ranting and raving about it… until the officer in charge politely pointed out that these two liberty-takers were wanted for a large number of street robberies and that there were many witnesses ready to identify them.

In the circumstances, the father had no choice but to agree to a deal: if they didn't press charges against us, the two muggers could walk too and all they'd have to suffer for their crimes was a good beating and a broken jaw. If they did press charges, they'd be done as well. So they dropped the charges.

For the first time ever in an Old Bill shop, we had been treated with respect.

So that was a near miss but it was just the shape of things to come. There was to be a lot more trouble with the law after that.

CHAPTER TWELVE

Sniffers In The Night

E ven though we'd had records in the charts, we still felt that
the music business was an alien world, that we were like
urchins in some Dickensian book who'd strayed into a party
uninvited when we were only fit to stay outside with our noses
pressed against the windows. Most of the people we met in the
rock business were conmen and liars, frauds and fakes. But there
were some decent folk, too. Through Garry Bushell we met Ross
Halfin, a wart-encrusted hobgoblin of a rock photographer, and
through him we got to know the guys at Rhodes Music, a top
guitar shop which was then in Denmark Street, and the legendary
UFO. They were a huge hard-rock band at the end of the
seventies. They were playing stadiums in the US and were
absolutely at the top of their game.

As well as being considered 'a bad influence' on Ozzy Osbourne
by Sharon, Pete Way was the most exciting bass-player you'd ever
seen. He played the bass as aggressively as a lead. Pete was the

main influence on Iron Maiden's Steve Harris. We met them and befriended them and they in turn introduced us to whole world of drugs and rock'n'roll excess.

We were massive fans of UFO before we even knew them. In Britain, they were an album act. They'd had a minor hit in early 1979 with 'Doctor Doctor' but it was their live double album *Strangers In The Night* that sold shed-loads here and worldwide. Just after we signed to EMI, we booked in to a little eight-track studio near the Green Gate pub in Custom House and recorded our own demo version of 'Doctor Doctor'; only we called it 'Tony Gordon Please': 'Tony Gordon, please, I want my money fast...' He wasn't impressed.

When UFO's *No Place To Run* album came out, they did five nights at Hammersmith Odeon. Knowing we were fans, Ross Halfin took us backstage to meet them and even though the two bands had no musical affiliation with each other a great friendship developed from that moment. They were all really good geezers. Phil Mogg, the singer, was a real gentleman. Tonka Chapman, the guitarist was a diamond. But Pete Way made the strongest impression on me. He was one of the biggest characters that I've ever met in my life and always will be. On stage he's an animal, but when you speak to him off stage he's like this softly spoken Frank Spencer of rock; wild in his own way but without causing offence to people, and a genuinely funny man. I was amazed by the contrast. I mean, they were a huge band – five nights at Hammersmith was massive – but they were all such down-to-earth geezers. They took us backstage, looked after us, we signed a copy of our album for Phil Mogg. It probably wasn't his cup of tea but they loved it. Mick and Vince in particular started to lig about with them. They saw them play all over the country and went partying with them. At one stage we started to do 'Doctor

Doctor' live. That was down to Ross. Garry Bushell had come along to see us at Nuneaton for the second gig of our first tour and Ross pleaded with us to play 'Doctor Doctor'. It went down like a lead balloon with our punk audience. The crowd went from being in a frenzy at the front of the stage to trooping off to the bar en masse to buy lagers.

We had an influence on UFO, too, though; they wrote the song 'Profession Of Violence' about East End gangsters through meeting us. But mostly the education was one way. We regarded them as how a band should be set up. They had armies of roadies, guitar techs and all the right equipment but they still had that wild edge. They were the biggest, heaviest band in America at the time. They made us look like amateur hour.

Unfortunately, UFO were also a very bad influence on us when it came to the old recreational use of pharmaceuticals. I was never into drugs back then, it wasn't until later in the eighties when I went to pot a bit, and started getting into puff. But that was really the only thing I was ever into. Vince and Mick got into the hard stuff. There were always blues – amphetamines – flying about at our gigs, but none of us had ever done cocaine. UFO used to snort it by the bucket load. They'd do huge US tours, generate fortunes and come back with fuck-all, and they'd oversleep through partying and have to hire private jets to take them to the next gig. It was madness. You know that scene in *Scarface* with Al Pacino and the mountain of coke on his desk? That was UFO backstage.

But drugs started creeping in with us. There was a lot of puff floating about. Kevin Wells used to bring it up from Grays in Essex; he knew the dealers down there. It wasn't a big thing then on our manor but it started coming in. And really, after hooking up with UFO, from about 1981 there was a lot of Charlie going up noses, and near the end a lot of smack being snorted, too. It was no good for anyone. Yet we'd fallen out with Andy Scott because of his nasty habits, which was a shame 'cos he was a good drummer. But him, his brother Kenny and that Wasted Youth lot were fond of excess. We were in a rehearsal studio in Poplar practising for the first tour and Scotty seemed so mangled that it showed. Vince was furious 'cos we had a lot of work to do. He exploded at him. 'If you wanna be in this band, get your fucking act together,' he said. 'You don't turn up drunk and you don't turn up drugged up. This is serious.' But Scotty couldn't even answer him. He just sat there, slumped in a corner, which made Vince even madder. He turned on Scotty's drum kit and kicked it everywhere. Then he picked up the bass drum and smashed it over his head. He was a pathetic sight, lying there, dribbling, with a bottle of Special Brew in his hand spilling everywhere and his bass drum parked over his head. Vince said, 'You fucking soppy cunt, you can get your drum kit together 'cos we're off.' We drove off in the hire van and left him there.

A couple of nights later we got together at the Bridge House, which we used as a band meeting point. Glen Murphy came over and told us we were barred for smashing up his drum kit. We explained why we'd done it, that Scotty was on drugs and we were against that. We spoke to Terry, too. There was no animosity. We just made our point. OK maybe we shouldn't have smashed his kit but we didn't approve of him popping downers either. Terry was very anti-drugs too, so he was in a moral dilemma of his own, but his boy was in Wasted Youth and they were signed to his label so he had to do something. In the end he said that, although he understood why we'd done it, we'd be barred until we'd paid for the kit. We said, fair enough, we don't really agree with your thinking but Scotty is out the band as of now. We don't want him. Wasted Youth is welcome to him.

We had the hump about it, obviously. Our first reaction was

SNIFFERS IN THE NIGHT

bollocks, fuck 'em. But we loved the Bridge House so much that after about a week we went back down there and handed over £250 quid, shook Scotty's hand, and that was it, no hard feelings. Terry and Glen were good as gold about it and just said, 'Forget it ever happened,' and we did. Except now we needed a drummer. Our first UK tour began in about a month and we were desperate.

Hoxton Tom's girlfriend Lesley, now his wife, knew a drummer called Nigel Wolfe from Dagenham who played in a Mod band called Back To Zero. She said he was half skinhead, half Mod, so we were a bit dubious, but H said he was OK so we arranged to meet him at the Barge in Barking. And he was fine, a nice enough bloke, smartly turned out with a crop. Just really quiet, but then most drummers are.

Nigel was a shoe salesman. He worked up in the City, but he quit his job to join the band. He was only with us for eight months. We were never really happy with the way he played. He wasn't particularly strong or versatile. He always did the same drum roll. We tried to get him to learn 'Headbanger 'but he could never master the beat at the beginning so we couldn't play it live. He was a nightmare on tour for a couple of reasons. Firstly, because he fell in love with every groupie he slept with: Mickey and Vince had to give him a beer shower to separate him from one. And more importantly, he kept making mistakes when we played live. Sometimes we'd come off stage fuming with him. But he did the job and he looked the part. We were lucky we'd already recorded the album because it wouldn't have sounded the same with Nigel behind the drum kit.

He wasn't our Pete Best. Pete Worst, I would have said.

He went on to drum on two of the 4-Skins songs, 'Wonderful World' and 'Chaos'. Both are on the classic street-punk compilation *Oi – The Album*.

CHAPTER THIRTEEN

Fight Club

I started prize-fighting by accident. It was a week before The Cockney Rejects went on our first tour, in February 1980, and I'd been playing football for Tarana over at Seven Kings in Romford, Essex. It was a miserable, overcast Sunday morning and we got beat about 5–0. So no change there. Afterwards, we went over to this big pub called the Seven Kings Hotel for dinner. Everyone knew the Seven Kings; it was renowned for prize-fighting. Roy Shaw fought there, so did Lenny McLean, Johnny Waldren, Cliffie Fields, all the big names. It was a legendary place. Mickey Pugh the Cockney comedian used to compere. At one stage they even brought in a boxing kangaroo to take on all-comers.

I was fifteen at the time, but I was with my brother Steve's mob who were all in their late twenties and early thirties. There was Steve, a fella called Gus, Barry Sudell, Ian Saville, Richie Webb, a little mob of us. So we'd had a couple of pints and the Sunday

103

dinnertime boxing thing started up. The MC was another Cockney comic called Harry Scott and he began inviting people up into the ring to fight. The challenge was to last three rounds with a Hungarian geezer called Colombo. If you did it, you got twenty-five quid, which must be the equivalent of about a ton nowadays. Colombo must have been in his late thirties, maybe forty. He was small but stocky, as solid as an ox, and he had a real name as a pugilist. He'd fought a few of the real faces. In those days you saw his name on every unlicensed bill. He was a good journeyman, he'd fight anyone. And so was Danny Chipperfield, who it turned out was the referee.

Twenty-five quid was a good purse back then for nine minutes and quite a few geezers fancied their chances. But Colombo was good. He belted one geezer, then another. They didn't have a clue. He was knocking them senseless. Then Harry Scott said, 'Right, who's next?' and Barry Sudell turned round and pointed at me. 'He's next,' he shouted. 'He'll have some of him.'

I said no, but they all started jeering at me to get up. I looked to my brother Steve to back me up but he just laughed and said, 'Fucking get up there.' So I thought, Bollocks, why not? I'm fifteen, I've had three pints and now I've got to fight this geezer! Unbelievable. Before I knew it, I was in the ring and stripped off, standing there in just a pair of jeans and Doctor Martens. I was built like a fucking hair-pin! Me shadow weighed more than I did. They put gloves on me and the crowd were pissing themselves laughing. I looked ridiculous. I thought, What am I gonna do? There was only one thing to do: go for it!

Harry Scott introduced Colombo and then he said, 'Who's the skinny young man?'

I said, 'Stinky Turner from Custom House.' Then I took the

mic off him and started singing 'I'm Forever Blowing Bubbles'. The crowd loved it. They were all cheering and singing along.

They got the mic off me and Harry said, 'You're going to go three rounds with Colombo.' Now no one knew me at all. They thought I was just some div who'd come up from the audience. But as soon as that bell went I was in there jabbing and moving and bobbing and weaving. The crowd were crazy for it. My team-mates couldn't believe it. They thought I was going to get a pasting but, to start with, Colombo couldn't lay a glove on me.

The first round went great, the second round came and went and I was doing all right. The crowd was going nuts, but I could tell Colombo wasn't happy.

We went in for the third, we were about a minute from the finish, and then he really started to come at me. I thought to myself, He's not going to fuck about now, and he didn't. He started landing big punches on me. I kept thinking, Whatever you do, don't go fucking down. The crowd was loving this, they were up on their feet, cheering and chanting. I'm fucking moving him around, keeping out of his reach. At one point he got me into a corner and I thought, Just grab him, fuckin' grab hold of him, push him off. He couldn't put me down. The bell went and the place went absolutely mad. It was like we'd won the cup. Absolutely brilliant. On top of that they counted out twenty-five quid in notes into my hand in the ring. But that wasn't the end of it. They let me get dressed – I had a UK Subs T-shirt on, and a black leather jacket – and then they took me into a back room in the pub. Sitting there was this portly geezer wreathed in cigar smoke. He had a dicky bow, a big cheroot in his fingers which were like sausages, all the bling, and, in a voice that sounded like he'd been gargling with gravel, he went, 'You done really well there, son.'

'I was a bit surprised. 'Did I?' I said. My eye was busted and me guts had taken a pounding. 'Yeah,' I went. 'I've really done well. I'm glad I've got me twenty-five quid, that'll keep me in sweets for a couple of weeks.'

The fella said, 'How would you like to come and fight for me for money?' I told him I was only fifteen. He said, 'Well, we can make out you're eighteen. Do you fancy it?'

I hesitated, but only for a second. Because I knew exactly what my dad's reaction would be. I was polite. I said, 'I don't think me dad will be too happy about it. I'm going to have to talk to him first.'

The fella shrugged. He said, 'Well, you get back to me.' He gave me a ticket for the next week. 'You come and see me any time,' he said.

It was never going to happen. I got home that afternoon and me old man clocked me eye. I told him what had happened and he hit the fucking roof. He really went into one with my brother Steve. He was raging, he accused him of just standing around and letting his mates talk me into it. But it wasn't Steve's fault. He was just carried away with the buzz of it all. And to be fair he didn't think it was going to go the distance. I don't think any of them did.

Dad said, 'If I ever hear that you've gone up there again, I'll be up there and I'll have something to say about it.'

I said, 'Dad, I didn't wanna go back there anyway. I didn't want to do it in the first place, I just got press ganged into it.'

And that was it. The prize-fighting route out of the East End was abruptly closed. Some people might have been tempted to go back 'cos the money was good. But I never went there ever again. In future, all my fights had a punk rock soundtrack.

CHAPTER FOURTEEN

With the Boys on Tour

Our first-ever UK tour kicked off at one of Britain's least exotic venues, the Bradford Royal Standard on 24 February 1980. There were nine dates, ending in Dudley on 7 March. We were promoting our new single, 'Bad Man'. The Kidz Next Door were supporting. They were another one of Tony Gordon's stable, with our old mate Grant Fleming on bass. Jimmy Pursey's kid brother Robbie was in the band. Pursey, who was lost in a fantasy world most of the time, always used to tell us his brother was a nutter; and yet he turned out to be this nice, quiet kid. But because Pursey had given him this big build-up it was like a red rag to Mick and the others. We hadn't even reached the Watford Gap before they started on him. Rob was sitting up the front of the tour van next to the driver and all of a sudden he's got someone's hand on his hand and another hand on his knee and Mick's whispering in his ear, 'Never mind, Robbie, we're gonna look after you tonight.' The poor sod puked up. I felt sorry for him. He was only the same age as me, but he seemed much younger mentally. He was this wide-eyed innocent from suburbia and he'd found himself on a bus with all these lunatics.

There were fifteen of us to start with; the two bands, our road crew and some of our loyal entourage: Danny Harrison, H, and Binnsy, plus John Bong, Luggsy and Crank who were ex-Glory Boys. We met up at Plaistow tube station and set off for Bradford. Wellsy was driving. It was not a well-planned expedition. We had enough trouble trying to find the M1, let alone the North. We might as well have been looking for the fucking Antarctic; but we had a laugh all the way up there, it was a riot.

Bradford was brilliant. It was a tiny little pub with no backstage area but the atmosphere was cooking. We pulled in, had our sound check and then went and checked in to our bed-and-breakfast. A few years later I was reading a book called *The Ripper Case-Book* about the Yorkshire Ripper and it turned out that his favourite haunt was the Royal Standard. There's a photo of the pub in the book and on a blackboard outside written in chalk is a sign saying 'Tonight, the Cockney Rejects'. He might even have been in there that night; although the only murdering going on was us murdering 'Roadrunner'. Besides, with us it was a case of, if the Ripper don't get you, the roadies will.

It was a great night. The place was absolutely crammed. We started with 'Ready To Ruck' and the crowd were going crazy from the opening chords. There was an Asian punk down the front with green hair who was getting a bit crushed. While we were playing, he got out a bag full of glue and started sniffing it. In the end he passed out and we had to have him laid out on the stage so he didn't get trampled. 'Hey, mate,' I said. 'Have you got a backstage pass?' Vince did try to kick him off at one point but there was nowhere for him to go, the crowd just rolled him back.

And that was it; our first gig outside London had been a big success. Mickey celebrated with some serious drinking. Mick, Grant and Danny Harrison ended up exploding all the fire extinguishers in the lift, which cost us about £500.

One fan had travelled up from the Kent coast to see us, this big doughnut of a bloke called Folkestone Joe. He was like Johnny Vegas without the charm. He did this fanzine in our honour called *Ready To Ruck* and he wanted to hang out with us. We didn't really like the bloke, though, because he was a ponce. He was just a leech, scrounging beer and food and hotel rooms off us. We didn't even know him. So we dough-nutted him out of there before the night was over and never saw him again. It was a case of 'where did you come from, where did you go, never come back again, Folkestone Joe'. That's the way we were, we didn't suffer any fools.

The next night was Nuneaton, the 77 club. I think it was called that 'cos that was its capacity. It was only a little dive. It was pissing down that night, but we still had a good crowd in. No trouble. Garry Bushell and Halfin came up to cover the gig for *Sounds*. The gig went well, until Ross persuaded us to play a cover of UFO's 'Doctor Doctor', which went down like a lead balloon.

We were in some shitty guest-house but Bushell and Halfin were living it up on EMI's largesse in the Holiday Inn. Bushell had the room next door to Annie Lennox and, as I recall, Halfin got pissed and smeared shit all over her and Dave Stewart's door handles. He ordered them 6.00 am fry-ups, too. He then spent the night going through the local phone book, making offensive phone calls to strangers.

Gross Halfwit Bushell called him. He behaved worse than we did.

He was all right though, Ross, I suppose, in small doses. He was a funny little fella. He liked giving out stick but he couldn't take it. That was the night he took the picture of me that made the *Sounds* front cover. He got me in the changing room and said, 'Be as ugly as you can.' I already had a tooth missing, which helped, so I proceeded to pull a face that could have scared moss off a rock. A wrong move for me as regards attracting women punters, but it was a great picture. *Sounds* used it on their advertising posters on the tube, so suddenly my face was everywhere. It was amazing exposure. Unfortunately, me dad had to go back into hospital for major heart surgery at the time and someone showed him the photo. He refused to believe it was me at first, then, when he found out it was, he was disgusted. It definitely prolonged his stay in hospital.

Bushell did us a great spread in *Sounds* from that night, a big piece titled 'Harder Than The Rest'. It was our second feature – the first one was 'The Cockney Rejects and the Rise of New Punk' by Bushell and Dave McCullough the previous August. It was all very positive.

We played Branigans in Leeds on 28 February. Another good, trouble-free gig with a great atmosphere. We got a review in the local paper which said 'Stinky Turner could only muster three words between songs and they were "Oi, Oi, Oi".' So that was the springboard for the next song we wrote, 'Oi Oi Oi'. It also gave a name to the new, real punk movement that grew up behind us and the Angelic Upstarts, the working-class punk phenomenon Garry Bushell dubbed Oi.

The following night we played Grimsby Community Hall. The gig was red-hot but the action off stage was even steamier. We'd left two of the roadies, H and Danny Harrison, at the gig beforehand while we'd gone back to our digs. When we got back, we went backstage, opened the dressing-room door, and found H lying there stark naked with this bird giving him a blow-job. I was fifteen and still a virgin, I'd never seen anything like it. She wasn't at all bothered. She seemed to like the audience. There was a bit of banter and then everyone started saying, 'She wants the singer.' I was pushed down there into this little pit, with everyone standing there watching – Wellsy, Binnsy, Danny Harrison, about ten of them in all. I got my jeans off and lay down on top of her. I didn't have a clue what to do. I just went for it. I couldn't believe what was happening. I'm getting my end away with everyone cheering me on. It was my first-ever sexual experience and, due to the circumstances, a bit of a wash-out. All the next day I was thinking, Is that it? Is that what it's all about? I'd had ten of them watching me and I was absolutely useless. One stroke at a time, sweet Jesus.

She had a few more of us before the gig, too; her total tally ended up in double figures. She was a very game girl.

About ten minutes before we were due to go on stage, we couldn't get into the changing room to tune the guitars. The door was locked and Mick was nowhere to be found. I was starting to worry. After a while, a couple of us took a running leap and kicked open the door. There was my brother lying there stark bollock naked on top of a bird and they're having a sixty-niner. I thought, I know that face. While she was noshing my brother he was going down on the same girl that ten of us had already been through! Mick didn't seem to care. It was madness, but that's what our first tour was like.

There was no fighting to begin with, just lots of shagging. It was an eye-opener for me. Obviously, I'd heard tales about what occurred on tours with groupies but I'd never experienced it before. Now I'd been there, got the T-shirt and was lucky I didn't need a check-up as well. She was a nice girl anyway. She must have been. She's probably on her fifth marriage by now, or at least living off the state with six or seven by different geezers.

We had two days off in York. Kevin Wells booked us into another crap-hole of a hotel. We went into a little pub, and there was about thirteen of us. We'd had a few beers and then gone on to this steak-house next door to it called The Schooner Inn. We weren't misbehaving, just having a laugh, but the owner didn't like the look of us. He was a little Northern geezer in Ronnie Corbett glasses. He came straight over and said, 'If you don't shut your mouths, you're out.'

When we asked him what he was going on about he really started getting out of his pram. So Mick stood up, said, 'Don't talk to me like that, you silly little Northern bastard,' and gave him a back-hander, which left his glasses hanging off one ear. The fella was livid. He said, 'I won't let you get away with that, I'll have you nicked', but we just said bollocks and fucked off back to the hotel.

Half-an-hour later the Old Bill turned up demanding to know which four of us had assaulted the bloke. We told them what had really happened, they took a few notes and went off to check our version with his. They didn't come back, so the bright sparks amongst us went out on the town with their spray-cans. When we went out the next day there was graffiti everywhere. I mean, how thick can you get? We had to spend another day there. We walked over to the steak-house which was shut 'cos it was a Sunday and sprayed right across the front was: 'Don't mess with Cockneys, you four-eyed cunt.' How stupid is that? We walked round the town and decided to go and have a look at York Cathedral, and all over the doors and on the walls there were crossed hammers sprayed everywhere, 'ICF' and 'Cockney Rejects', all over the cathedral. Stupid bastards. We had to leave York immediately. We pissed off and stayed somewhere in Leeds.

While we were in York, we saw a funny thing on the TV. We were watching some documentary on BBC2 about Telford, the most boring town in the world. There were all these kids sniffing glue and one of them, some skinhead with a bumfluff beard, says to the camera, 'Stinky Turner, come to Telford, come and save us, Stinky.'

I have no idea what he thought I could do to save the place. We never played there, though; we'd seen the documentary. It was a shit-hole.

The tour went on. I remember thinking how poor everyone seemed in Grimsby. It wasn't like the Bromley Contingent and Chelsea set punks with their affluent mums and dads. The Grimsby punks looked absolutely potless. There was one geezer up there who came to the gig wrapped in bin bags.

The day after, we drove down to Penzance, pirate country, for a gig at the Demelzas club. I suppose it was always going to be too much to hope that the tour would pass without trouble. We got to the gig for the sound check, we were about twelve-handed by now – 'cos we'd sent Luggsy and Crank back to London for misbehaving – and we found they had a boxing ring set up there. The place was used by an amateur boxing club during the day, and they had this hopeful who was their local champ working out with his trainer. The fella asked if anyone wanted to spar with him and Vince immediately volunteered me. I thought, Why me? I'm here to do a fucking sound check. I don't need to fight no one. I had the hump. I didn't want to do it but I couldn't duck the challenge.

This trainer went, 'All right, boy,' in this West Country accent. 'Get up here and have a go with him.' He sounded like one of the

Wurzels. So there I was in me DMs, putting me gloves on and off we went.

As soon as we started, this geezer tried to get a bit rough. He was older than me, about eighteen or nineteen, and he came out hitting hard, which you don't do when you're sparring. He done me on the nose, so that was it. I absolutely splattered him. I opened him up and gave him a proper pasting. The trainer had to jump in and stop the fight. I had him on the ropes and was giving it to him. They had to pull me off him. It was his own fault, he'd tried to take liberties.

The trainer said, 'That was a bit uncalled for.'
I said, 'Well, you asked me to come up and spar, mate, and he tried to get nasty. So, as far as I'm concerned, that's it.'

The word obviously circulated because when we came back for the gig there were a lot of bouncers in and you could tell they wanted to clump us. They were giving us the old dead eye, glaring at us, virtually growling in fact, but we weren't bothered.

In those days we used to have a concoction bucket for use on hecklers. It was our ultimate deterrent, the bucket of doom. We'd fill it with rotten fruit, piss, vomit, shit, gravy, eggs, sauce, whatever we could get our hands on, and leave it at the side of the stage. When we started playing we got a bad reception, the worst of the tour, all because I'd hit the local hero. You could see the bouncers were egging the crowd on, they wanted them to give us grief. We had one geezer at the front of the stage who wouldn't stop heckling. He was a portly geezer, fat, not a punk; he had a normal haircut. He was wearing a Fred Perry shirt. He had a big fat mouth too; he kept on and on: 'You fuckin' wankers, fuckin' wankers, get awf the fuckin' stage,' he said in this Jethro accent.

And I was saying, 'Yeah, fuck you, I was like that after me first pint, you cunt', but he wouldn't shut up. He had this peroxide punkette with him with a Blondie haircut and she was joining in the heckling, too. Every time we finished a song they were off again. So the decision was made, we were gonna have to do him.

Between songs I said, 'We've got something for you, me deario.' And old Jethro went, 'Oh right, have you got oi a badge or a T-shirt?' I said, 'It's better than that', and I turned to Ricky Meakin in the wings and said, 'Pass the concoction bucket.' And Jethro was standing there with his bird, all expectant. I said, 'I've got this for you,' and, wallop, I covered the two of them from head to foot. Eggs, flour and piss all over them. He went Garrity. I said, 'Who looks the fucking mug now?'

But all the bouncers immediately started coming round. They got to the front and one of them said, 'What was all that about? Look what you've done.'

I said, 'Bollocks, he's fucking heckling, he had it coming. If he's paid his money to come in and be a big mouth, that's what he gets.' And they backed away.

It was nearly the end of the set anyway. We played the last two songs. Didn't do an encore and that was it. I was sitting backstage relaxing while Mick and Grant hit the bar. They had a couple of girls on the go, when one of the bouncers came up and told Mickey to get out. He said Mick was too young to be in the club. Vince saw it happen. He said Mick started to explain that he was the guitarist with the band, and the bouncer just grabbed hold of his arm. Mick stepped back and went, 'crack', hit him with a left hook and knocked him straight on the deck.

Now I didn't know this was going on. I was sitting backstage while the roadies loaded up the gear. All of a sudden the backstage door caved in and there was this big commotion. All these dicky-bow bouncers piled in mouthing off, demanding to know who'd upped their mate. And they're looking around pointing at Vince, 'cos he was the big one. Mick was only nine-and-a-half stone so they couldn't say it was him who knocked out their fifteen-stone buddy. It would have been an embarrassment. Then a load of locals came backstage too, to back up the bouncers, and they all wanted to row with us. They were about thirty-handed. We had twelve, but that's including the Kidz Next Door, so the odds were realistically three-to-one against us. We were game, but we had to be a bit careful.

The club manager came in just as the head bouncer was complaining that his best man had been carried off to hospital. The manager was as good as gold, though. He said, 'Well, if he's done that to your top boy with one left hook, I wouldn't pick another row with them if I were you.' He went on, 'The way I hear it, he deserved what he got. What are you moaning about?' He was great about it, and that was it.

So we carried on getting all of our gear out of the gig. But now more locals had turned up, about fifty of them, chanting, 'You fucking Cockney wankers' in their West Country accents.

The odds weren't good at all. I thought we were going to cop it. The numbers were insurmountable – twelve of us against fifty of them. But I also thought, their top boy had been knocked out, if they were real hard men, they'd just come and decimate us, but not one of them made a move. All that happened was after we'd loaded all the gear in the van and started driving off, a few of them ran up and kicked the back of the van. That was the best they could do. I just wound down the window and said, 'You fucking mugs, see ya later.' They've had two geezers take a good hiding, and one a shower of gunge, and we ain't had nothing. They didn't even try and follow us back to the hotel.

The next day we set off for Plymouth, the Clones club. It was

Tuesday night and a crap venue. They had to put boards on top of milk crates for the stage. I think Stiff Little Fingers were playing somewhere else in town and we had about sixty people in, including a geezer with his dog. It was a really odd gig. As we were playing, people in the audience were doing pile-ons; that's where someone lies down and everyone else jumps on top of them. So naturally I got involved in a couple of pile-ons too. It was a really crazy night. The bar staff and the management went missing, so we were just climbing behind the bar and helping ourselves to pints and spirits all night.

The following day we played Exeter Roots club, which was OK. The only bit of excitement came after the show. Vince and Mickey pulled these two birds. Mick had a big fat one and when he took her back to his room the road crew steamed in to catch them at it. They found Mick in the bog while his delightful companion was crouching over the sink in his room having a piss. Mick came out the khazi, saw what was going on and hit the roof. He chucked her out in just her knickers. It was freezing outside and I think one of the boys took pity on her and gave her something to cover herself up.

On 6 March we played Swansea, which was an absolute shit-hole of a place. We were booked into this little hotel, one of those where you got silver teapots in each room. We all congregated in one of the rooms, and Ricky Meakin was passing round the teapot. I poured out a cup and took a sip and spat it out everywhere. Before he'd made the tea, the dirty bastard had shit in the pot. We went out to see the sights – it looked like down-town Albania – and the hotel owner found the teapot with the turd still inside. When we got back he kicked us out.

Now we had nowhere to stay. We went to the venue, Circles, for the sound check but the gates were locked. It was about 5.00

pm. We waited and waited, and started getting the hump. Then Vince had a bright idea. He remembered that Jimmy Pursey was in Monmouth, recording his solo album in Rockfield Studios. It was only about eighty miles away. Vince suggested we fuck the gig off and go down there. It seemed like a top-notch idea. So Wellsy went up and pinned a note on the door saying we'd waited an hour for the gates to open and now we were fucking off. Then we just got in the van and drove. It was a shame to let the fans down but it was no way to treat a band. It was 6.00 pm when we left, most sound checks were at four or five. We never had any comeback about it either 'cos in our contract it said we were due to sound check at 5.00 pm. It turned out the manager didn't show up until 7.00 pm so he didn't have a leg to stand on.

So we jogged on down to Rockfield and surprised Pursey. He played us some of the tracks and they were absolutely awful. He had two geezers in from Generation X, the drummer Mark Laff and the guitarist Derwood Rockfield was a splendid place with stables, the works and a big fuck-off forty-eight-track studio. Jimmy was chuffed to see us and decided we'd all go into Monmouth for a drink. The trouble was, West Ham had just knocked Swansea out of the FA Cup and as we were having a beer we started to get a few looks. We weren't looking for any agg at all. All of a sudden a geezer came over in a black and white Swansea top. He said, 'I know you, Cockney Rejects.'

He was speaking to Danny Harrison, who said, 'That's right, mate.'

The bloke went, 'West Ham are all wankers and you're all shit.' Harrison just said, 'Go on, fuck off.'

There were all these big rugby geezers on the other side of the bar staring. I thought, Here we go. Pursey was oblivious to it all.

A big, fat geezer, he must have been six foot tall and sixteen stone, shouted out, 'All you Cockneys are wankers.'

I'd had enough. I got up and walked to the middle of the bar and he came towards me. I said, 'Who are you fucking talking to?' Now all of our lot had come up behind me and his lot was behind him. It was a stand-off. We were just waiting for someone to make the first move. It was me. I just went 'bosh', upped him and the whole pub erupted. It was like a saloon-bar brawl in a Western. They kept coming back with more people but we were doing them. The geezer who started it all took a kicking. Then I looked round and three of them had Kevin Wells. They had his jumper over his head and they were giving him a hiding. We sorted them out, then it was on to the next incident.

I saw little Robbie Pursey's face: he was nearly crying, poor fucker, he was shitting himself.

Because we were winning the day, the Welsh broke out the tools. They started using glasses, stools, pool cues, a fire extinguisher. It was a miracle they didn't start throwing darts at us. So Danny Harrison got an ashtray and smashed it right into a geezer's face. Anything they could do, we could do better. It was turning nasty, nastier than I'd ever seen it.

To my right, I saw Mick on top of a geezer hitting him. This fella had hush puppies on and where his trousers had ridden up you could see he was wearing pink socks. He looked ridiculous. So, in the middle of all this carnage, I started laughing. Funnier than that, though, when it looked like we were winning the day, Jimmy Pursey decided to get into the fray. As he stood up, in his tartan coat, this big Welsh fella just went 'smack' and Pursey hit the floor like a sack of spuds. He was in and out the frame within five seconds. And these two poor bastards from Generation X were just sitting there with their half pints of lager thinking, What the fuck have we got into here?

It was a massive row, it must have gone on for fifteen minutes.

Then, just as Vince was smashing into one of their ring leaders, the guv'nor emerged and said the Old Bill were coming and we'd better fuck off. He didn't try and keep us there, which was decent of him. The fighting stopped. There were a few casualties on the floor, a bit of spilled blood, we had a couple who were bloodied up. We had to pick Pursey up off the carpet, but we got together and trooped out; and as we left one of these Welsh geezers said, 'Well done, lads, good row!'

When we were back in Monmouth that summer, four of us went for a drink in another pub and a geezer came over and asked to shake Mickey's hand. He said, 'You knocked my teeth out in March, what do you wanna drink?' Fantastic.

We all piled into the tour bus and headed back to the studio. Pursey was very subdued on the way back, but we said, 'Well done, Jim, you got up there, you stood your ground.'

'Yes,' he said, 'you should have seen me, I was on top of this geezer.'

He was just a fantasist. Harmless, really.

We stayed the night at Rockfield then went on to the last gig of the tour at Dudley JB's which was John Bonham's club. I was really looking forward to this one, being a Led Zeppelin fan. Vince had already warned us we had to watch ourselves because Bonham had these Swan Song bouncers who were supposed to be really useful. Like Zeppelin's manager Peter Grant they had an awesome reputation. You didn't mess with these fuckers. They'd tear you apart.

The gig was as good as gold; the only problem was our chief roadie, Binnsy. It was his twenty-second birthday and he'd drunk so much he couldn't organise a thing. He was throwing up at the gig and was so out of it he lost the money we were paid. That was to be his last gig with any responsibility.

We got back to the hotel quite elated, looking forward to an end-of-tour party. There were ten of these Swan Song bouncers waiting for us in reception, great big hairy fuckers they were. They said someone had nicked one of their leather jackets and there was a wallet in it. They were spitting blood. I said, 'Hold your horses, I'll round everyone up and we'll sort it,' because it was news to me.

I got everyone together and went back to reception. One of the bouncers was really giving it the big 'un. Mick was acting as spokesman and, diplomatic as ever, he said, 'Listen here, if someone's fucking nicked your jacket we'll sort it out 'cos that's a liberty, but we're the Rejects and we don't give a fuck about you being Swan Song bouncers or Peter Grant. We don't give a fuck for all that. If you come to us giving it the big 'un and wanting to row, we'll have a row with yous.'

There was a tense moment as they exchanged glances. Eventually one big cunt said, 'We don't want a row, we want the jacket back.'

Mick replied, 'Yeah and rightly so; if it was one of us who nicked it, we'll get it back for you but don't come here swearing and shouting your mouth off 'cos we'll go outside now and go at you anyway you want.'

We were only kids, the oldest would have been Wellsy, who was twenty-three. The Swan Song bouncers were men, in their late twenties, thirties.

But that was how we left it. It turned out one of our lot, John Bong, a petty thief from Benfleet who'd come down to join us, had nicked the jacket. He handed it over and we returned it. We told them it had got mixed up with our gear and left in the van. No one would have nicked the jacket, we said. They were OK about it. We shook hands all round and that was it. Everyone was happy. 'Good gig, lads,' they said and walked out.

I thought, Thank fuck for that, 'cos they were big lumps. Looking back, they had every right to come after us and have the hump.

We got John Bong and I told him, 'You're on the first train home tomorrow, you fucking liberty-taker. You could have caused carnage.'

If it had come to blows, I think we would have come off worse. We were as game as anything but they were proper hard geezers. But Mick's way was just to front them. He didn't give a fuck. He probably thought we would cane them because we hadn't lost a battle like that. I'm proud we stood up to them. We never showed fear. We never backed down. We stood our ground and sorted things out on our terms. And then we got the night porter out to celebrate. We'd notched up our first tour and it hadn't gone too badly. The album was in the Top Thirty, we had the new single to record. Things were on a roll.

The greatest coup of the whole tour, though, was the van. When we hired it, we said we were using it to go on a beano to Clacton, and we drove it all round the country. Of course, we fiddled the mileage before we gave it back.

CHAPTER FIFTEEN

Star Wars

The rock weekly *Sounds* played a big part in making us known. It was a much better paper than the *NME*. The *NME* was for students, *Sounds* was the people's paper. In 1980 *Sounds* started to outsell the *NME* and it was easy to see why. *Sounds* wrote about things that were happening at street level: 2-Tone, punk, New Mod, Oi, proper reggae and the New Wave of British Heavy Metal. The *NME* was full of pretentious shit about long raincoat bands written by posers with their heads up their arse-holes.

I really loved going to the *Sounds* offices. To me, it seemed magical. That's why one of the few things I regret is the trouble we got into up there one time. As always. We were provoked.

The staff there were divided about us. Half the writers loved us, but there was an element of resentment too. Pete Silverton was one of those who didn't take to us. One lunchtime, he came back to the office and Mickey was sitting in his chair. Silverton rolled up and said, 'Get outta my chair.' No please or nothing. He was just very dismissive.

Mick said, 'No, I'm not getting out, if you ask me like that. Ask me properly and I'll get up.'

Silverton started shaking. 'Oh,' he said, 'I just need my chair.'

Mick said, 'OK, you can have your chair.' And as he stood up he gave Silverton a couple of back-handers. 'You fucking wimp,' he said. 'You little wanker. Talk to me like that again and I'll fuckin' kill ya.' A few people got up and Mick said, 'Yeah, anyone else want it?' And of course no one did. I thought, Oh no, we're gonna get banned.

Alan Lewis, the editor, asked Garry Bushell to make us leave shortly after and we did. We were banned from the office, but it didn't last long. Mick didn't hurt Silverton, he just shook him up a bit, taught him some manners.

There was another incident with Pat Marc who was a Chelsea fan. He was a big lump with peroxide hair and Sid Vicious tattooed in his head. He was nothing really, just a face about town, but he had this reputation. How or why, I'll never know. One afternoon, we came up to the *Sounds* editorial floor and Pat Marc happened to be sitting in there. I had a feeling in my bones that something bad was going to happen. I suppose I should have suggested going elsewhere, but I didn't. We sat away from him, minding our own business, but you could see he was desperate to talk to us. He swivelled his chair around and asked when we were playing next. And I knew that 'cos he was Chelsea and he was mouthy that Mick would take it the wrong way. And he did. Mick said, 'Why do you wanna know?'

Pat Marc replied, 'I just wanted to know, I might come up there with a few boys.' It was an unfortunate choice of words.

Mick's back went up. 'What do you mean, come up there with a few boys?' he said. 'Is that a threat? We've got a few boys of our own.'

Then Pat Marc made a comment about West Ham, something to the effect of 'Your lot ain't doing too well nowadays.' And that was it. Mick was up out of his seat like a fighter pilot who'd just hit the ejector button. Smack, smack, smack. He hit Pat Marc, with a quick one-two and he collapsed. Just went down on the floor.

'Leave it Mick,' I said.

Mick was growling. 'You cunt,' he said. 'I'll fuckin' have ya.'

Pat Marc was just laying dazed on the floor; for a big fella he didn't want to know. We restrained Mick. Pat Marc got up, said, 'What was all that about?' and ran out of the *Sounds* office with a look of terror on his face.

One of the *Sounds* writers tried to get in the middle of it all, but Vince, who didn't look like the friendliest of geezers at the best of times, told him to sit down or go through the window. Really, it was a liberty for us to go up there and do that. Looking back now, I can see we must have put Garry Bushell in a terrible position. I don't know why we were like it. I think we had an in-built hatred for middle-class music posers. Alan Lewis was a good bloke; so was Deaf Barton. Eric Fuller liked us – 'Eric Fuller-shit', Garry Bushell called him. He once described us as 'family entertainment – Kray family entertainment'. A nice line, but it didn't go down well with Vince because of his McVitie family connection. Alan Moore, the brilliant cartoonist who went on to create *Swamp Thing*, included the twins in a *Sounds* illustration he once drew for us, too.

Robbi Millar was another fan. I remember her coming to interview us at home, walking down Prince Regent Lane in see-through plastic trousers. You'd never seen anything like it. Dave McCullough was all right, too, until he went a bit funny and got into all those divvy raincoat bands. He was quite excited about us to begin with. He thought we were a breath of fresh air. That Mark E. Smith from The Fall once told him, 'Don't rope us up with The Cockney Rejects, they're like fucking Max Bygraves.'

I thought, I'd love to get my hands on you, ya div. I'll do a cowpuncher's cantata on your fucking head. Yeah, we want to be roped in with you, don't we? They weren't half as big as we were, going 'Don't rope us in with The Cockney Rejects'. Ridiculous. But the Pat Marc thing, we knew that was a bad incident. We were in the wrong. We knew we'd got Garry Bushell in trouble so we decided we couldn't go up to the *Sounds* office again.

The problem was, looking back, that we never left our Custom House attitude behind. There was a way of life in the East End, a code of conduct if you like, that people adhered to. You treated people with a certain respect. But in other circles people seemed to think they could talk to anyone any way they wanted and there would be no repercussions. It led to a lot of fall-outs, even with people we liked. For example, before we signed to EMI we were on our way to Polydor Studios to see Pursey and we saw Billy Idol coming towards us eating an ice-cream. He was an ice-cream, that bloke, wasn't he? I really liked Generation X as a band but he looked like a right fucking poof. He had a shoulder bag and he was mincing along, licking the nuts off a large Neapolitan.

I said, 'There's Billy Idol there.'

Mick looked and he went, 'All right, Bill, how's it going?'

He just lifted his eyes, sneered at us and carried on walking.

We walked on a couple of yards but then it started to bother me. We'd showed out to the bloke and he blanked us. I said, 'The cunt, he's half given it the big 'un rather than talk to us.'

Mick said, 'Yeah, he has. I'm gonna have a fucking word with him.' And I thought, Oh, no…

Mick ran back, caught up with Billy Idol and said, 'Oi, you, I fucking talked to you and you blanked us, who the fuck do you think you are? You're fucking nothing anyway.' Then he kicked Idol up the arse. I'll never forget it. Billy Idol had a pair of jeans on and as Mick kicked him all this dust came off of his pants.

He said, 'What was all that about?'

Mick replied, 'You fucking cunt, blanking us, you're lucky you got away with that.' Then he turned to me and went, 'Come on, bruv, let's fuck off up Polydor, see Pursey, a real star.'

I looked at Billy Idol; he was standing there holding his ice-cream in one hand and his arse in the other.

A few months later, we were sitting in EMI and Sheena Easton came in with a couple of minders. We said, 'All right, Sheena? Nice to meet you.' Very pleasantly.

She said something really derogatory and flash. She was really horrible.

I said, 'Who the fuck are you talking to? Who are you being rude to?'

She gave me a bit of verbal again and got a mouthful of abuse back. Her minders kept quiet. There was just no need to treat people like that.

We had a run-in with the Madness hangers-on in June 1979. Mick had gone to a party in Islington with a fella called Terry Johnson, who wasn't a fighter, he was just a normal kid. They went there with Robbi Millar. Brendan Smythe, Chas Smash's brother, was there with his entourage. They were eyeballing Mick and Terry all night. When they went to leave, eight of these blokes tried to block their way. And Brendan was right at the hub of it. Mick said, 'Look, fuck off, we're going home.' But one of them threw a punch, so Mick said, 'Come on then, have a go outside.'

It was two against fucking eight, and the lot of them joined in.

Mick's having a go, but his mate is on the floor. The Old Bill turned up and Smythe and his gang all fucked off, so they nicked Mick and Terry Johnson for threatening behaviour. They got banged up all night, just because a gang had taken liberties with them at a party for no reason. How can you get nicked for defending yourself? It wasn't right and it played on his mind for months. Mick never forgot it and he never swallowed it. Mick never would. He vowed that, if he ever saw Brendan Smythe again, he was going to give it to him. Lo and behold, nine months later he did.

It was April 1980 when Mick got his own back. We were in Rhodes Music in Denmark Street. Kevin Ireland ran it, lovely fella. He always helped us out with back-line and new guitars. Mick was in there trying out some guitar when he looked up and saw Smythe and a skinhead mate walk past. Mick wasn't going to miss this chance. This was pay-back time. We shot outside just as they got to the end of Denmark Street and for some reason they decided to turn around and come back towards us. They hadn't seen us and they were about a yard away, when Mick stepped forward and said, 'Remember me cunt?' As Smythe looked at him, Mick hit with a right hander. It had such force it knocked his head against a shop window. Then he hit him with a left hook and knocked him clean out on the floor.

The other skinhead went to step in and I went, 'Yeah, do you fuckin' want some of me? I'll fuckin' have you.'

He said, 'No, no trouble.'

Brendan Smythe was on the floor with his tongue hanging out.

Mick leaned over and said, 'My name is Mickey Geggus and you took a liberty with me, you and your fuckin' firm, about eight months ago. Well, you ain't so fuckin' big now. You want me, that's me fuckin' name. Get whoever you want, and I'll fucking see you any time, you fucking prick.'

Brendan never said a word. He was just sparked out on the floor.

About four months later I was in the TPA, the Tin Pan Alley Club, over the road with Kevin Ireland, and Smythe was in there with a little entourage. I thought, Here we go. I wouldn't have minded fighting him one-on-one, but he had a little firm with him including a few older geezers, knocking back vodkas.

But Brendan came over and apologised. He said he was sorry about what happened at the party and put it down to the drink. 'Tell Mick I didn't mean it,' he said. 'We're all in together, we're all Londoners.'

So I shook his hand and said, 'Fair enough, but, if your little firm are thinking of any agg, you can take me outside the lot of you and kick the fuck out of me but it'll be the worse thing you've ever done, because we know where you are.'

He went, 'No, I don't want nothing like that.'

He bought us both a drink and that was that. The next I heard of him he'd joined the Foreign Legion. Chas Smash had to go out and get him back. He topped himself after that.

There was always a thing between us and Madness. We knew that when we played the Electric Ballroom their North London firm, the Clock End Skins, would be there, but that was the end of that particular feud.

Another great rivalry was between us and the 4be2s, a band Johnny Rotten's brother Jimmy Lydon formed, and who had a large Arsenal following. Someone had the bright idea of booking them as our support at an Electric Ballroom gig in 1980. They had quite a lot of mouth at the time; we kept hearing things come back about them being the top boys in London, and the East End were all wankers, so we were quite pleased they were on our bill. They had this fella called Dave Archer who was their mouthpiece; Jock MacDonald managed them. We were up at EMI a week before the gig and Archer was swanning about with his pony-tail. I decided to have a word with him, so I went up and pulled his pony-tail with a 'ding-dong', like the Avon Lady. I introduced myself and told him straight that if his mob dared to show up at the gig we'd batter the fuck out of them. He went white. 'Make sure you give them the message,' I said. And he must have done, 'cos suffice to say on the day of the gig they never showed. We were well up for it, though. Just as well Lydon never showed. He only had one eye, and he wouldn't have been seeing much out of the other one.

We were always determined not to let anyone from the music business, however big they were, take liberties with us.

We finished the first tour on 7 March and started a second one on 5 April. In between we recorded the new single, 'The Greatest Cockney Rip Off'. We had a warm-up gig at the Electric Ballroom on 3 March. Slaughter & The Dogs asked us to support them. I don't know why we did it 'cos their star was definitely fading. They'd had one decent single on Decca back in 1977, 'Where Have All The Boot Boys Gone?', but that hadn't charted. They were nobodys really, a punk Status Quo. But their guitarist Mike Rossi thought he was some kind of rock star. We did the gig reluctantly. I'm pleased to say we did forty minutes and blew them off stage. We were the dogs' that night and we absolutely slaughtered them. Not a whiff of trouble either.

Mike Rossi hasn't changed that much. We played with them at a big punk festival in Spain in 2000 and Rossi had lost his Manchester accent and was talking like a Californian, saying how he was making films in LA and had these big projects on the go.

And I thought, If you've got all these big projects in LA why the fuck are you flying over to Spain for £500 to go on stage at one in the morning?

The second Cockney Rejects tour kicked off in Manchester, a place called The New Osborne Club, which was run by Mike Rossi's brother Ray. They were like chalk and cheese, though. Ray was a real character, as mad as a March hare. We were determined the second tour was going to be a good one, and that there'd be less trouble. The first day, Man U were playing Liverpool at home and the place was crawling with Cockney Reds, but we didn't get involved in any of that.

The show was fine, and afterwards Ray Rossi said he was going to take us all for a meal. He laid on two cars. We got into one with him and he shot off like a maniac. After five minutes, he pulled over sharpish. 'Hang on,' he said. 'See that cunt over there? He owes me money.' He leaped out of the car, took a baseball bat out of the boot and ran over to these two geezers, swinging the bat around, demanding cash. They started running for their lives with him after them like Captain Caveman swinging his club.
We were sitting in the car, watching. It was like *The Sweeney*.

They managed to get away from him, and he came back, put the baseball bat away and just said, 'Wankers, I'll get 'em another time. Now, where do you wanna eat?'

So, obviously we took to him and went on to work with him again. He was a good laugh.

The next night was our first-ever Scottish gig, at the Bungalow Bar in Paisley. We drove through Glasgow to get there, through the Gorbals and it didn't look all that to me. It had this reputation but the place wasn't any different to Poplar or Mile End. The Bungalow Bar was one of smallest gigs we ever played. It probably held a hundred people but there must have been 200 there. They were packed in like pilchards, literally hanging off the chandeliers. The stage was only two inches off the floor. It was more cramped than a rush-hour tube train but there was no trouble. There was a bit of football chanting before we played so I went on and said, 'Listen, I don't give a fuck about football, but if anyone wants some, I'm Cowdenbeath.' And everyone laughed. I'd used me noodle, broken the ice and defused the tension.

The following night's gig was at Aberdeen Music Hall, another good 'un. Scotland was absolutely brilliant for us. Then we played Forfar, which was one of the tiniest towns I'd ever been in; the local football club Forfar Athletic had a pitch like you'd find on Hackney Marshes. But they stuck us in this massive place called Reid Hall with a 1,500 capacity; massive great stage. I thought we'd be playing to about fifty people, but Dundee was just up the road and we got about 500 in.

We were sitting backstage before the show, and this Scottish punk walked in wearing tartan bondage trousers and started helping himself to drinks. We weren't hostile to him, we thought we'd show him a bit of hospitality, maybe this is the custom up here. But this Jock started getting more and more obnoxious. He was rude, he was swearing, and then he started jabbing his finger at me. 'You fucking bastard,' he said. 'You've sold out. You're just the same as Pursey and the Clash.'

We asked him to leave 'cos we had to tune up and change strings ready to go on, but he wouldn't stop shouting his mouth off. So I said, 'I think it's best you fuck off. I ain't gonna take any more of this shit off you.'

He went, 'What are you gonna do, you fucking big boy? What are you going to do?' He kept on and on and on.

In the end I said, 'I'll show you what I'll do.' And I absolutely lashed him all over the changing rooms. I must have broken his nose, knocked him out cold. They had to carry him out. My first thought was, I hope he's OK, my second one was, Shit, I could get nicked here.

We went on stage and it was at the back of my mind. I was starting to feel bad about it. We got to the third number, which was 'Bad Man', and I looked down and this figure had materialised at the front, his nose smashed across his face, claret everywhere. It was him. He was jumping up and down going, 'Ya fuckin' brilliant,' pogoing about like a mad man, loving it. He didn't come back to the changing room afterwards, though.

We had one more gig in Scotland, Edinburgh Astoria, on the ninth. I'd had a call from a local band called The Exploited before the tour asking if we could help them out and I'd offered them a support slot in Edinburgh. We met up with them before the gig and went to the pub with them. They had an entourage with them who were all heavy-duty Loyalists. I had trouble following their accents but they were as good as gold. We had no agg off them at all. But, as the night progressed, we must have given them our address, because for months afterwards we were getting Loyalist gear through the post: magazines, wallets, earrings and watches all embellished with the red hand of Ulster. They were OK people and we had a good laugh with them, but I didn't want to get involved in all that. I knew Mensi was into the Loyalist songs and the Red Hand Brigade but it didn't seem to have much to do with East London. We had enough people to fight as it was.

After Edinburgh it was back to England. We had a date in Hull, then Retford Porterhouse. We had the entourage come up from London for that. We had quite a posh hotel, the poshest we'd ever stayed in. The car park was full of Bentleys and Rollers. Terry Scott and June Whitfield were staying there that night, too, and I'm afraid to say we lowered the tone considerably. I was sitting in my room relaxing and the first thing I heard was H come out of his room singing, 'I've shagged, I've shagged.' Turns out they had some little punk bird called Sarah in there and a few of the entourage had been through her: Butler, Leachy, Wellsy, and she'd absolutely loved it, couldn't get enough. She told H that Pursey had been giving her one, and she'd gone round his house in Hersham and shagged Pursey and Mike Read and that Pursey had made a video of Mike Read in stockings and suspenders getting stuck into her. She was a very game girl. Sarah had a blonde mate with her, who proved a lot more discerning to start with. Wellsy set his sights on her and after half a bottle of Scotch he had his wicked way with her. In fact, after a few more Scotches she was most obliging to about fourteen of us. Not me, I hasten to add. They ended up shaving her pubes in the bath, which she seemed to enjoy. Unfortunately, they were doing it in Binnsy's room. He came in and got most irate and ended up slinging her out of his window. She fell about ten feet into some rose bushes. It was terrible. This was all going on *before* we got to the gig.

Johnny Butler shot straight down there to help her out. Terry Scott and June Whitfield were downstairs having dinner at the time, and as we left for the venue we saw this girl stark bollock naked in the forecourt giving Johnny Butler a blow-job in full view of the dining room. Everyone in there could see it. I don't know if June thought it was absolutely fabulous but the pair of them didn't give a fuck. Butler had done it deliberately. He backed her up until he knew they could be seen and then said, 'Come on, do it here, this'll be the best place.' The filthy animal.

Something similar happened on another tour but they got too cocky. Wellsy was screwing Vince's bird from behind by the hotel window and as she looked down she saw Vince in the grounds a floor below waving up at them. She wasn't happy...

The tour finished back at Bradford Royal Standard, the Ripper's retreat. It was fucking brilliant. We'd got through the tour with next-to-no trouble, had loads of laughs and the album was riding high. It got to twenty-two and stayed in the charts for three months. That's the way it should always have been.

We had fallen out with Jimmy Pursey over the single, though. 'The Greatest Cockney Rip Off', our first Top Thirty hit, came out at the end of April. It was a piss-take of Sham's song 'Hersham Boys' with a bit of 'The Greatest Rock 'n' Roll Swindle' thrown in. We were booked in with Pursey to record it, but we had it all written and we knew this was the song that was going to get us into the charts. To put it in perspective, this was a tough time for Pursey. He'd dissolved Sham to form a super-group with Paul Cook and Steve Jones, the Sham Pistols, but that went nowhere. And now he was doing a solo album which was absolute cobblers, with songs about frogs and bats and animals. It must have occurred to him that he was basically washed up, while we were going from strength to strength.

We went in and recorded the music OK, but then we started arguing about my lyrics. I'd written it all but Pursey wanted to change the words again like he'd done with 'I'm Not A Fool'. I said to Mickey, 'I'm not having it.' Never again would I let him muck about with my words. The lyrics Pursey came up with were absolutely unbelievable. He had these lines, 'When I was at school, I was a fool but now I'm Joe Cool.' Then he had another bit: 'If you don't like it, go away and bike it.' It was rubbish and I refused point blank to sing it. He said just try it, but I said, 'No, not this time, this ain't the fuckin' Walton Hop, no one talks like that in the East End.'

Pursey started getting really uptight and taking it personally. 'Without me you'd be nothing,' he said. 'I've made you.'

I said, 'Look, Jim, we know that you've helped us and we're grateful for that but you can't go writing our songs.'

He was adamant. He said either we listened to him or he was going. I think he was just a bit fucked up at the time. He said the song would go nowhere without his changes and that we'd have another flop on your hands. We said flop or not, we'll do it our way. Pursey said it again, 'If you don't do it my way, I'm gonna go.'

Vince just shrugged. 'Go on then, fuck off,' he said. As blunt as ever.

And Pursey left. We thought, Thank God for that. Five minutes later there was a knock on the door and he came back in crying. 'I fucking love you,' he said. 'I love you, but you don't listen to me. I know what I'm doing.'

Vince just sat there going, 'Yeah, we don't listen, bye bye, go on, fuck off.'

Pursey stood there getting more and more upset. In the end, Mick took him to one side and said, 'Listen, mate, we don't want to fall out but we can't work like this. We can't have an atmosphere in the studio, we need to work. You're having a breakdown, you need to get away and rest and get some help.'

And that seemed to get through. Pursey got his stuff, thanked Mick, said sorry and left. He was Joe Cool about it. And that was the last time we ever worked with him.

I think he was gutted when 'Rip Off' charted 'cos it proved he was wrong and that we didn't need him. But I did feel a tinge of sadness for him because he'd been an all-right geezer and he'd lost the plot. I'd see him up at Tony Gordon's office and he'd be wearing a Clint Eastwood poncho all the time and a fucking beret. He ended up Skint Eastwood too. Fame didn't do him many favours. He seemed to go into free fall after that. Sham were a big band, he had Top Ten singles at a time when you really had to sell a lot of records to do that. His downfall came when he started to see himself as a Messiah for 'the kids'. He started thinking he was something other than just a normal bloke who shits and pisses and cleans his teeth like anybody else. And when it got nasty at the gigs, at Hatfield and at the Rainbow, he just couldn't handle it. It wasn't his background. It sent him over the edge. What could he do? He'd got roped up with this big house in Surrey with a grand piano which he couldn't play. He was smoking a lot of weed and he just lost it. Shame really. Shame 69.

CHAPTER SEVENTEEN

Class War at Cambridge – Punt City Rockers

'Oi is bootboy music for the working class and if you ain't working class you'll get a kick in the bollocks.'

(STINKY TURNER, *SOUNDS*)

Mickey Geggus remembers: The Rejects went high society in 1980. Ray Rossi had a few spare tickets for the Cambridge May Ball. Elvis Costello was playing, so we took a crew down there. It was like stepping back in time. As soon as we got there, we saw these toffs all swanning about in Edwardian dress and talking in cut-glass accents. There were punch bowls, canapés and fancy cutlery. It was ever so la-de-dah. We went in to one marquee and a few of these Hooray Henrys were fighting each other, so we thought we'll have some of that. We just walked up and waded in, but of course we were really hurting them, laying them out; so the security men ushered us out and we ended up down at the riverside where they were all punting. The temptation was too great. We jumped in a couple of punts, loaded 'em up with bottles and just pelted everyone else off the river. Just like Elvis, our aim was true! We were punt rockers that day. All their punts were overturned, the chinless wonders were swimming for safety, struggling to get their heads above water. It was chaos, like watching an Ealing comedy unfold, hilarious anarchy of the first order. Then the Cambridge boys all gathered on the riverbanks, braying abuse at us, so we came ashore and steamed into them. There were only twelve of us, including Grant, Vince, Danny Harrison, Swallow and Kevin Wells, but we gave them a proper seeing-to. It was bad, but it was what you did at the time. Poor old Rossi had his head in his hands.

In the thick of it, this hulking great Scotsman emerged in his kilt. He was about six foot five with a huge red beard; he looked like a cross between James Robertson Justice and Lurch from the *Addams Family*. 'Right, laddies,' he growled. 'Who's up for a fight then?'

I said to Harrison, 'Come on, we'll steam him, one, two, three…'

We chinned him simultaneously. They were good punches too. The geezer didn't budge. He just looked at us. He was about forty but he was as hard as a cold slab. Then he went into action and he was swinging us about. It took six of us to put him down, but we did him in the end. He was a boy, though. He took some stopping.

In the midst of all this chaos there was even time for a couple of nicely brought-up Cambridge girls to succumb to some tattooed rough-boy charm. I had a few words with Elvis Costello that night, too. Vince was a quality ligger and he'd managed to smarm his way into Costello's hospitality tent. I walked up and saw Vince sitting on a crate of beer. I went to walk in and join him and the bouncer put his arm on my chest. 'You'd better remove that,' I said.

He said, 'Think you can do anything about it?'

That was it. I grabbed him, shoved him out of the way and told him to fuck right off.

Elvis came over. 'There's no need for that, Mick,' he said. 'Everyone's welcome here.'

'Bollocks,' I said. 'Poke it.' As I walked away I heard Vince say, 'Typical...' Turncoat! Anything for a free beer...

Finally the authorities called the Old Bill who chased us from one end of the university campus to the other, and then out into Cambridge Market Square where they finally nicked the lot of us. They slung us in the cells for the night. We sang football songs from dusk to dawn and by breakfast they'd had a bellyful of us. They let us out with a caution. Paul Weller might have lost out to the Eton Rifles but we made the Cambridge toffs see stars, and they weren't footlights.

CHAPTER EIGHTEEN

The Postman Always Shock Twice

Even though The Cockney Rejects were taking up a lot of my time, I always made room for my other band, The Postmen. For a band that didn't really exist outside of our schoolboy imaginations, we did pretty well. We had Peel sessions, reviews in *Sounds*, we recorded for EMI and to this day even our demo tapes have been known to surface on ebay.

The Postmen were the band I formed at school. There was me on guitar and vocals, Terry King on buckets, Johnny Matthews on globe and vocals, and Stevie Stone on whatever he could lay his hands on. We were all from Custom House, all the same age and from the same sort of backgrounds. But because none of us could play any instruments and we were never going to get the money together to buy keyboards or proper gear, we had to come up with a radically different approach to music. We were post-punk if you like, or more accurately beyond boring old-fashioned concepts like structured music. Some music-press pseudo once referred to us as 'a post-modern unit deconstructing pop sensibilities'. Silly cunt. We were just kids having a laugh.

My mate Terry King used to write a lot of the lyrics. He'd come to rehearsals with all these great phrases like 'Welcome to the machine', which I thought he was writing himself. It wasn't until later that I found out he was lifting them from his older brother's Pink Floyd albums. I'd never listened to Pink Floyd, so lines like 'Have a cigar' just sounded really fresh and nutty. 'Have a cigar… or TAKE A FAG!' I thought it was excellent.

For other lyrics we'd get a copy of *Smash Hits*, write down a line from every song in there and slice them all together into Postmen songs. There might be a line from Genesis mixed with something from Siouxsie & The Banshees. I wanted it to mean absolutely nothing.

We did our version of the Banshees' 'Happy House', which became 'Hairy House', and our song 'Calling Plaistow' was a mad echo of 'London Calling'.

In November 1980, we went in to record two tracks for the first *Oi!* album which EMI released. That was our finest hour. We had an electric guitar, an acoustic guitar, the school recorder, a globe and an old steel comb which we'd covered in Izal bog paper and played like a mouth organ. We went into the EMI studios and set up our buckets. The engineer said, 'What the fuck's going on?'

I said, 'We don't play drums, we play buckets,' and looked at him like he was a twat for not knowing.

We got him to mike up the buckets. One of our songs, 'Bonfire Night', was going well. I decided to add a keyboard over-dub, using my sister's little Bontempi organ. We miked it up and did a take. Mad Stevie Stone had the backing track playing through his earphones and when it came to the keyboard passage he just started smashing it, head-butting keys.

It made a right horrible racket. The engineer just looked at us. He said, 'Is that it?'

I said, 'Yeah, that's a take, now we want him to go in with his steel comb.' And we got this poor cunt miking it up! It was an absolute piss-take being in EMI doing that.

Two of the songs made the album, though. 'Have A Cigar 'and 'Beardsman', which was about our geography teacher. His name was Vallis; he came from Plumstead in South-East London and had the biggest beard you'd ever seen. We used to call him Beardsman. We had the most fun I ever had in his class. We'd just sing all lesson and make up songs. That was where unrecorded classics like 'Day-Trip To Baghdad' and 'Peter The Poofter' were written. 'Beardsman' was a name we had for anyone with whiskers. We were fascinated by people with beards.

Good old John Peel heard our two tracks on *Oi! – The Album* and he loved us. He offered us a session. We got the call in December, a month after the album came out and I decided to record the session on my own. I went to Rhodes Music shop to borrow an acoustic guitar from Kevin Ireland and I took it and some other little goodies with me: a school recorder, some spoons and various coat hangers. I got to Radio One at Langham Place, they sent me to the studio and, what with it being near Christmas, the engineer was as drunk as a cunt. He looked up and said, 'Whossh The Postmen?'

I said, 'It's me.'

He miked up the guitar, I only played the top string, and I laid down the riff to a song called 'Mouse', then did a spoon over-dub on the globe. The engineer was loving it! He got me a megaphone and we got all these weird effects on it. I was just standing in there singing 'Mouse... bat' on the megaphone with the riff playing in the background.

I did a song called 'Uncle' next. They had a grand piano in there, so we miked it up. I could only play a few chords, but I got a *Smash Hits* and went through the first line of every song, a bit of Elvis Costello, some Genesis, the first line from a Blondie number and that became 'Uncle'. The third song I recorded was like a marching song. There was some gravel in the studio, and I got him to put a microphone by it, then we just marched on the gravel doing a kind of Munich beer-swilling thing.

At the end, the engineer said it was the best fun he'd ever had. I don't know if that was because he was pissed or 'cos he wanted to seem hip. There was a lot of that Emperor's New Clothes thing about the new wave bands. Maybe he genuinely liked it. But it always made me laugh that The Postmen did a Peel session but John Peel turned down the Police and U2. My only regret is that we never made the Festive Fifty. We must have been bubbling under at 51, just behind Wah! Heat.

Peel never knew who I was. I left my name as Jeff Geggus, my real name. A bit later his producer, the late great John Walters, needed to get in touch with The Postmen and rang me mum and she said, 'Oh no, he's not here, he's away recording with the Rejects.'

He was amazed. 'The Rejects?' he said.

Me mum said, 'Yeah, The Cockney Rejects.'

He went 'Bastard!' and then he roared with laughter. He didn't have a fucking clue, he thought we were some surreal band they'd discovered.

Mind you, they paid me £480 for doing the session on me own. For stamping on gravel, drinking beer, saying the first line that came into me head through a megaphone and thumping chords on the piano. £480 for a load of old bollocks. John Peel broadcast it too. It was hilarious hearing 'Mouse... bat' and this

146

little riff being picked out on the top string with all these spoons and buckets being played. I was in tears. And afterwards he said, 'Yeah, hmm, very, very Pink Floyd influenced.' The great man took us seriously, which made it even more of a result. Fucking brilliant.

We only ever played one gig as The Postmen, which was in May 1979 for Vince's twenty-first birthday. That was in me brother's old Elkington Road flat, 'Elkington Studios' as we called it. I shudder now when I think of it. It was billed as 'A special night with The Postmen' and Garry Bushell reviewed it. He gave it a great review in *Sounds*! Bushell even said we had more potential than the Rejects! Terry King just sat there playing these buckets with a football net over his head 'cos he thought that was punk rock. He didn't have a clue. Maybe Bushell was right, maybe we could have gone further than the Rejects. We were making more money. My only regret was that we never went on tour with the Gonads and the Orgasm Guerrillas. That would have been the ultimate swindle.

CHAPTER NINETEEN

We Can't Do Anything

The first time I met Andy Swallow I remember thinking what a lovely geezer he was. It was April 1980 and West Ham was playing away at Cambridge. Grant Fleming had an old white Cortina, and he volunteered to drive me there. But he had to go to Stratford first and pick up these two fellas. One was Johnny Turner, the other was Swallow. They got in the car, we shook hands, and had a laugh all the way up there. Swallow was a funny bloke but if anything he seemed quite quiet, sensible really.

We drove up to Cambridge and went to a car park. I thought nothing of it, but waiting for us was a little firm from Grays and Tilbury: Tony Barker and his mob of Essex boys. Now I didn't know this but Cambridge had a little firm – I suppose they came on their pushbikes with little baskets on the front. The word had got out that they wanted to have a go and I'd inadvertently been roped in as part of the West Ham vanguard whose job it was to sort them. We got out of the car and shook hands with Barker and the rest. It still didn't dawn on me what was happening. Then Swallow, this nice geezer that I'd just met – went to the boot and said, 'Everything's in here.'

They opened the boot and it was rammo with weaponry; there were hammers in there, crow-bars, machetes, iron bars, knuckle-dusters, the lot. We were better armed than Saddam's Republican Guard.

I just looked at this arsenal and thought, Fuck me, this is heavier than anything I'd ever been used to. I didn't want to get involved. I said, 'Listen, if they're coming to meet us, let's just leave the armoury in the boot for back-up. They're probably nothing and we're about forty-handed.'

It was agreed. We went to the meeting point and thankfully there was a no-show from the fearsome Cambridge crew so we won the day without throwing a punch. But that was the day I met Swallow and learned he was one of the new top dogs. He was only a youngster, he must have been nineteen or twenty, but he went on to become the top boy in the ICF. Later, he moved in to the rave scene, started his own record label and gave the Artful Dodger his first break. He's a successful businessman now, and totally respectable.

Through meeting me, Andy Swallow became part of the band's following. He brought a lot of other Essex boys with him, people like Johnny Turner, Billy Eve and John Simmonds. The next time we toured, the entourage who came on the road with us were the new young hardcore of the Inter City Firm. We already had the older lot with us, Johnny Butler, Dickle and Carlton Leach, plus the little Poplar firm, Andy Russell who was known as Skully, and Terry Hayes.

The Rejects' away team had doubled in strength overnight. I was easy with it at the time 'cos we felt we needed a big firm to deal with the kind of shit we'd had in Monmouth. I'd been getting more involved with the hooligan element at football anyway. We were bold enough now to go into the West Side and the West Side Boys were the top firm. We'd gone from fucking about in an eight-track studio singing about a kid wearing flares and slippers to writing songs like 'West Side Boys', singing about taking the Shed and the Kop; all in the space of a year. We'd started to feel invincible. We even wrote on the back of the second album: 'From Scotland down to Cornwall, we done the lot, we took 'em all.' That's how we felt. Looking back on it now, it seems like a death wish.

It was a recipe for disaster, of course. Our third tour became the tour to end all tours – literally. It pretty much killed us stone dead as a touring band, and the irony was 1980 had been looking like our year. We'd had two singles in the Top Thirty, we'd done *Top Of The Pops*, we'd had two Peel sessions, a hit album and West Ham had won the Cup. We started to feel like we could do anything – and what better title for the next single? We headlined the Electric Ballroom in May, and the next day we were due to record at Rockfield, only Mick went and got nicked at the Cambridge May Ball, an absolutely classic moment in ruck'n'roll history that is related elsewhere in this book.

Rockfield was lovely, a beautiful house out in the country with cows and sheep everywhere. The first thing we did when we got there was rig up in a field, plug in and play naked to the cows. It was fantastic, and an odd place to record 'War On The Terraces'. We had four new songs ready to record, and that was the most belligerent. It was a celebration of football hooliganism reinventing itself: 'So you look out on the terrace/And a smile it breaks your face/'Cos soon the younger generation/Will be there to take your place.' It wasn't the next single, but it was the first track on the second album, *Greatest Hits Vol 2*, which came out in October, so it was kind of a definitive statement.

We decided the single should be 'We Can Do Anything', which we really had high hopes for because it was away from the 'Rip Off' and the 'Bubbles' thing. It was poppier with a good catchy chorus and a great big sing-along hook. We'd already parted company with Pursey so Pete Wilson produced it. Bless him. Pete was a lovely geezer, but he was an old hippy. He'd driven down in this old mini and, after we finished recording, just as a parting shot, we let down all the tyres on his car and covered it in food: salad dressing, beans, jacket spuds. We smeared it everywhere and just fucked off and left him in the middle of Wales.

No wonder we had bad luck, pulling stunts like that.

'We Can Do Anything' bombed. It came out in July, hit the charts at sixty-five, dropped a couple of places and then vanished. It was gone. I don't know why 'cos it was a good song, maybe it seemed a bit arrogant because it was our V-sign to all the people who were knocking us. It got no airplay and we didn't get *Top Of The Pops* 'cos it went down in the second week. I'm not sure they'd have had us back anyway. The only people who played us were John Peel and Mike Read.

And because the record flopped we were still known by the last hit, which was 'Bubbles', and the West Ham thing proved to be our downfall. As the third tour was booked for June 1980, I started to get a feeling in my guts that it was going to be a disaster. It was. A bloody disaster we never recovered from. The vision of us in our claret and blue was burned into the retinas of every soccer yob in the country. It was a red rag to a hell of a lot of bulls. I don't think we'd thought it through. I mean, say a band from Leeds that kept going on about the Service Crew had come along and played in the East End. They would've got slashed. But I was too thick to work that out beforehand and no one from EMI ever took us to one side and said, 'Listen, boys, maybe you ought to play down the violence thing, yah.' Quite the opposite; they'd actually put 'West Side Boys' on the B-side of the single and they couldn't say they didn't know what it was about because all the EMI execs were on it singing the backing vocals. I don't think they gave a toss about us really. To them we were a cash cow with two years' life at the most and then as far as they were concerned we could all fuck off back to obscurity.

We should never have done that third tour. Rat Scabies had asked us to support The Damned on their European tour at the same time. They were playing in Italy, Germany and France. It would have been great, but Tony Gordon wouldn't let us go because tour support slots cost money. Well, they do, but they're also an investment. They take you to a brand-new audience and get you promoted in the European media. It would have been a shrewd long-term move and it would certainly have proved far less costly than the third UK tour, which ruined us. We should have had a break and let the West Ham thing die away. But as it turned out, when we set out on that third tour our entourage was younger, stronger and more aggressively West Ham than ever.

It kicked off in Port Talbot. It was one of the biggest shit-holes you can imagine; all cranes and gas works. The only thing it had going for it was this big fairground on the front. EMI asked us to take this Aussie journalist called Brett along to cover the opening dates. He was going to review us in one of the music papers, *New Music News*. He didn't seem too bad to start with. We left him at the Post House hotel and did the sound check in the Double Diamond club. When we got back he was at the hotel bar cracking on with all these big Welsh rugby players. You always think that Aussies can drink but this prick has had two pints and he's pissed as a fart. He was as good as gold in the van but not any more. He'd started insulting these Taffs, calling them sheep-shaggers and being generally obnoxious. Kevin Wells had to have a little word with him. He said, 'Listen, mate, when Englishmen drink, we know how to hold it so just fucking behave yourself.'

The Welshmen were fine, though, they said, 'Don't worry, lads, we know he's a prick.'

We told Brett to sober up in his room. He started up, 'You can't bar me, I'm an Aussie.'

We told him to fuck off and he did, but by now he'd annoyed us. We marched up to his room, knocked on his door, barged in and stripped him off. 'We'll show you,' we said. We held him down on the bed, got some scissors and gave his pubes a haircut. Then someone stuck some chewed-up Wrigley's Spearmint gum in whatever he had left. At one stage, we turned him over and someone said, 'We've got a surprise for you.' He tried to clench his buttocks, but we opened them up and stuck a tube of SR toothpaste up his arse and squirted it. He had a ring of confidence all right. We should have used Pepsident, then we could have sung: 'You wonder where the yellow went...'

The poor sod didn't know what was happening. He was squealing, 'What are you doing to me?'

We even wrote a song about it, 'With The Boys on Tour': 'We're all thugs/Let it pass/Toothpaste coming up your arse.' Then we tied him up, nicked all his clothes, and went to our rooms before going on to the gig.

We couldn't have tied him up properly, because he got to the phone and called the Old Bill. Half an hour later, we were in our room watching TV and the Welsh Filth turned up to investigate a reported assault and robbery.

We told the coppers what had happened, and said it was only a laugh. Luckily, Brett didn't want to press charges, he just wanted his gear back. But when the cops took us to his room, he started mouthing again. We just shrugged and said, 'You should learn to hold your beer, old son.'

The coppers said they'd escort him off the premises and drop him at the station but somehow they managed to lose him 'cos a bit later we heard him outside the hotel shouting, 'You fuckin' English wankers, I fuckin' hate you fuckin' Pommy bastards.'

Swallow and others were in the next room. All of a sudden, I saw a window open up and cups, saucers, an electric kettle and a toaster started to rain down on him. He got pelted. 'Fuck off, you whingeing cunt,' they said. 'If it wasn't for the Old Bill in the corner, we'd smash you to fuck.'

So Brett beat a retreat and the Old Bill got him, put him in the car, took him to the station and put him on the train. A week later, the *New Music News* came out and he'd given us a brilliant review. Not a word about what had happened, just a glowing write-up.

We never got to play Port Talbot. There was a row going on at the gig before we arrived. When we got there we found a big mob of about a hundred skinheads and eighty-odd punks outside who couldn't get in because they were wearing DM boots. The club would only let them in if they could confiscate their boots. I was looking for an excuse not to play because I fancied going to the fairground. I told the manager we wouldn't play unless he let the skins in with their boots on. He refused, saying it was company policy. So we declined to play, sacked the gig and went to the fair. It had rollercoasters, bumper cars, hot dogs, the works. It was a thoroughly unprofessional way to start the tour, but it was a bloody good laugh and we'd shown solidarity with our fans. Little did I know the next night we'd have hell to pay with another firm of skinheads.

CHAPTER TWENTY

The Battle of Birmingham

B y default, the first gig of the tour was at the Birmingham Cedar club. The violence that night was the worst I have ever seen at a rock concert. It was brutal and relentless. It made Sham 69 at Hendon or the Finsbury Park Rainbow look like day-trips to Alton Towers. The night ended with umpteen casualties, including my brother Mickey. There were people being cut, bottled and glassed, the PA was utterly destroyed, there was claret everywhere. Men and women were in tears. It was the rock'n'roll equivalent of Rorke's Drift, only instead of 140 redcoats with guns facing 4,000 Zulus, we were twenty-odd Cockneys battling more than 200 Midlands skinheads in vicious hand-to-hand fighting.

We got to Birmingham with two vanloads of mates who'd come up purely for the crack. There was Johnny Butler, Dickle, H, Swallow, Danny Harrison, Danny Meakin, John O'Connor, Bruce who was one of the Ancient Brit crew, Brett Tidman. It was a good firm, but no one was expecting trouble. We were all in the mood for a party. We had the Kidz Next Door with us too, of course, but you couldn't count on them when you calculate the odds.

We did the sound check in the afternoon, which was fine, and got back to the gig just after seven. Kevin Rowland, from Dexy's Midnight Runners, owned the club and he was there on the night. It was an odd place, very poorly designed. The stage was right at the back but there was no backstage area. There were stairs in the middle of the venue which went up to the changing room, so you had to walk through the crowd to reach the stage.

We were due on at 9.00 pm. As soon as we got there, we could sense there was a hostile atmosphere. It was packed to capacity, with 500 or so crammed in. A lot of the crowd was skinheads but there were a lot of straight football hooligans there, too; a mixture of Villa and Birmingham City, which in itself was strange because normally they hate each other's guts. It was like West Ham and Millwall coming together to face a common foe, which was unimaginable to us. At that time it would never have happened, the hatred between South and East London was too great.

We had to walk through the body of the crowd to play the gig. As soon as they saw us, they started gobbing at us, and not it a punky way. It was pure loathing. 'Fuck off,' they were going. 'Fuck off, you Cockney cunts.' The atmosphere was poisonous, the worst I'd ever experienced. The entourage came with us as usual and stood at the back of the stage behind us. There was a pair of steps that went down to two exit doors at the back. The only other way to leave that club was through the crowd.

We started playing. Some of the crowd was clearly in to it, but a big belligerent section wasn't. They were just verballing us from the off, they didn't want to know. There were a lot of people at the front going, 'Come on, you wankers, come on, you cunts.' I couldn't really focus on performing because I could tell it was going to go off. One particular bonehead sticks in the memory. He was down the front wearing a Fred Perry shirt and he had an Aston Villa tattoo on his arm. All he did was screw us, saying, 'Come on, come on', offering us out with his hands. I looked at Mick. We both really wanted to get down there and give it to them, but we were trying to keep calm.

We were in the middle of 'Where The Hell Is Babylon', probably the fourth number, when the first pint glass came flying over. I reacted in the worst way possible. I stopped the set and said, 'Whoever chucked that glass, fight your way to the front of the stage and we'll go outside one-to-one. We'll see who's fucking big then.'

I should never have said it. Suddenly the air was filled with things being slung at us: fag packets, coins, beer. Nothing too heavy, but there were a few more glasses in the bombardment, too.

I remember seeing Mick in his yellow vest – we used to call him the Canary – exchanging a few words with the boneheads down the front.

We finished the song, and Vince started tuning his bass. I turned round to see how he was getting on, and the next minute I heard a commotion. I looked and Mick wasn't standing next to me any more. He was in the audience on his own just having it with this mob. So that was it. We all jumped down and it was proper going off, we were battling these skinheads. Vince swung his boot as he leaped in from the stage and kicked some gobby geezer right in the mouth. Knocked him spark-out.

There were only twenty-odd of us, and initially there were about eighty of these Brummies who wanted to know but we pushed them right back to the bar. We were beating 'em no problem and that was when I saw a geezer take a glass and stick it right in Danny Harrison's face. There was blood everywhere. Over to my right, Johnny Butler was cut as well. Some of the opposition already had tools and where we had pushed them back to the bar the others were getting their hands on glasses and bottles. Armed, they started to turn the tide of battle. We were forced back towards the stage, stepping over their casualties on the floor.

I looked back and H was standing up on the stage. Some huge bonehead came from the side and smashed him right in the mouth. He was lucky he never broke H's jaw. But H didn't even go over; he just turned round and upped him.

We reached the stage and starting pulling over the PA equipment to throw at them. There was nowhere else to retreat to. We had to make a stand. We could have gone through the exit but that would have meant defeat and we couldn't contemplate that, we couldn't give in. We were on that stage trying to hit them with everything we could lay our hands on, the bass drum, the stool, the mic stand, the lot. The shower of bottles started up again. I looked up and saw what seemed like a UFO spinning over. It appeared to be moving in slow motion. It was a big glass ashtray and it bounced off Mickey's forehead. The claret poured out of his head like a waterfall. But that only made me madder, and I punched my way back into the melee.

At this stage, the bouncers finally decided to make a show. They pushed their way up to the stage and started shoving us through one of the exit doors into a small corridor. The bouncers locked us in with one of their blokes to keep us in check. We looked around and realised that Mick, Andy Swallow and three others were still in the club.

I told the bouncer to open the door. He didn't move. I lost me rag: 'Open that fucking door now,' I shouted. 'We've got five men out there.'

He was a big geezer, but not that old, probably twenty-six, twenty-seven. He was shitting himself. Vince said, 'If you don't fucking open that door now, we're gonna do you.'

The geezer started crying. He said, 'I can't take no more of this.' He went to pieces.

We pushed him to one side and kicked the door out. There were bits of iron in the room from disassembled clothes rails; not heavy, but, if you whacked someone round the head with one, they'd know all about it. We grabbed what we could carry and went back into the fray. Our five were still on their feet holding the fort. They'd dragged a couple of big tables on stage to use as a shield. There were people unconscious all over the floor. There was broken glass everywhere, the PA was smashed to fuck. The row had been going on for about twenty minutes. We had to finish it. It was do or die time. We burst back into action giving it everything we'd got. We were smashing them, cutting them, hitting them. We drove them back through the club, past the bar and clean out of the venue.

As they were retreating, they were all shitting themselves, which just shows what wankers they were. We'd fought our toughest battle, we'd fought as a firm against the odds, and we'd won. They had all showed so much heart and bottle to stand their ground like that. If it had happened in wartime and we'd been wearing uniforms, we'd have got the VC for it.

At the moment of victory, about thirty Old Bill arrived, which was just as well because it calmed things down. I looked at my brother's face and it was ruined. He had claret everywhere, a gaping head wound. Danny Harrison was bleeding, Johnny

Butler was cut badly. The place looked like a battlefield, there were geezers being stretchered out. Poor Robbie Pursey was as white as a sheet. He was the same age as me, but I was used to it. All the Kidz Next Door came from cosy little places around Hersham. They'd had nice up-bringings. They must have thought, What the fuck are were we doing here?

As soon as the cops got there, they wanted to nick Mick. For some reason they always seemed to go for him. I was livid. I said, 'There's twenty of us and all that fucking scum start on us and you wanna arrest one of ours? What were we supposed to do?'

The Old Bill were speechless. Give Kevin Rowland his due, he never complained, he backed us up. He said, 'You had to do what you had to do.' He was apologising to us. The poor sod was shell-shocked. His bouncers were useless. The only show they made was when they cordoned us off on the stage and pushed us through the exit door. But they didn't do a thing about the row.

Looking back now, there's no doubt that Birmingham was the beginning of the end for us. It was a horrible night. Bouncers crying, birds crying, geezers I looked up to had been cut to bits but they wouldn't go to hospital because they wanted to go round the town looking for the other side. I was sixteen. I don't know if the experience toughened me up or fucked me up. I really don't. Once the adrenalin wore off, I realised it was just terrible. A lot of people probably never got over it. I don't think Mick ever did. Within four years, he'd lost all his hair. Baldness does run in my family, but not that early. It was traumatic, it wasn't like the kind of 'riots' at venues the music press wrote about. It was a fight for survival. It was vicious and nasty and our songs were the main cause of it.

We saw mates getting glassed. These were geezers who always stood together and never gave in, geezers you thought were invincible, yet they were vulnerable, too. They could be stabbed and cut like anybody else. We were lucky no one died.

CHAPTER TWENTY-ONE

The Aftermath

The cops let Grant Fleming rush Mickey to hospital. They had to, his forehead was hanging off. As soon as they'd finished with us, eight of us tooled up and got straight in the minibus. Even Nigel Wolfe was game. We drove round looking for any skinheads we could find on their way back from the gig. We had pick-axe handles, iron bars, the lot. Whenever we spotted a mob of them, we pulled up, piled out and ran 'em everywhere. Every mob we found shit themselves. None of them wanted to know.

After half-an-hour or so, we spotted the mouthy bastard with the Aston Villa tattoo. I jumped out of the van with a baseball bat and said, 'Right, you cunt…' He had a bird with him and, as soon as he saw me, he put his arms round her and pulled her in front of him. I said, 'Look at you, you fucking coward.' He didn't say a word, he just trembled.

We went back to the venue. Grant had brought his cousin

along who none of us knew. When we told them what we'd been doing, this cousin started mouthing off. 'What's it all about?' he hollered. 'What have you got to do things like that for?' He was shouting and screaming.

Vince got hold of him and smacked him in the mouth twice. We had to pull Vince off him. 'Go on, fuck off out of here,' we told the cousin. 'Fuck off before we cut you to bits.' Tempers were running high.

Meanwhile, Mick had got to the hospital. They'd put stitches in his head wound that looked like a Fred Perry design. You can still see the bump to this day. While he was in there, though, the casualty department started filling up with boneheads; refugees from the gig all trooping in with various injuries, broken limbs, cuts and bruises. Some came in on stretchers with drips. And of course they immediately clocked Mick and Grant. With numbers on their side, the Brummie boneheads started massing outside the procedure room where Mick was having his stitches done. There were scores of them, and they were grabbing hold of scalpels, tooling up. Mick had to tell the doc to finish the stitches there and then so he and Grant could get out the window – a fourth-floor window by the way – and shinny down a drainpipe to get away. That's why his wound scarred so badly. They had to get out 'cos the Brummies would have killed them. Somehow they found their way back to the hotel.

When I saw Mick, it all hit home to me. He looked such a mess. I thought, Has it come to this? We'd gone from the gentle fun of 'Flares 'N' Slippers' to total war. Partly it was our fault, we'd given it large and if you talk the talk you have to walk the walk. Half of me thought we're going to have to pack it in. But then the other half of me, the hooligan, was thinking, We've come here and kicked the fuck out of them, let's get on to the next place.

But even then it wasn't over. We had an Edwin Shirley truck parked round the back of the hotel, ready to drive on to the King George's Hall in Blackburn for the next gig. When we got up the next morning someone had bolt-cropped the truck and all the gear had gone: the drum-kit, the amps, the guitars. So we had to go to Blackburn, to a hall which held about 2,000 people, and use the Kidz Next Door's equipment. I went off in one van with Vince, Wellsy, Brett Tidman, Dickle and Butler; and Mick, Johnny Turner, Grant and Swallow were in the other van driven by Mark Reynolds, the drummer from Kidz Next Door. They weren't over the battle, anyway, and now the gear had been half-inched they wanted revenge.

They were on the outskirts of Walsall when they spotted a big congregation of skins and Mods. Knowing the skins had been tooled up the night before, our lads were armed as well. They stopped the van, went up to them and started asking 'em about the stolen gear. There was a bit of verbal. One of the skins tried to pull a tool, and that was it. Mick produced an iron bar and splattered him. They battered the lot of them. It didn't get the gear back but it made them feel better.

We got to Blackburn, met up and went down to the gig. On the way, Mark Reynolds accidentally cut up a carload of blokes. Because the van had darkened windows, these blokes couldn't see who was in it. They pulled up in front of Mark, thinking he was alone, got out of their car and started shouting and hollering at him. They were going to do this and that. They were big geezers, four of them in jean jackets, all in their thirties. Well, this was too much. We kicked the doors open and we battered them all over this shopping centre. We kicked the shit out of them. It didn't bother me 'cos they were bullies. It was the day after Birmingham, Mick had stitches in his head, and him and me were fighting in the doorway to WH Smiths over who was going to hit one of these geezers!

The gig was fine, though.

The next week we played an Asian cinema in Derby; all the blokes working at the venue were in turbans. There was a big mob from Ilkeston there but they were fans, which was a relief. I wasn't ready for another battle yet. This geezer from West Ham had come up, a fucking wally. He used to wear a gum-shield to football. He was an idiot, he was the chairman of the Who's-he? Club. He brought his cousin up to Derby. We hadn't invited either of them. The gig was packed out, we had 800 in and a really good atmosphere. All of a sudden this cousin walked on stage and booted a skinhead in the mouth for no reason whatsoever. The kid had just been dancing and enjoying himself. We stopped the gig, and H walked over, got this cousin by the scruff of the neck and knocked two of his teeth out. The crowd started cheering; but then they went a bit nuts and began to smash up chairs so we cut the gig short. We only did forty-five minutes.

Some DJ from Hull came back to the hotel with us but he was a fucking nuisance, so he got the toothpaste treatment.

Huddersfield was next. Ray Rossi had given us an Asian bouncer for extra security and you had to feel sorry for the poor bloke getting shoved in with us. The gig was at a black club called Cleopatra's. It was mostly fine except for this little mob who called themselves the Huddersfield Skins and who were trying to cause trouble. They weren't even worth bothering with, but we told the bouncer he had to earn his keep and sort them out. There were forty of the scruffy cunts mouthing off at us at the end, and Carlton said to the Asian fella, 'Come on, son, earn your money,' and pushed him off the stage slap-bang into the middle of them. They didn't hurt him – if they had done, we'd have jumped in –

but all you could see was this poor geezer trying to haul himself back up on stage. We pulled him up but we were pissing ourselves. This was the gig when one of the twats in the audience started trying to take the piss out of Vince while we were playing. Vince reacted in the usual way, he blew kisses at him and then got his dick out and waved it at him. The geezer went mad. He turned to Wellsy and said, 'Let me get him.' Wellsy obligingly lifted him on to the stage and Vince hit him on the head with his bass. Knocked him right out.

After the gig, everyone was relaxing at the hotel, shagging, puffing and whatever. All of a sudden there was a call to arms. This same little firm of nuisance skins from the show had turned up looking for us. We rushed down the stairs at them and they turned around and fled. We went outside thinking the van would have been destroyed. They'd bent one of the side mirrors. Pathetic.

The next night was Northampton, which went well, and we drove on for Sheffield where we were due to play a 1.00 pm matinee at the Limit club the following afternoon. I was rooming with Vince and Wellsy and at 5.00 am the next morning some cunt started kicking at the door, saying, 'CID, open up.'

I thought it was a joke; that if I opened the door I'd find Meakin standing there with a bucket of piss. 'Fuck off,' I said. 'We're asleep.'

But they kept on hammering. It was the CID and they nicked all three of us. We thought it was to do with Swallow. He and the others had got up to such high-jinks in their room that the owner had chucked them out and maybe they'd broken back in. But it was to do with Walsall a week or two before, when Mickey had done the skins with an iron bar the morning after the Battle of Birmingham.

They tried to nick me for it. This cozzer said I'd been identified from the picture of me with no tooth on the cover of 'The Greatest Cockney Rip Off' but there wasn't a picture like that on the cover and I hadn't even been in Walsall. I'd been in the other van going to Blackburn, so I knew he was bullshitting.

Mickey was charged and the rest of us were taken down the Old Bill shop where they interrogated us individually; no one gave anything away. Give him his due, Andy Swallow offered to give himself up so the rest of us could get out but I said no way. Then they pulled someone else, who wasn't one of us lot, in and he named everyone who had been in the van with Mick. He grassed the lot of them.

We had the sold-out show at the Limit club that afternoon. The owner phoned and asked the police if they'd release Mick but they refused, and they said the charges were too serious; they didn't even know if they would give him bail. Mickey had been charged with GBH, malicious wounding and causing an affray. It made the papers. The *Daily Mirror* called us notorious. Mickey was looking at a five-year stretch.

I had to drive back to the gig and tell the audience what had happened. I offered them their money back or the chance to use their tickets at a gig we'd rescheduled for the following Saturday if Mick got out.

Mick was banged up for the whole weekend. My mum and dad were devastated. Mum said, 'I told you not to go into this game.' Dad was disgusted. This wasn't how he'd brought us up. I think they felt we'd let them down. Tony Gordon was shocked initially.

When Mick did get out on bail, we weren't on good terms. We didn't even speak to each other. I kind of held him responsible for the nicking, and probably for the entourage. I felt the whole band was in jeopardy because of what he'd done in Walsall, and it was.

We did the gig the following Saturday and we started rowing

with each other while we were playing, threatening to knock each other's teeth out. It was all going out over the mic. I don't know what the crowd must have thought. We went backstage. He took his guitar off. I took me shirt off and I just hit him. Then it went off. It was a full-scale row. We both got cut, there was blood everywhere. It went on for five minutes and I was getting upped and it was just as well H and Wellsy kicked the door in and pulled us apart. If it had gone on any longer, I don't think I'd be here now. When they broke in, they said they found us holding on to each other like terriers.

It had to happen because of the tension that had built up between us during the tour. Afterwards we shook hands, got in the hire car and drove home to plan our next move. It was time to reflect, and make the second album before Mickey went on trial.

CHAPTER TWENTY-TWO

Liverpool: You'll Never Walk Again

We went back to Rockfield to make the second album and in another dumb move agreed to have Chris Briggs from EMI as the producer. He probably wanted to keep us reined in as well, although he didn't exercise any calming influence on the content. The first track was guaranteed to stoke up more trouble: 'War On The Terraces', our hymn to the claret and blue fight club. It was madness really. We hadn't learned a thing.

I got lazy with that album, I didn't write a single song, I just left the lyrics to Mick. But it sold well, it got to number twenty-three in the charts and even had a good review in *Melody Maker*. But to me, the album doesn't stand up as well as *Volume One*. It doesn't stand the test of time and Nigel Wolfe's drumming was shit. Probably the most significant track was 'Oi Oi Oi' which became the anthem of the whole Oi! movement. One line summed it up: 'The kids they come from everywhere, the East End's all around', 'cos this music wasn't just for West Ham fans, Oi! was for working-class kids everywhere.

The sound Chris Biggs got for us was disastrous and we began to terrorise him. He walked out once because someone had a five-knuckle shuffle in his bed, which seemed unreasonable. He said, 'Who's had a laugh and a prank in my bed? There's spunk everywhere. I don't expect this when I come away with people.' He wouldn't shake anyone's hand that night. Briggs hated it when H stripped off and streaked across the dinner table, too, but for us that was quite restrained.

Simple Minds were there at the same time. Jim Kerr had some posh bird in tow. Me and Vince were outside having a joint while she was horse-riding. Kerr was watching her all gooey-eyed. 'Look at me, James,' she said in her hoity-toity voice. As she spoke the horse threw her, but her foot got caught in the stirrup and she was being dragged all over the court. Jim Kerr was panicking, running after her like a headless chicken. He kept looking over to us for help, but we were too stoned; we just stood there laughing our heads off. He didn't say anything; he knew who we were.

The single 'We Can Do Anything' came out at this time but it flopped. The next one, 'We Are The Firm', did better; we tried to get back to the 'Rip Off' with a bit of 'Threes-up Mother Brown' in there and we nicked the chorus chant from *Quadrophenia*. 'War On The Terraces' was the B-side. It went in at fifty-four; it need to go into the Top Fifty in the second week for us to get *Top Of The Pops* but it peaked at fifty-one and that was our last hit.

We played 'War On The Terraces' live for the first time when we headlined the Ballroom in July 1980. There were rumours that Arsenal were going to turn up. Dave Smith was supposed to be bringing his firm down to smash the gig up. He was going to make this big stand. But they never got inside. Smith and his firm were tracked down by the ICF and sent packing before they even reached the venue. The only trouble we had inside was from a

Chelsea skin who came backstage before the show and started slagging West Ham off. He must have had a death wish. I just launched into him. He came in giving it large and went out like a plate of jelly.

We came on to 'Ride Of The Valkyries', a bit of Wagner to set the mood. The Ballroom was packed. You couldn't move in there. There were hundreds of people outside who couldn't get tickets. Our first number was 'War On The Terraces' and the place erupted. It was awesome. The Stray Cats were in the audience; it was the first gig they ever went to in London. They said they'd never been so frightened in their lives, and that was one that went off peacefully.

Our next gig was at the Bridge House. It was a Prisoners' Rights benefit concert organised by Garry Bushell and Hoxton Tom. With a five-stretch hanging over Mickey, maybe we thought it was insurance. The place was packed to the rafters and Johnny Butler turned up in a load of convict chains. It was fantastic; it was probably the best gig we ever did.

We had the second album ready to go, and EMI wanted us to do a fourth tour to support it. But we knew we had to get rid of Nigel because his drumming was so basic. Very basic... he was basically shit. And he was so boring too. He had to go. We'd been chatting up Keith Warrington, better known as Sticks, from the Angelic Upstarts. They were on the slide a bit and he fancied jumping ship. We were planning to sack Wolfie but hadn't quite got round to it, then Garry Bushell wrote an article in *Sounds*, saying we'd been asked to play a Save The Whale Gig and that 'Apparently Nigel Wolfe has been "seen later".' It was our way of saying he'd been sacked but it was the first poor old Nigel knew about it.

He rang us up and said, 'What's all this about? It says here I've been sacked.'

Mick said, "Fraid so, mate, back to the shoe shop for you.'

I celebrated by having my first tattoo done. It was about time I joined the club. I went to Dennis Cockle in North London and had a Union Jack on my arm with 'England' written underneath it, because that was before the cross of St George came to prominence. I had to hide it from me mum. I pretended I'd hurt myself playing football. It was only about ten days before Mum worked it out for herself. She shook her head and said, 'Where did you go wrong?' Then Mick designed a boxing-glove tattoo which we both had done. Later, I had a bulldog put on me arm. I think Cockle's eyes were going, though, 'cos it's fucking terrible.

While Mick was in and out of the solicitors about his case, EMI replaced Rob Warr with a fellow called Ashley Goodall. You only had to look at the geezer to know he wasn't on our wavelength. He had a curly blonde perm. He used to come in and go, 'Hey, Stinky, have you been playing with young girls' titties this week?'. EMI were doing *Oi! – The Album* with Garry Bushell that October and as we had time to kill we went into their studios a lot, doing demos. It was costing us £500 a day but it was worth it 'cos we were really dedicating ourselves to our music, learning to play better, trying to master Aerosmith songs, writing different stuff. We were finding ourselves as a band. Mick was really maturing as a guitarist. He'd grown up as a musician. He wrote a song called 'England', an acoustic instrumental, which he played to Paul Weller, and they recorded a version with Weller singing and Pete Way from UFO playing bass on it. It was never released, although it's been out on a bootleg; someone snided it from somewhere and brought it out as Paul Weller featuring The Cockney Rejects. Mick was fuming. It wasn't Weller featuring him; it was the other way round.

The hook-up with Weller came about through Grant Fleming.

We loved The Jam but we'd never met them. Maybe Weller wouldn't thank me for reminding him, but at this time, 1980, he and Mick became good mates. I never really mixed with him. I met him once at a rehearsal studio in Shepherd's Bush, and thought he was an all-right geezer, but I was not one for ligging. UFO were great geezers and Mick and Vince loved hanging about with them but it wasn't my scene. I was never comfortable with the backstage thing. I was happier going for a beer with Garry Bushell in Charlton or on the Ferrier Estate.

The only downer about working at EMI was we couldn't stop ourselves from thieving. Capital Records was right next door and all their stock ended up walking. All the Sammy Hagar T-shirts and albums came my way, 'cos I was such a fan. He was an ex-boxer, a really cool guy. Why I wanted the T-shirts I have no idea. I gave them away to people. I wasn't like Vince and nor was Mick. Vince was a seasoned thief, the only thing we'd ever done before was nick some Fruit Salad and Black Jacks from the Co-op. Even then I was so frightened when I did it that I went and put them back. I was only about eight.

We got the dates through for the new October tour. We were booked in for another gig in Birmingham. I don't know why. Maybe I should have had misgivings after the way the previous tour had gone pear-shaped but my attitude was, 'Fuck it, we'll go out there and have it.' As soon as the dates came through, I went round West Ham spreading the word: Birmingham is on.

We played Huddersfield for the second time and then Grimsby and there was no agg. The next date was Brady's in Liverpool on the Thursday with Birmingham on the Friday. Everyone was geared up for it. There was going to be a mass turn-out of the ICF, a three-line whip. Nobody was worried about Liverpool. We turned up there eight-handed. We stayed in the Holiday Inn and had that bloke Ashley Goodall from EMI with us. We had to suffer him in our hotel.

We got to the gig for the sound check. The great Ray Rossi was there, Shotgun Ray they called him, as promoter. I liked him a lot but as we were setting the gear up he had a few words with me, like he half meant it. He made this saucy comment. I said something saucy back and he bit. So I said, 'Do you want to row then or what?'

He said, 'All right then.'

So they roped an area off and I must have rowed with him for about ten minutes. I threw him all over the place, mangled him, but it wasn't fists. There was needle in it but it was half-joking. In the end, I was sitting on top of him.

He said, 'I've had enough now.'

I said, 'Yeah, you better have done.'

He was a geezer, I was only sixteen, but I threw him every where. I'm not sure why he got like that. It was probably because he was having a lot of hassle about money from Tony Gordon, but it was nothing to do with us. We shook hands afterwards and we've got on ever since.

We went back to the hotel and found out there had been a commotion. Vince, Wellsy and Danny Harrison had come back and found eight Scousers mobbed up outside. They told Vince and Kevin Wells to hand over their Harrington jackets and, when Wellsy told them to fuck off, one of them tried to slash his face with a Stanley knife. Our boys gave them some verbal and then went into the Holiday Inn. What else could they do against a mob with knives? They weren't super-heroes. The hotel called the Old Bill. We shrugged it off, but Ashley Goodall got on his high horse and demanded a police escort to the gig. How fucking ridiculous

Rockstars! Me and brother Mick in front of my boxing trophies at home – a right pair of posers!

Top left: Having a beer after a recording at Rockfield studios in Wales. It was here that we cut *Greatest Hits Volume 2* and *The Power and the Glory*. (*Clockwise from top left*: Mick, Vince, Kevin Wells, me, and Danny Meakin)

Top right: Life's a beach, but not in Grimsby! Here we are around 1980, still in the early days.

Bottom: Times were changing for us in 1982. In London, during our wild heavy metal phase.

Tough times.

We went to the states full of dreams, but the biggest thing we achieved was being paid to leave! The top picture shows us at the beginning of a disastrous 1985 tour (*Left to right*: Ian Campbell (bass), Keith Sticks Warrington, Mick and me), and the bottom shows me at the end, a lost teenage hippy at his lowest ebb.

After the nightmare of America, we staged a comeback gig in 1987 (*top left*) with Vince (*pictured*) back on bass. It went off. The Rejects were back on the map, but by May 1989 we were ready to hang up our gloves. These are the photos from out last gig (*top right* and *bottom*). It was the end of an era of crazy highs and terrible lows, and the time was right to move on … or so we thought!

On the road again. Music's in the blood – we just had to play again. Here's the line-up for our comeback gig in San Francisco, in 2001 (*pictured top, left to right*): Mick, Tony Frater on bass, Les Cobb drums, and me as Stinky Turner again!

Bottom: In Summer 2003 we played to 40,000 at the Full Force Rock Festival in Leipzig, Germany. Fantastic is the only word for it.

Family. My kids mean the world to me. Up top is my daughter Chantelle on holiday in Devon, 1996. Below on the train with (*left to right*) Chantelle and my sons Jeff and Jay.

Top: With Karon, the love of my life.

Bottom: As I am today, outside 137 Varley Road, the house I was born in. Me mum still lives there now.

Top: Friends for life. All of us together in Madrid 2004. (*From left to right*) Me, Karon, Mick , Tony, Lesley and Nobbie live it up Spanish Style.

Bottom: The Cockney Rejects as we are now, still doing it.

was that? It made us look like pricks. But the EMI man insisted and so we had two cars and an escort, only I couldn't fit in one of the cars. I had to walk half a mile to the gig with Danny Meakin which kind of defeated the object.

Of course, when we got there, there were all these Scousers, skinheads and terrace geezers near the entrance and they were all verballing me. 'You fucking Cockney wanker.' I kept walking. One of them said, 'Do you want a knuckle sandwich?' On my life!

I said, 'You've been watching too much *Grange Hill,* you cunt. A fucking knuckle sandwich? We used to say that in the infants, go on, fuck off.' I thought, Just be brave and go through it, expecting to get a clump at any minute.

Then a massive bouncer bowled right through and slung an arm round me. He said, 'Stinky Turner? Come with me.' He told the mob to back off and they all did. The bouncers seemed well prepared. Once we were inside they pulled out all these coshes and billy-clubs, saying, 'Don't worry lads, you'll be all right tonight.'

I thought, Good men. We were only eight-handed and if it had kicked off we wouldn't have stood a chance.

It wasn't a good gig. We had a worse reception than Robert Kilroy-Silk at an Arab Friendship rally. As soon as we went on stage, we were hit with a barrage of abuse, it was relentless, and they were chucking things at us, too. So right away we knew how it was going to go. We just gave it the big 'un back. There was a steel barrier up to keep the audience at bay, and all the bouncers were at the side. Two songs in, the crowd sent a shower of bottles over us. The bouncers came on stage and stopped the gig. We had to wait backstage while they calmed them down. I remember thinking, Fuck me, I've got to go back out there. It was going to be really hard work. After five minutes, the bouncers told us to get back on. Mick was playing a new red BC Rich, which he'd borrowed from Tonka

Chapman. We were into the fourth song, still getting loads of verbal, and I saw Mick take off Tonka's guitar and smash it into the audience. He did two geezers straight over the head with £1,000 worth of axe. Slaughtered them. We all rushed to the front of the stage, but you couldn't really reach over it with your hands.

The bouncers leaped in and pulled us back. They started appealing for calm but the Scousers were fuming. They should have just pulled us off stage. After ten minutes of commotion, they put us back on. There was this great fat doughnut down the front who'd been verballing us all the time. Before we even played, he was hurling abuse. So I got the mic, went over to him and said, 'We've got a song for you, my Scouse friend, and we're going to play it. It's called "You're A Fat Man",' and Mick started up the riff to 'Bad Man'. The fat cunt was fuming, and when it got to the chorus I was singing it to his face 'You're a fat man.' All of a sudden, the bouncers came on stage fuming and stopped us mid-song. One of them told me to come over. He had this big cosh in his hand and, as I was waltzing over to him, I thought, He's gonna put it over my head. Instead, he started telling me to tone it down – in front of the whole audience. Of course, they were loving it, the fat cunt was laughing at me, because I'd been told off by the bouncer.

We started playing again, giving it loads of front. The bottles had stopped coming but all of a sudden from nowhere a pint pot came flying through the air and caught me right in the Jacobs. I couldn't help myself, I had to go down on one knee. It took the wind right out of me sails. I got up and thought, Right, don't get mad, get even. I got the mike and I said, 'It's Thursday night, you've all paid a fiver to get in, you've got to go home by taxi 'cos the trains have stopped running and you're gonna get in at two o'clock in the morning and then get up at six to go to work. We've taken a grand for this gig and we're fucking off to the Holiday Inn to drink Tequilas, goodnight.'

And with that we went backstage. Well, they went mental. The bouncers had to come round to protect us. You could see the backstage area from the stairwell and all these dirty Scousers were gobbing and pelting things down at us. But I'll give the bouncers their due, they stood their ground. The punters mobbed up outside. In the end, the bouncers had to go out en masse to disperse them 'cos they wanted to kill us. They took us round to the cars, looked after us, but even as we walked through you could see the Scousers lining the streets, glaring.

We made it back to the Holiday Inn. I don't even know why we started staying at places like the Holiday Inn. I suppose it felt more rock starry, but I preferred the little Colwyn Bay guest-house-type places: Jean's Bed & Breakfasts and all that. Being in the Holiday Inn encouraged bad behaviour. These plush places were just a waste of money. We were paying for all the entourage and people ran amok, letting off fire extinguishers. We got a £2,000 bill for one night in Bradford. It was crazy. When we got back to the Liverpool hotel, there were the usual high-jinks with beer and birds but I just went to bed. All I could think about was the next day. The night we'd just been through had been hell but we didn't have anything nice to look forward to. Tomorrow was Birmingham.

We got to the venue – incredibly it was the Cedar club again! How crazy was that? We did the sound-check. A lot of the West Ham boys were already there and the mood was belligerent. It was only four months since the riot and they wanted to teach these Birmingham skins another lesson. H was so hyped up he even clumped one of The Exploited, who were supporting us. Feelings were running high. There were twenty-five ICF up already with loads more on the way. We would have been sixty-handed by the evening.

We drove over to the Holiday Inn to check in only to find the Old Bill waiting outside. They came over as soon as we parked up. This inspector did all the talking. 'Cockney Rejects?' he said. 'You're not checking in here, you're not doing anything in Birmingham. You're going to get into that van, we're going to escort you to the M6, and you're going back to London because you won't be playing a gig here tonight.'

I thought, What a touch, because, to be honest, the more I thought about the gig the less I wanted to do it. The mood our boys were in, it would have kicked off even if the locals hadn't started.

The cops had one car in front of us and another one behind. They took us to the M6 and then on to the M1. The rest of the dates were pulled as well because the PA company withdrew their equipment. I remember thinking, Maybe this is the end, we may never tour again. If we could have got ourselves on *Top Of The Pops* at this time, when everything was going wrong, we might have been able to turn things round. But it wasn't to be.

CHAPTER TWENTY-THREE

Ww've Been Framed

W e were down but we weren't out. As a band we'd taken some heavy punches. Mick had his court case hanging over him like the sword of Damocles, we'd missed out on *Top Of The Pops*, the tour had been pulled and to top it all Red Ken's GLC slapped a ban on us. We would no longer be allowed to play London venues because of 'gig violence', even though the trouble at gigs was happening far away in places like Liverpool and Birmingham. A more inspired manager might have packed us off to the USA or Europe – we found out years later that we were selling masses on the Continent. We felt things could have been different for us.

The opportunity came up to do an ITV programme called *TV Eye*. The producer called EMI and said they wanted to feature us in a show about football violence. You might have thought a clued-up record company would have told them where to go, but, no, they advised us to do the programme. So like the mugs we were, we agreed. The trigger for it had been a recent League Cup match. West Ham had played Tottenham at home, and there had been a full-scale invasion of the Spurs end; it had gone proper off.

Terry Murphy let us hire the Bridge House for a private function one Saturday dinnertime before the next home game so ITV could film us in front of an invited crowd of mates. They were all there, Tony Barker, Hoxton Tom, Grant, Swallow. They filmed us playing a couple of numbers – 'Fighting In The Street' and 'War On The Terraces' – then some arty-farty bird interviewed us backstage.

Mick was our spokesman. She started by asking about the Tottenham game and football violence in general. We told her it was getting worse and that there was no end in sight because there were a lot of little firms on the rise. We predicted it was going to spread to Europe, and she was nodding in agreement.

Then she changed tack. 'What do you think of right-wing politics entering into your music?' she asked.

Mick said, 'Hang on, love, we're not here to talk about politics. We're not involved in politics, we don't talk politics. We're here to talk about football.'

She got the ball rolling again, asked a few more questions about fighting at football and then it was: 'What do you think of the rise of British Movement at your gigs?'

It was ridiculous because there was no BM trouble or even any BM activity at our gigs. It wasn't what we were about. Mick said, 'We don't get British Movement trouble, my old man fought in World War Two, we aren't Nazis, we hate Nazis, right? Leave it out.'

Reluctantly she changed the subject and went back to football.

The programme went out the following Thursday and, as you've probably guessed, it turned out that the show wasn't about football violence, it was about the British Movement and how they had infiltrated the terraces. None of the interview with us was shown. Instead, the programme claimed that the band was at the forefront of BM activity and that we were using our gigs for BM recruitment drives. Then they cut to a ten-second clip of us playing 'War on the Terraces'. It was absolute bollocks, the biggest load of lies you'd ever seen. We were livid because none of it was true. We were never a political band. We weren't socialists like the Upstarts or hippy anarchists like Crass. We had nothing but contempt for politicians. We were anti-politics from the start. Our songs were about the realities of our lives, our hopes, our dreams, our battles, police brutality and discrimination. One of my first songs, 'Fighting In The Streets', sums up my attitude to politicians. The lyrics say: 'Wankers hand out leaflets/They never ever let it be/I don't care what they do/But they better not come near me.' Another part of the same song goes: 'You all look for solutions/But you can rack your brains/No matter what the government does/It's never ever gonna change.'

Yes, as a band we were all patriotic like most decent people are, but we were patriotic for our country and our community. We weren't obsessed with another country's evil, failed past. But, because of who and what we were, we got attacked by left and right, by the middle-class media and crackpot Hitlerites alike.

The next morning, we went straight over to Tony Gordon and demanded he sue them. He just shrugged and said, 'Well, the damage is done now.'

I went, 'What do you mean "the damage is done"? They've libelled us, they've lied, they've fucking ruined us, done us like kippers, let's take them to court and fight them.'

He refused point blank. He said, 'You've got yourself into your own mess, you shouldn't have done it.'

I said, 'Well, where was your advice? You're our fucking manager, ain't ya?' I was shouting. I wanted to get him by the throat.

But he just said, 'No, the money's not in the bank to sue.'

We'd had two Top Thirty albums and five Top Seventy singles that year, we'd sold merchandise by the lorryload and we were with EMI, the world's biggest record company, but apparently there was no money in the bank. It was crazy. If we'd issued a solicitor's letter, we'd have got an out-of-court settlement at the very least. We would have beaten them hands down, because they didn't have a leg to stand on. But we couldn't persuade him to act.

You could ask why we didn't sue them ourselves, but we were kids. We were out of our depth with solicitors and all that shit. We were relying on our manager to fight our corner and he just turned his back on us.

To make it worse, a week later we asked him to try and get the GLC to waive the ban so we could play the Lyceum. He said, 'You're joking, no one's going to give you a licence after that show.'

John Curd the promoter wanted to put us on, but Curd couldn't go in the face of the ban, or he would have lost his licence. So, from that moment, the band was effectively shagged. There was nowhere to go. We'd been framed by ITV, absolutely tucked up. And, of course, the *NME* jumped on it and repeated the lies, probably just to have a pop at *Sounds*. They wanted to see us destroyed. We were too real for those cunts.

In the end, it was down to us to prove where we stood with the Movement. There was a show-down between our firm and the BM at Barking station; and, as at the Electric Ballroom, we decimated them. It started when their mob followed us from the Barge Aground pub in Barking. There were twenty of us and about twenty-five of them. They were putting things about, saying how they were going to do to us what they did to Sham.

They thought because they were older than us we'd back down, but we stood our ground. As the two mobs squared up, H turned round and smashed their leader Dick Barton. He went down in a heap and the rest of the master race immediately shit their pants and took off. It was the greatest Nazi retreat since the battle of Stalingrad. And, just like in 1943, they'd had a field marshal captured by the enemy.

If we'd been having problems with the Far Left, they would have had the same treatment. We had no time for cranks.

In 1982, the ICF took the BM out of the frame for good as a force in East London. Our one-time roadie Skully and other ICF chaps had organised a march protesting about the jailing of Cass Pennant, who was like a black Del Boy and was staunch ICF. The BM started threatening people, trying to pressure them to cancel this 'march for a nigger'. Word got around and people were up in arms. The ICF had been planning to take on Tottenham fans the following Monday, as West Ham were playing Spurs that night. Instead, they hunted the BM down to the Boleyn Arms and smashed them to fuck. They never gave us any agg again. Cass went on to become our manager for a while; until we caught the cheeky chappie flogging bootleg Rejects videos on his stall.

CHAPTER TWENTY-FOUR

Forrest Clumped

W'd never been prone to depression. As far as I was concerned it was something that had happened in the 1930s. But even the most positive-thinking optimist would have to acknowledge that we'd now hit rock-bottom and that there was nowhere else to go. He'd be wrong to think that, though. As it happened, we still had a lot further to go. We were going to keep on going down, down, deeper and down like Status Quo on a waterslide. Things just got steadily worse. I was in my first proper relationship with a pretty local girl called Debbie, which I suppose helped keep me steady. But the overwhelming feeling among the band was abject gloom and apprehension. Mick's trial was coming up in January, it was hanging over us like a cloud. We were convinced he'd be going away for many years; so we only had a couple of months to try and salvage something. The solution was to throw ourselves into a new album. We started writing *The Power & The Glory*, which turned out to be our finest album to date. We'd already demoed some of the songs and we wanted to make it the business. But before we went into Air Studio, more disaster struck.

I'd been ill with flu and Debbie had come round to see me at my mum's. I still felt wobbly but I said I'd walk her home. At the top of Varley Road there were garages where Ronan Point, the notorious exploding tower block, had once stood. As we got to this little alleyway, three big geezers came straight towards us. I tried to move us to one side, but one of them barged straight into Debbie, and pushed her out of the way. I snapped of course. 'What the fuck are you doing?' I snarled.

They just laughed at me. 'Do you want some?' they said. I was just a kid to them. Debbie was shitting herself.

They were all about eighteen, but I recognised one. He was a hefty lump called Forrest, and I knew where he hung out, round Sark Walk where my sister lived. They were heading that way and as I knew Mick was round at my sister's that night I backed off. 'All right,' I said. 'We'll leave it for now. It's three on to one, there's nothing I can do.' We carried on walking, but as soon as we got round the corner I told Debbie to get off home while I ran off to my sister's the back way.

I told Mick what had happened and we immediately went out looking for this Forrest and his cronies. Mick picked up a lump of wood as a tool. We found them all standing round on a street corner. Never one to mess about, Mick went straight up to Forrest, smashed him in the face with the wood and leaped on to him. I steamed into the other two but they took off.

Mick got Forrest on the floor but Forrest sunk his teeth into Mick's thumb like an animal and wouldn't let go. Mick kept hitting him but his choppers were clamped on like a vice. I picked up a milk bottle. 'Let go, you cunt, or I'll do this right over your head,' I said. Forrest didn't react, so I carried out the threat and smashed the bottle over his head. He let go all right.

I kicked him a couple of times and left him lying there on the floor. Mick went back to me sister's like nothing had happened. I headed back towards Varley Road. Mick rang me dad, and me old man went round and disposed of the glass. He also got hold of the lump of wood and burned it in the front-room fire.

Forrest ID'ed us and the Old Bill came round me old woman's house with a warrant for our arrest, for assault with a weapon. Mum said we'd gone and she didn't know where. With Mickey's trial coming up, we felt we had no choice but to take off. Most people on the run at this time jetted off Marbella. Not us. Mick jumped in a cab to Danny Meakin's house at Manor Park, while I got a train down to the Costa del Canvey… Canvey Island, where Meakin's mum had a caravan. The only problem was the camp was about to shut up for winter so I knew I couldn't stay long. Every time I phoned home, Mum was begging me to give myself up. Dad said, 'How can you stay there when the electric's shut off? You've gotta come back and face the music.'

The Old Bill suspected we were in contact with our parents and they promised Mum and Dad that if they got us back home they'd just turn up and nick us. There'd be no rough stuff, no melodrama. So reluctantly we came back. I was worried, not for me but for Mick. It was another assault charge and once again they said he'd used a weapon. On top of Birmingham, it didn't seem possible that he wouldn't go down. The thought made me feel ill.

It happened almost as the Old Bill promised. They didn't slap us about but they did go in for some maximum theatrics. We were round me old woman's house as agreed, and at 7.00 pm, with all the neighbours looking, a vanload of cozzers turned up, nicked us and slapped the cuffs straight on for dramatic exit.

Then they banged us up in the cells. This local CID bod called Denton really had it in for me and Mick, he wanted to nick us bad. We refused to make statements. We were sitting there eating and Denton opened the door and sneered: 'Police car, eh? You hate the Old Bill, don'tcha, you little lot.'

Mick said, 'Yeah, that's right.'

Denton said, 'You're going to be here a long while. I tell you what, if I give you a guitar, maybe that'll help pass the time.' He was smirking.

Mick said, 'Yeah, you're fucking clever, ain't ya?'

Denton went, 'Don't worry about this, you're gonna go away for this one.'

They kept us in there for seven hours, and then Mick was charged with GBH and wounding with intent. I was just charged with GBH. They gave us bail, and we went straight to the solicitor. Then it was back to the studio to do *The Power & The Glory*. How we got through it, I'll never know. How Mick didn't have a breakdown is beyond me.

The only thing that seemed to be going right in my life at this time was my football. I was still turning out for Terrana and I was starting to play really well. We knew this character called Ricky Webb, who we used to call Foghorn Leghorn and who knew a scout for Millwall. I was rank West Ham obviously but I pestered him to get them to take a look at me. I thought it would generate publicity for the band. 'Iron signs for Lions', that kind of thing.

The trouble is, scouts tend to turn up unannounced. This particular Sunday morning I'd been out drinking until 3.00 am. I got up to play, but I was in a foul mood. My head was throbbing like a dick at a lap-dancing club. We were playing a team called Struttons FC. Five minutes into the game, one of their players pushed me over in our area. I went down on my teeth. That was it. I steamed into him and gave him a good caning in our penalty area. Everyone got involved, pulling me off him, and the referee had no choice but to send me off. He called me a fucking disgrace and I was. I'd given away a penalty, which the other team scored from. But at the time I wasn't in the mood to bite the bullet and walk away quietly. I was effing and blinding, shouting at the ref, really giving it to him. I eventually walked off, changed, and said, 'Fuck the lot of yous', and walked home.

A couple of hours later I got a phone call from Ricky Webb. 'Thanks a lot,' he said.

I didn't know what he was on about. Inevitably, the Millwall scout had been there. He was livid. He told Ricky, 'Don't ever, ever, ever, waste my time with untalented, hopeless people like that again. I have never been so insulted in all my life.' I never did get that trial.

Ricky said he hadn't told me the fella was coming because he hadn't wanted to put me off my game. Laugh? I almost bought a round. That was the end of any dream of a professional football career. And I was in the dog-house as far as Foghorn Leghorn was concerned. We still carried on playing, though. There was no stopping Terrana.

CHAPTER TWENTY-FIVE

Dancing With The Devil

W e wanted to make *The Power & The Glory* special because it looked like being the last album the band would ever make.

UFO had recorded *The Wild, The Willing & The Innocent* at Air Studios in London's Oxford Street and that's where we insisted on working. It was about £1.60 a minute to record in there but, fuck it, if we were going out, it'd be in a blaze of glory. We got this little fella called Steve Churchyard as producer because he'd worked as UFO's engineer. The studios were great; loads of famous faces were floating about. Linda McCartney was there at the same time as us. Marvin Gaye's studio was there, too, but for some reason he'd abandoned it. He hadn't been in there for ages so we had a snoop about to see what we could thieve and it was like Christmas. We found a bag of coke in there. There must have been a quarter of an ounce of really pure gear. There was a bit of Jack Straw in there, too, so that went as well.

We consciously tried to come up with a more mature album. The title track was real ballsy punk-pop in The Professionals mould. It was a defining anthem, about being East London and working class:

> From the bombs that flew through World War Two
> From Albert Docks to Bow
> We could never show our fear
> The world could never know
> And the fat-cats sat in office blocks and said:
> 'Look we won the war'
> And the tears we shed over our dead
> Made us hate them all the more
> The Power & The Glory
> The power and the pain
> Ain't no matter what they say
> We will rise again.

We did a couple of acoustic numbers, too. We wanted the sound of a waterfall on one track. The only way we could get it was by miking up the men's khazi and taping us pissing into the latrine. We should have called it 'Golden Shower'.

We finished the album off in Rockfield, and that's when we put the wind up the devil. Ozzy Osbourne was staying in the area, so we decided to make some mischief. We loved Ozzy, absolutely thought he was the bollocks, but that didn't mean he was safe. Especially as we figured the Prince of Darkness would be out of his satanic skull on drink and drugs.

They had clay-pigeon shooting at Rockfield and big white sheets on the bed. One night, after a lot of dope and lager, we got the sheets, cut out eye-holes, grabbed some twelve-bore shotguns and headed for Ozzy's place dressed as the Ku Klux Klan. 'We'll give him fucking Satan,' said Mick. 'We'll freak him right out.'

Ozzy was staying up the road in a big mansion. The four of us got there, sheeted up, and started dancing around on the grounds in front of the house, chanting odes. All of a sudden Vince said, 'I'll wake the bastard up.' He got one of the shotguns and let off a round into the air.

All the lights came on, and suddenly the top window flew open. It was Ozzy, wild-eyed and demented. He looked mad, like we'd interrupted him in mid-trip. The great man stood there screeching and moaning at us. 'You fuckers,' he shouted. 'Get out or I'll fucking kill ya,' in his Brummy accent. Then he started intoning all this Latin shit, magical spells, incantations and all that.

There was more activity in the house so we let off another couple of shells and scarpered before the roadies came and got us.

Ozzy had seen these four mysterious, robed figures brandishing twelve-bores looking like ghostly apparition from 19th-century Alabama in a field in the middle of nowhere in Wales. And, with whatever shit he was on at the time, it absolutely freaked him out. It might even have been our fault that he started shaking.

When Ozzy found out it was us, he told Ross Halfin, 'Tell them Cockney cunts that if they ever, ever try a trick like that with me again, I'll blow their fucking legs off.'

But he did laugh about it, and later we got the message back via Garry Bushell that he thought we were 'men after his own heart', which was a fine compliment. It had been a brilliant wind-up. Mission accomplished. After all the shit we'd been through, much of it self-inflicted, we were starting to enjoy ourselves again. Unfortunately, we'd gone massively over-budget. Our first album had cost about two thousand pounds. This one cost twenty-seven grand!

We got up to a lot of mischief at Rockfield. One freelance rock photographer really copped it. He'd turned up uninvited and wanted to stay for a few days. He was about thirty, posh accent, camera, long black hair like Alice Cooper, cowboy boots. He looked like he should have been in Iron Maiden. He said he lived in a car. The lads took him down the local pub and apparently he wouldn't stand his round, so from there on in he was fair game. Ricky Meakin and Danny Harrison would bring him food, but they'd stick the chocolate biscuits up their arses before they gave them to him and rubbed ham and cheese round their knobs. Horrible. And yet he ate the lot, wolfed it down. A finger of fudge was not enough to give the cowboy a treat. Then he had a midnight visit from masked men with the concoction bucket. Give him his due, he came after them with a fire extinguisher – chased them into the kitchen and got brought down with a hail of eggs, spuds and flour. And that's when we noticed he'd come down bare-footed. The cowboy boots were still in the room. At one stage he ran into the night, into the pitch black, and seconds later we heard a terrible scream where he'd run into a water tank and broken his nose. We brought him back in, mopped him up and tended to his nose. Everyone was sweet, he knew it was an accident. We helped him upstairs to his bedroom. We left him at the door, and just as he walked in we heard more screams: someone had taken a Tom Tit in his cowboy boots.

We stopped recording over Christmas and went home. The day before Christmas Eve I met up with H, Frankie Hamilton, another bod and a geezer called Billy Challenger, who was known as Moth, and we decided to pop into EMI. We got on the piss at The Horn of Plenty in Mile End at 11.00 am and by half-one we were on the train up to Bond Street to have some 'Freddie Freeman's' – free booze, courtesy of the record company. We were already pissed. H was walking up and down the carriage annoying people, getting in their faces, trying to make them sing carols. If I'd had any sense, I'd have diverted them from EMI. But, of course, I didn't. We got there and they put us in a little hospitality room with a load of beers. At about 4.00 pm one of the silly fuckers decided to punch a window through.

EMI were supplying us with gratis booze and that was how he decided to repay them. Obviously we were asked to leave. We came out of the building singing 'Bubbles', full of Christmas spirit. There were two geezers walking across the road, older than us, one of them had a bottle of wine in his hand. 'Fuck off, you cunts,' one of them shouted. 'West Ham? You wankers, we're fuckin' Arsenal.'

We went over to confront them with a few choice words. 'Fucking telling us to stop singing "Bubbles", you're nothing,' we said. 'The shit on our shoes. Arsenal couldn't make the show in the Cup Final and you don't show here.'

The trappy one went to throw a right hander, so we steamed into them, not too hard, just giving them a slap. Suddenly, this tall, blond geezer wearing a Parka coat appeared out of nowhere and dived in to the fray. He looked about thirty. I chinned him and as he hit the deck he pulled out a radio. He was a plain-clothes copper. We just scattered.

I knew all the back streets really well, and I made my escape to Rhodes Music in Denmark Street. I told Kevin Ireland what had happened. I said, 'I think I'm nicked, again.' It had happened right outside EMI and we'd been seen leaving the building. All the Filth had to do was go into the record company and they'd be able to ID me, if not any of the others. And that's how it went down.

I was already up on a GBH charge for Forrest; I was due for Committal in January. It was a mess and I was genuinely worried that I'd go down for it. Kev sympathised. I sat in the shop strumming a guitar as a dark cloud came over me. Phil Daniels the actor was there. He'd heard everything I'd said and he tried to lift my spirits. 'Don't matter, mate,' he said. 'You'll be all right, you just go home, it'll be fine in the morning, everything will be cushty.'

I thanked him for the advice and kind words but I knew it wasn't going to go away that easily. In the end I rang EMI 'cos I was worried so much. I got through to Ashley Goodall's phone and a fella called Malcolm answered it. He said, 'Stinky, you're in big shit. This has happened right outside EMI, the others have been nicked. You assaulted a plain-clothes policeman and unfortunately someone at the company has given your name.' It was just as I feared. He went on, 'I think it's best if you come up and turn yourself in.'

My gut reaction was 'no way', but this Malcolm made me realise there was no way out of it. I was bang to rights. The next day was Christmas Eve. What were me old man and old woman going to? Debbie was working in Bond Street. I was supposed to meet her after work. It was a mess. I went to EMI, and meekly turned myself in at Marylebone nick. All my previous dealings with the cops hadn't prepared me for what happened next. Four cozzers grabbed hold of me and literally threw me into a cell. One big bastard started going into one, shouting in my face, 'We'll fucking have you for this. You assault one of our lot and we'll make you pay. Who the fuck do you think you are, you cocky bastard?'

I was allowed one phone call to a solicitor, and I was stuck in a cell on me Todd. I had no idea what the others had said, but the plan was: deny everything.

After about fifteen minutes, three Old Bill came in and told me to strip off for a full body search. This big burly cop with a beard told me to bend over so they could examine my arse. Trying to lighten the situation, I said, 'If you've got the guts to look up there, mate, good luck to you.' Then I noticed the beardsman was holding a badminton racket.

They went through the motions of peering up me chad. 'Pull your cheeks apart,' the burly one said. 'We can't see a thing.' And as I did he rammed the handle of the racket right up me rectum. I cried out in agony. 'Stop making that racket,' the twisted cunt said. The other two laughed at his sick joke. 'You fucking bastard,' he went. 'We've got a good mind to kick you all round here.'

I said, 'I don't know what you're fucking talking about.'

They were screaming and shouting at me. They kept me in there for what felt like an eternity. It must have been five hours. I didn't have a lawyer, or a cigarette. I was going up the wall. Then, finally, they brought me out to start questioning me.

In the meantime, they had contacted my old man who somehow had got in contact with Debbie and they both came up to the station. The cops said I wasn't getting bail and that I was being done for assaulting a policeman and for robbery.

Dad said, 'Robbery? He's never robbed anyone in his life.'

They tried to make out that after hitting the copper and the two Arsenal divs I took their bottle of wine, and that was robbery. Now, why the fuck would I be stealing wine in the middle of a row? I didn't even drink wine.

I was kept in there overnight. They charged me with ABH and robbery, and let me out in the morning. I couldn't believe it. I went and saw Tony Gordon immediately but he didn't want to know; he just said I'd have to get my own brief and get on with it. It didn't seem fair. OK, we'd been boisterous, but the Arsenal geezers started the row, they'd thrown the first punch. And the copper never announced who he was, he'd just dived in. Of course he was going to get hit.

They reckoned I'd beaten this thirty-year-old plod to a pulp. We saw him the next day and he didn't have a mark on him. I had murders with Mum and Dad. Mick and me now had two serious court cases to look forward to. The only good thing we had going on was *The Power & The Glory* album. It was our best work to date but I couldn't be sure now that it would ever see the light of day: as this latest tear-up had happened outside EMI who would have blamed them if they'd binned us? Happy Christmas. What a way to end the year.

CHAPTER TWENTY-SIX

Stay Free

It was New Year 1981, and I had some auld acquaintances that couldn't be forgot; the first being Forrest. We'd been committed for trial, so we knew it wouldn't be heard in a magistrates court. It was too serious for that. Before that, I had to go before the Marlborough Street Magistrates over the bashed plain-clothes copper. Frankie Hamilton and Billy Challenger had their charges dropped to drunken disorderly and got a £5 fine each. I got stuck with assaulting the cop and a robbery charge, and H was charged with ABH; we were both committed for trial. I found out later that Frankie, this Moth geezer, had grassed me up. When that got out, he vanished and has never been seen on our manor since. His name was just filth.

To let off steam we booked two gigs at the Bridge House for the end of January. The first one was absolutely rammo. It was just like coming home, an absolutely fantastic tonic. The second night was even better, I'd never seen so many people in there. We went down a storm, then, just after the second encore, the side doors came flying open and the Old Bill raided the gig. Thirty uniformed plod were trying to pour in with their truncheons drawn, having to almost fight their way through the fans. Something told me they hadn't come for our autographs. I thought to myself, What the fuck have we done now?

They started turning everything over, going through our flight cases. They wouldn't tell us why, just told us to stay put. They kept us waiting there for over an hour until we found out they'd come to nick Danny Harrison over something that had happened in Sheffield back in October. He'd been accused of nicking a gold ring and the Old Bill thought they'd be clever and nick him at our gig and ruin our night as a bonus.

With Mick's trial for Birmingham imminent, EMI decided to have us record a live album before he went down. They were sure he was going to get five years, we all were. So this was their snidey way of making sure they got the contracted four albums out of us; especially as *The Power & The Glory* wasn't 100 per cent finished. They stuck us in Abbey Road studios in front of an invited audience of 400. We actually recorded *Greatest Hits Vol 3* on a Sunday night and the very next day Mick's trial started. How's that for timing?

Our hearts weren't really in it. I can't listen to it now, but not for that reason. What really ruins it is the audience. Rather than record the crowd that we had in there, Ashley Goodall dubbed on the audience from the London Symphony Orchestra. So you hear us finish a song like 'Police Car', and then there's all this polite clapping and posh people saying, 'Jolly good!' It's fucking embarrassing. I mean if he'd wanted a big crowd we could have invited more or he could have dubbed on Thin Lizzy's reception at Hammersmith Odeon, for fuck's sake. It's unlistenable. Mick tried to fake gastroenteritis by taking Ex-Lax and crapping in the hotel swimming pool, just to get his trial postponed so we could finish *The Power & The Glory*. It didn't work.

I couldn't face going to Birmingham with Mickey. I felt so fearful about the outcome I couldn't bear to sit through it. I was ill with worry.

Mickey had been told by his barrister, Mr Chin, to expect a five-year sentence. In the end, though, I think it was me mum going up in the box than swung the judge and jury. She turned on the waterworks and really came through for Mickey. She said we'd been through a hell of a lot to make it in the music game, that we were provoked everywhere we went; that we weren't bad kids; that we'd done a lot of boxing and tried to carve out a decent life for ourselves. And, although she knew we were our own worst enemies when it came to diplomacy, I honestly think that in her heart-of-hearts it really was what she thought of us. The tears were pure drama, though. She should have won a BAFTA. Mickey pleaded guilty on two counts, assault and causing an affray, and they dropped the malicious wounding. He got a £2,000 fine and a two-year suspended sentence. He was as lucky as fuck, especially with his previous.

Well, that was one case out of the way, but we both still had to face another GBH charge.

My main worry for myself was that I still had a suspended sentence hanging over me for the time I'd been done for demanding money with menaces a couple of years before. With two charges to face I was convinced I was definitely going away. We couldn't both be that lucky.

With Mick given a temporary lease of freedom, we could at least finish off *The Power & The Glory*. I think the album stands the test of time, but the later songs we recorded were the weaker ones. Things had changed. We'd lost our impetus; the stuffing had been knocked right out of us and it just wasn't the same. We recorded 'On The Streets' as a single. It was a good song but musically it was softer, maybe too mellow – Garry Bushell slated it in *Sounds*.

We wanted EMI to bring out this album before the live one. The plan was release *The Power & The Glory* and book in another tour before the next trial. But EMI vetoed the idea. They wanted the live album out first, even though there were tracks on it which had never been heard because they were from *The Power & The Glory*. They put us back on the road. We played six gigs to put our toe in the water: Brighton, Grimsby, Hemel Hempstead, Scarborough, Bradford and Bolton. There wasn't one hint of trouble. There were no firms looking to fight us, no nickable offences, nothing. *Greatest Hits Vol 3* went straight into the Top Thirty, too, so I started to think we might have turned a corner.

The Power & The Glory release was put back to July and we planned a full-scale tour to promote it, avoiding trouble-spots like Birmingham and Liverpool. That was assuming we got through the Forrest trial; everything now hinged on that.

The trial was set for the end of April at Snaresbrook Crown Court. We had good solicitors and a black barrister called Mr Evans who was absolutely brilliant, well spoken and as sharp as you like. He got Forrest in the stand and he couldn't even tell them his full name. Evans asked him how big the lump of wood had been. Forrest said about six inches. Evans said, 'Well, what damage could that have done?' Forrest changed his mind and said it had been a yard long. He made himself look a pillock. His two cronies were brought in as prosecution witnesses but they had to admit they hadn't really seen anything because they'd legged it. Debbie went in the box, then me sister, then Mum; then it was our turn.

The prosecutor said to Mick, 'I put it to you, Mr Geggus, that you got a lump of wood with a nail in it and smashed it in Mr Forrest's face.'

Mick said to the judge, 'I can assure you, Your Honour, that I am a musician not a thug.'

There was quite a few cheers and the odd titter from the public gallery, which was packed out with punks.

I had my turn the next day and everything went fine. After two days, the prosecutor summed up; he was two-bob, absolute shit. Then Mr Evans got up and slaughtered them; he just tore their case to shreds. Usually you go to the cells while the jury deliberate, but the judge said we were free to leave the building and have some lunch. That's when we knew for sure we were going to have a result. We went out and had a celebratory fry-up. It felt good and it was – we both got a not guilty. We were free to go.

As we came out we saw Denton the copper sitting there. He was fuming. We went up and tried to shake his hand. He just glared at us. 'I tell you what,' he said. 'I might not have had you this time but I'll get you next time.'

Mick just slapped him round the cheeks and said, 'You don't half look like Gary Dickle, you could be his double, mate.'

Denton was livid. You could tell he wanted to kick the fuck out of us. It was beautiful. We knew he wouldn't dare.

This meant Mick was in the clear; he'd got through both trials unscathed. I had one more to go, but in the meantime we went back on the road to promote *The Power & The Glory* album in July. We were back on track. Nothing could stop us now.

CHAPTER TWENTY-SEVEN

Oi – The Backlash

We were determined to stay out of trouble. To keep our noses clean, we stayed away from football. We even stopped going to gigs. And it worked. We were on our best behaviour. Hard as it might be to believe, I actually dipped a toe into luvviedom. Terry Murphy had started to put on plays at the Bridge House around this time. His son Glen had taken up acting and he invited us to come and watch him. The Mayor of Newham was going to be there and it was all very respectable. So we went along on this Sunday and they'd converted the stage into a Roman temple for some biblical epic about Jesus. What a laugh that was! Unintentionally, mind. Glen was a hard bastard and to see him come lumbering out wearing a loin-cloth and a silly helmet was hysterical. He was coming out with all this flowery dialogue about the stars in the heavens. It was so out of place I wanted to piss myself. It was the worse play I'd ever seen in my life, it was cringeworthy. I tried to slip out at the end but I got cornered and had to pretend to Glen and his dad that I'd thought he was brilliant. 'You've gotta do more of it,' I said. I didn't have the courage to tell him the truth. Perhaps if I had, he might have jacked it in, but there again maybe he went on to become a TV star because of my few words of encouragement. Possibly the Mayor of Newham told him a few diplomatic porkies too. The fact remained that every time I saw him on *London's Burning* after that I remembered him in his loin-cloth with his big, squashed boxer's nose trying to sound poetic.

Things were looking good for us again. The album was finished, at a final cost of £30,000, so we knew we had to make the tour a good one. Everything was booked. Our biggest tour yet, with EMI promoting the album hard. They had lined up displays in HMV and Virgin. The feedback was good. Things were really changing,we could feel it. We were going to have a song given away with the magazine *Flexipop*, and all the other pop magazines wanted interviews and features, too. It wasn't just the rock press covering us any more. Then, two weeks before we were due to kick off the tour, I woke up one Saturday morning, turned on the radio, and the news was dominated by just one story: Southall was in flames.

The 4-Skins, The Business and The Last Resort had played the Hamborough Tavern in Southall, Middlesex. The local Asian youths, stirred up by agitators, had burned the pub to the ground with a handy stockpile of petrol bombs. Typically the bands got the blame.

The Southall riot seemed to ignite trouble all over the country. The riots spread to Toxteth in Liverpool and Handsworth in Birmingham. Talk about timing. The press was looking for scapegoats, the *Daily Mail* in particular got it all arse-about-face, and suddenly bands like us and the Angelic Upstarts were being roped in. *Sounds*, which had more black-music coverage than any other UK rock weekly, was pathetically labelled the 'fascist bible of hate' by a *Mail* reporter. The *Observer* even had a pop at Rose Tattoo, quoting the great Australian band's lyrics as evidence of a new violent rock trend and conveniently forgetting that 'Street Fighting Man' had been a hit for the Stones a decade before.

It was ludicrous. Ironically enough, the only paper which reported the Oi scene fairly at the time was the *Guardian*. Twenty-odd years later, a 4-Skins tribute album came out on US indie label Workers United; their songs were covered by bands like The Bolsheviks. Does that sound very fascist to you?

But, at the time, reality counted for nothing. Oi was drowning in press lies fuelled by class prejudice and there was no way to swim away from it. Tony Gordon called us in for a crisis meeting. He said that HMV and Virgin were refusing to promote and publicise the new album. All the window displays were being returned. To top it all the tour had to be cancelled. Every promoter who'd booked us had pulled out. Things were just too hot out there. I was devastated. Southall was nothing to do with us. We weren't even on the new *Oi* album; our sound had moved away from that. It was a complete kick in the bollocks. Mickey and me has walked away free from two things we had done but lost the tour through something that had nothing to do with us.

With everything up in the air, the inner cities in turmoil and the press full of hysterical bullshit, you would have thought someone at the record label would have thought about delaying the album release until things had settled down. Not EMI. They stuck that fucking album out and it bombed. It was a major change of direction for us, it needed to be listened to and judged on its own merits and it needed a tour to sell it. It didn't happen. EMI pulled the rug from under our feet. They said, 'Your album has bombed, you've assaulted the police, you've been involved in this, that and the other, there's the door, see you later.' It was an easy way out for them.

The Power & The Glory got good reviews in *Sounds* and *Melody Maker*. *Sounds* said side two was too sedate but still gave it four stars. Surprisingly, *Melody Maker* was even more positive. But it entered the charts at ninety-one then belly-flopped out again. The single, 'On The Streets', went nowhere. 'Blando' Garry Bushell called it, but others liked it. It didn't even make the Top 100.

Then we got the call we were half-expecting from Tony Gordon to say that EMI had pulled the plug. They were wiping their hands of us and they put it down to me and the Copper In Disguise I'd 'assaulted' outside their building. That was the final straw, they said. If that was the case, why hadn't they sacked us on Christmas Eve? They got their pound of flesh out of us first. They got another two albums out of us then kicked us in the bollocks. I can't lie about it: that sacking shattered me. To me it was the end of the world. Where could we go after EMI? The only way was down. We were still on Tony Gordon's payroll and drawing a wage, 'cos there was still money in the pot, but we didn't know for how much longer and we didn't know which way to turn. Everybody in the music game seemed to be against us. I didn't have a clue what to do next. And, to add to the party atmosphere, my trial date came through.

CHAPTER TWENTY-EIGHT

Rumpole To The Rescue

My trial was to be held at the Old Bailey in September. I'd made the big league. I took off to Spain with Debbie to try and clear my head – I had to get special permission to leave the country. I wasn't much fun to be with because I knew that when we got back I would be just a day's notice away from being up in court and I was ill with worry about it. I hardly slept. I couldn't eat. I only managed to hold down a few tubs of ice-cream in the whole fortnight. I got sunstroke too. Even me mum didn't recognise me when I got back. And yet the funny thing was this prosecution was the least serious of all the things I'd ever been accused of. The whole case was ridiculous. The copper had never declared who he was and so I wasn't knowingly assaulting the police, and I certainly hadn't nicked any wine.

Three days after we landed I got a call saying I was on trial the next day. Me and H had to grit our teeth and face the music. I hired my brilliant barrister Mr Evans from the Forrest trial again;

I had real faith in him. To me he was like Rumpole and Perry Mason rolled into one. I was relying on him. I had no eye-witnesses to substantiate my story, just a few character witnesses. My beloved manager, Tony Gordon, refused to even write a letter on my behalf, but Garry Bushell gave me one and so did Kevin Ireland. And that was it. It was all down to Evans.

That morning, before we went into the court, he took me and H to one side. He looked grim and we really didn't like what he had to say. 'I've made a plea bargain,' he said. 'Here's why: you don't have one witness between you and, if you plead not guilty, I'm telling you, they will find you guilty on both counts. It will take four or five days' trial and you, Jeff, will probably get six months, and you, Mr Harmer, will get twelve to eighteen.' Have that! I gulped. H started to argue the toss.

Mr Evans then said he'd been giving us the bad news first. He had another option. He explained that he'd made a plea bargain with them to save all the time. The Old Bill had agreed that, if we pleaded guilty to assaulting a policeman, they'd drop the robbery charge. The idea was to play it down and say it was Christmas high-jinks that got a bit out of hand and that it shouldn't be in a court of this magnitude. We went along with it, even though I knew that pleading guilty meant I was admitting breaking the terms of my previous discharge. What other choice did I have?

They got us in the dock at the Bailey. H was up first. Steven Harmer, no previous convictions… that was a turn-up, for a start! He got a £300 fine. Then it was my turn. They brought up my previous conviction, demanding money with menaces, and I thought I was sunk. This had to get me six months minimum. But then the eloquent Mr Evans came into play. He argued that it had all happened a long time before, when I was a kid. He asked the judge to take into account that I was nearly at the end of my discharge. 'He's seventeen,' he said. 'He deserves another chance. He's got big things happening with his band, he's on EMI [not knowing they'd just sacked us] and they're going to push them and keep him on the straight and narrow.'

It was a lovely pipe-dream, I even started to believe it myself. Incredibly, it worked. They whacked me with a £500 fine for assaulting the copper, and another £350 for breaking discharge. Then I got a new conditional discharge for two more years. I had an £850 bill on me plate, but I didn't give a fuck. What mattered was I wasn't going down. I could walk away.

Everyone was pleased, except me mum. She was fuming. '£850,' she said, 'and a two-year discharge for doing nothing. Where's that copper?'

I pointed him out.

She said, 'Right, I'm gonna go over there and smash him right in the mouth, so we can get our £850's worth.'

She meant it too. I told her to leave it. 'No,' she said. 'Where's the justice? Look at him, the big fucking lemon, standing up in court saying a sixteen-year-old has done this and that to him and he's standing there right as rain...'

We had to beg her not to hit him. Having seen him in action, if it had come to blows, she would have decked him, too.

I said, 'Let's pay the money and go, there's gonna be no trouble whatsoever any more. I'm finished with all that, I'm really tired with it. I just want to get out of here.'

And we got her out. She wasn't happy about it and I wasn't happy about having to cough up 850 notes, but at least I was at liberty.

A couple of nights later, a few of us went over to Hampstead to see the Kidz Next Door. Afterwards, they dropped me and Debbie off at the Mobil garage on the A13. It was about 1.00 am,

I'd had a skinful and I was with me bird. All I wanted to do was get some fags. I walked up to the counter and there were these two geezers coming towards me. I knew them, one was called Carter the other was Stan Waite. They were about the same age as me and both local.

Waite had obviously decided to make a name for himself by having a go at me. He was really screwing me out. I should have ignored him, but being half-cut I was easily wound up. I said, 'Are you fucking looking at me?'

'Yeah,' he said. 'Fucking want some?'

That was it. I steamed him and knocked the fuck out of the liberty-taking cunt right there and then in the garage.

His mate Carter said to Debbie, 'If he don't get off, I'm gonna have to do something about it.'

I didn't stop and so Carter jumped me from behind. I felt something go into my back. I turned round to fight him and as we exchanged punches Waite revived. Now I was trying to fight the two of them. I couldn't actually feel any pain at this point but I sensed something wasn't right. Debbie went and got a dustbin lid which she smashed over Carter's head and the little Asian geezer who ran the garage came out in a state telling us to leave it out.

The two of them fucked off. Then Debbie gasped. 'Jeff,' she said. 'Your back, your back.'

Blood was pouring out of me; the snidey little bastard had stabbed me. They wanted to call an ambulance and get me to hospital. I wouldn't have it. After all, I'd just put them through, I didn't want to put me old man and old woman through any more. So, instead, I made Debbie take me back to her mum's and they patched me up. They cleaned the wound and bandaged it. The injury wasn't too bad and I felt OK.

My gut reaction was to start thinking about taking revenge. But then another little voice inside me started to make more sense. Did I really need another battle, did I want to get sucked in to a running war on my own manor? As it happened, I did get my own back on one of them years later, but for now I thought this had to stop. I'd only been out of court for two days, now I was getting grief on my own doorstep and I'd never had that before. I could have found them and battered them but then, every time I left my house after that, I would have been looking over my shoulder to see when the next gutless cunt was going to come at me from behind with a blade. The game was changing. It wasn't fighting in the street any more. Now it was about Stan and Freddie (Stanley knives and Freddie Frasers, razors) and squirts (ammonia) and all that, and that was never for me. I've never used a knife in me life. I didn't want to get involved in that.

I knew I had to make a big decision about where my life was going. So, I sat down with Mick, thrashed it out and decided to pour everything we had into the band instead. We knew we had to get out of East London and away from punk and football violence. We had a meeting with the great Peter Way from UFO. Our aim, we decided, was to get a new deal if we could and move the band into the rock arena, move towards an AC/DC sort of sound. Rose Tattoo appealed to punks and skins as well as the *Kerrang* crowd, so did Mötorhead. There was something happening, a kind of fusion between punk and rock which was to fire and inspire bands like Guns N Roses. We had to grow up and become part of that.

Out of the blue, we got the news that another notorious character wanted to sign us to his record label NEMS: Patrick Meehan, the self-styled gangster of rock. Meehan had been involved with Don Arden; he'd managed Black Sabbath and Nazareth. And now he was into the Rejects.

We went to meet Pat at his little mews office near Victoria. We'd heard all these rumours about his gangster connections but when we met him he looked like Captain Pugwash. He was tall with thick grey hair and a beard, a bit like a heavier Dave Lee Travis, and he always wore a suit. He had all these cocaine sores round his face and kept disappearing into the khazi in between swigging from a bottle of brandy. He was quite a character. Of course, the danger signs were there from the start. We knew his reputation but what mattered to us was that he was interested in us and that he said he could get us a deal. He said, 'If you can get Pete Way to produce your new album, I'll give you twenty-five grand for it.' How bad was that?

Tony Gordon did the negotiations and suddenly we were signed to NEMS. A new chapter was beginning.

CHAPTER TWENTY-NINE

Dole Queue Rockers

*T*he *Wild Ones* was our first hard-rock album. Pete Way
produced it and it was an absolute departure from our punky
roots. We didn't try and bring our old audience with us gradually,
we just went right in with it. Wallop, have some of that. We
decided to go the Aerosmith, AC/DC route, and although the
album was a commercial flop it stands the test of time and it was
fun to make.

But leaving our old sound behind was to prove easier than
losing our appetite for destruction.

We recorded the album at Parkgate Studios near Battle in East
Sussex; Pete was obviously there with his fridge full of Special
Brew, and UFO's road manager, John Knowles, came down so it
was a good crack. There was another fella called Tony Chapman
who was basically Patrick Meehan's gofer and his role seemed to
be to tell everyone a bundle of lies while keeping us all supplied
with coke and beer. So we had a proper rock'n'roll entourage now.

One night we went into town to eat at a pub restaurant called the George Hotel. The geezer who owned it was from South London and kept going on about how he was a Cockney. We were sitting there trying to eat and he would come up to us banging on about being staunch Millwall, and how West Ham were shit. He was in his forties, old enough to know better, but he wouldn't let it rest. He kept getting louder and louder, he was a proper nuisance. In the end, Vince had words with him but the bloke was on a roll. Every few minutes he'd come back out with his chef's hat on, shouting 'Lions!' and giving it verbal, with us getting drunker and increasingly pissed off. Confrontation was inevitable. Finally in the face of prolonged provocation, Mick had enough. He walked up to him, gave him a couple of slaps and pushed him on the floor.

The geezer was flabbergasted. 'You can't do that,' he said. 'I'll call the police.' So he was a proper Cockney, was he? What kind of Millwall supporter calls the Old Bill?

I said, 'Listen, mate, you've been giving it mouth all night, he slapped you, pushed you over and now you want to call the police? You're pathetic.'

Pete Way was flapping about like an old woman with his long hair and his eyeliner, going, 'Please don't, please don't, calm down, they've 'ad a lot to drink, they don't mean anything...'

We drank up and left. The landlord's bike was parked outside. We knew it was his because that was one of the many subjects he'd been boring us about. For some reason, we decided the bike was coming with us. I don't know why. We stuck it in the boot and, as we were going down these little country lanes, me and Vince decided the time was right to road test it. We were like Butch Cassidy and The Sundance Kid. Vince was pedalling, I was sitting on the cross-bar singing 'Rain drops keep falling on me 'ead', as we made our way home on a pitch-black road, pissed as puddings. We didn't know where we were going. It took us an hour to find our digs, which had only been five minutes away from where we'd started. We dumped the bike outside, went in and crashed out. Ten o'clock the next morning two coppers came banging on the door. Here we go again, I thought, new album, new court case...

Mercifully, the geezer didn't want to press charges. All he wanted was his bike back. So we gave it to them, what was left of it. It looked like it had done the Tour de France with Dawn French sitting on it. It was buckled and twisted, and splattered with mud. But we never heard a word of complaint; we got away lightly with that one.

The other small problems around the album were with personnel. Pete had brought in John Fiddler from Medicine Head to work with us while we were rehearsing the new songs in West London. He was a big name, he'd been in the British Lions and the rehashed Yardbirds, too, but to me he was just a curly-haired bloke living in the sixties. Ray Major, the guitarist from Mott The Hoople, worked with us, too, but he was a lot more help and easier to get on with.

We'd used what money we had left to get all this fantastic gear. Sticks got a three-grand Ludwig kit with a double bass drum like Alex Van Halen. We had top guitars, Marshalls and Peavey bass amps, the lot. The irony was we had the best equipment we'd ever had but we weren't playing any gigs.

We got in to Parkgate in November 1981. Pete Way was as good as gold, although even he had his funny little ways. On the first day, he met me at Battle station in this beat-up old jalopy, a Citröen – a headmistress's car. It was so embarrassing. We went into a garage, Pete filled up then went in to pay. The next thing I knew he was tapping on the window, with a little purse in his hand. He'd overfilled by half a penny and didn't have enough; he wouldn't even knock the garage for a halfpenny! He couldn't do it. You had to love him.

Pete brought in Gary Edwards to engineer the album. He was a lovely Welsh fella who'd worked with Rainbow and the Scorpions, all the big bands. Phil Mogg had sacked him from the UFO album *The Wild, The Willing & The Innocent* 'cos he said Gary had come back pissed one day, which was very much a case of 'hello pot, meet kettle'. But he was shit hot, and he did a good job for us.

In December, we relocated to Redan Recording Studios in Queensway, London, and this is where the band's story takes another dramatic turn for the worse. And this is where Wilf Wright enters the picture.

Wright was UFO's manager but, in the middle of recording our album, Pete and Phil had plucked up the courage to sack him, and he took to coming down to Redan to try and woo Pete back in various ways. He was an odd bloke, another sixties throwback, a beardsman with long, permed hair. Wilf was big but very quiet, he hardly said a word, but he tried to give you the impression of hidden depths and limitless knowledge about the rock game. He'd also managed Robin Trower, who had done business in the States, and he claimed to be best mates with Rod McSween, the rock promoter. Wilf, it seemed, had all the right connections.

We were in the process of working out how to say 'see you later' to Tony Gordon. We knew that if we were going to make it in heavy rock we needed somebody who knew that end of the business inside-out.

So, Wilf Wright would be there every day with his bottle of

brandy and god knows what else, telling us where we should go and what we should do. And, even though we'd been warned about him, we were flattered that this rock guru was showing so much interest in us. Wilf said he loved what we were doing and that we needed him to manage the band. He said he'd take care of Tony Gordon and his contracts, that what he and EMI had done to us could be sorted out and that he'd get us money back. It would be easy to break with Gordon, he said. It was all music to our ears.

Ray Major sounded a note of caution. He saw us getting more and more involved with Wilf and said, 'Don't go with him, don't do it. After all you've been through, you're coming out of the frying pan into the fire.' Like fools, we ignored him.

Out of the blue, Gordon called us. He sounded very curt and off-hand. He said he needed to see us. He hadn't once come down to the studios to see how we were getting on, so we assumed he wanted to talk to us about where we were going with the record or something, but he just said, 'I've called you here to inform you that you're bankrupt. All the money is gone and I suggest that if you want to keep your heads above water you'll have to go out and get jobs.'

I couldn't believe it, we were only on £35 a week, how had the money gone? We'd just signed to NEMS for £25,000 two months before, that's the equivalent of about £100,000 now. It hadn't all gone on the album. Gordon said that we still owed Rockfield Studios £10,000 and someone else £15,000. I couldn't work out why these bills hadn't been paid. It was a crushing blow. We were in the middle of a new album, we were doing photo-shoots with Ross Halfin, Garry Bushell was publicising things, Geoff Barton loved it. Everything was on the up again. All of a sudden we were pot-less. I didn't know what to do. I had no money, no savings. It was only twenty months since we'd done *Top Of The Pops* and now we were looking at signing on the social. We weren't scroungers; we'd always had the work ethic, and now we were on the Nat King Cole. It felt awful. And to make it worse, it transpired that Gordon hadn't paid our National Insurance contributions, so we were getting something silly like £18 a week.

We had to go to the social in Freemasons Road every week and because we were so embarrassed about it we always went in disguise. We'd put big hats on, glasses, so nobody recognised us. We didn't want anyone to know we'd fallen so spectacularly. One day, there was this great, long queue and I found myself next to Perry Fenwick, who now plays Billy Mitchell in *EastEnders*. We ended up chatting. He was having trouble finding acting jobs, but he was more shocked to see me there 'cos he knew all about the band. He only came from a few streets away from me, we even went to the same school. He was a nice fella and it's great to see him doing well for himself. At the time we never imagined we'd be signing on for long because *The Wild Ones* would be coming out in a couple of months and we still had big plans; so it wasn't that much of a stigma. Little did we know…

We'd moved to Redan in January and the problems with John Fiddler reached a head. We just couldn't get on with the geezer. He wanted to sit behind the drums, or to play the guitar or be on the bass. He wanted to sing. He fell out with Pete about the sound. He was an absolute control freak; I don't know how we put up with him for so long. He always made such a nuisance of himself. After one of many disagreements, he did a Pursey and said, 'Do it my way or I'm going.'

And once again Vince said, 'Well, there's the door. Fuck off, and don't ever come back.'

And that was it. He was gone. It was a case of Fiddler on the hoof.

There were other problems, too. The album started getting delayed because Patrick Meehan's cheques were bouncing. We would be in there for a week, then out for a fortnight, then back in again. We actually finished it in March but, for reasons that were never made clear, Meehan didn't release it until September and the summer didn't half drag.

Wilf Wright had obviously got into us by this time, and he told us he was going to get us released from our management contract with Gordon. Gordon wanted that. There were lots of meetings between the two of them which we were never party to, so I don't know how he did it, but by the end of February 1982 Gordon was out of the picture and Wilf was firmly in charge.

I always remember the big plans he had for us. He knew Rod McSween at ITB – International Talent Booking – and he was going to contact Def Leppard's manager Peter Mensch and get us a tour support with them in the USA. He'd speak to us a lot about America, selling us a dream, and I developed a fascination for the place.

Everything he said sounded so good we were already hooked.

Around this time, the Bridge House was closing down and we were invited to play one last gig there. We decided to play the new stuff, hit the local faithful with a heavy metal set. Amazingly, it was really well received. It went down a storm with the audience and critics alike. There were quite a few rock writers in and we got good reviews. It seemed like a great omen for the future. Happy days had to be round the corner.

There was one small, dark diversion for me at the time. Debbie fell pregnant. I was still only seventeen, she was six months older; and this had happened in the middle of our money crisis. I knew it was the wrong time for us to have a kid. We were too young and too unsettled. I had to convince her to get rid of it. She went into a clinic in Brixton and had an abortion but I felt bad about it. It wasn't a comfortable thing to go through for either of us.

In April, Debbie fell out with her stepfather so she moved across the water to stay with her real dad in Charlton, in South-East London. As we'd just got engaged, I went with her. We lived with him for a couple of months then got our own flat there in Littleheath. We'd been together just over two years. We'd met in April 1980 in the Paul's Head pub in Canning Town just when the band was taking off, and now we were living together. I ended up doing seven years with her. It was like a jail sentence... for her.

You could still see Custom House if you looked from the top of Charlton Church Lane, but nobody on my old manor knew where I'd gone to. This was the start of my reclusive days. The plan was to hole up in South London and put everything into the band.

Wilf Wright was still talking everything up. He had an office in the Harrow Road, in North-West London. He was managing us properly, although as I remember it nothing was ever signed. He said that Gordon was releasing everything to him. He opened a band bank account and said that everything that came out would require two signatures, so no money could ever go astray.

In April, Wilf stuck us in to Ear Studios and told us to start rehearsing for a US tour. We were going to do twenty dates, he said. It sounded fantastic. We got in there and started rehearsing and Wilf would come down and say that Rod McSween was doing this and that and that the tour was only a couple of weeks off. It never happened. We were rehearsing for nothing.

To this day, I don't know why things didn't work out. But we still wanted to believe in Wilf. We'd sit in his office and make all our grand plans with him, plotting our American deal.

We were still in Ear Studios when the Clash turned up to start rehearsing for their Combat Rock tour. I got talking to Joe Strummer about various things and he stuck out as a really nice, genuine fella. He was definitely the one who was the most together. Topper just seemed out of it and so did Mick Jones. We decided to have a football match on the green. We had some mates with us and they had a few black minders. We took our gear off and had a seven-a-side, us against the Clash. They might have been a great band but they couldn't play football to save their lives. We beat them 10–1. Mick Jones was running about in a pair of Doc Marten's, he couldn't even kick a ball. It was a great day.

We'd just done the 'Total Noise' EP, but not as ourselves. We did a cover of the ZZ Top song 'Francine' as Dead Generation, and we recorded 'Tough & Tasty' with Garry Bushell as the Gonads. Mick even did a bit of poetry on it. We played it all back to Strummer and he loved it. He said 'Francine' sounded like the Stones and that 'Tough & Tasty' sounded like Charlie Harper sings heavy metal. We told him it was Bushell singing and he laughed. 'Good old Garry,' he said. He was very aware of the band and Oi.

And he had every right to tell us to fuck off because of the things we'd said about the Clash in print. I'd accused them of selling out and 'Join The Rejects' had a verse about Joe: 'Do you remember 1977/The Daddy of the gang said we'd go to heaven/Every word a lie and none the truth/So here's our answer to today's youth/Join the Rejects, get yerself killed.'

Amazingly, Strummer had a lot of time for us and he tried his best to put us right. He was wise, and helpful. I never agreed with his politics but as a geezer he was totally on the level. It was great to meet someone I'd looked up to and not be disappointed by them. Joe tried to give us advice about Wilf Wright. We had to tread carefully, he said. And if we weren't happy with Wilf we should walk, he said, because we still had all our gear and we had no legal contract with him. We did think about it seriously but Wilf kept filling our heads with dreams and promises about America. We were going to have swimming pools in LA, flash cars, stay in big hotels. He span a good yarn. He knew we were getting frustrated so he told us he had a deal in the offing with Atlantic Records in the States. He packed us off to Cornwall for a week, and Vince's last words were: 'Well I'm not coming back until we've got a deal.'

We stayed in a caravan park near Lands End. Rock stars, eh? We took photos of ourselves on the beach and sent them back to people saying we were in the South of France. The things you do to try and keep up your profile. In reality, we were still absolutely skint. There was a mini-mart on the site and we had to shoplift our supper out of there. We'd come out with fish fingers up our jumpers.

When we came back, there was still no deal. Wilf reckoned everything had gone pear-shaped with Atlantic and they'd pulled out at the last moment. All we had to look forward to was *The Wild Ones*' release.

It was a good album; it got rave reviews. Geoff Barton loved it. He took over from Tommy Vance for a week on Radio One, and he was playing tracks off the album and calling us 'the British Aerosmith'. I was listening in me flat in Charlton and I almost fell off a chair. Everyone we respected thought it was a great album but you couldn't get it in any shops. There was no poster campaign for it, no tour to promote it. It just died like a dog. All the time, effort, hope and money we'd put into that album had come to nothing. It was soul-destroying.

As incredible as it seems we still didn't break off with Wilf Wright. He managed us until 1984. We had believed in him for a long time.

Of course, by 1983 I'd started to dislike him as much as I'd disliked Gordon. I didn't trust him. Frustrated as we were, he would use the fantasy of America as a carrot to keep us sweet. We were promised tours and we'd wait by the phone for him to ring and it was always that he'd met Rod McSween, and he was going to get back to him in a month or so. Once he rang up and said we had to go to lunch with McSween the following Wednesday, that he wanted to put us on as support with AC/DC on a world tour. It sounded fantastic. So we turned up, but Rod never appeared. I never did get to meet him.

The gutting thing is I think, if we had been handled right, and if we had toured the States on a hard-rock bill, we might have cracked it. Who knows where it could have ended up. Instead, *The Wild Ones* was the last gasp of a dying band. After it came out, it all went downhill faster than Rik Waller on roller skates.

CHAPTER THIRTY

Twisted Mister

The Wild Ones did about as well as Paula Radcliffe in the Athens Marathon. It had everything going for it but it crashed out without getting anywhere, and that knocked the guts out of me. I was smoking more and more puff; I'd become a virtual recluse. I was still living in Charlton but the only time I left the house was to work with the band. I was all out of money, totally skint, I'd grown me hair long and I refused point blank even to venture over to Custom House. My whole life had become dedicated to resurrecting the band. I woke up and went to bed thinking about it, I even dreamed about it. I couldn't let go of it. I had come down so far that all I could think about was turning everything around and making the Rejects successful again.

The only people I spoke to were family and band members. By now we had lost touch with the firm entirely. That was down to Wilf Wright. Soon after he took over as manager, Wilf told us we had to lose the entourage. He made Mick move out of the place he was sharing in Manor Road Buildings with Grant and Andy Swallow. Wilf said we had to change our ways; nice respectable rock bands didn't turn up at gigs firm-handed. And it did seem to make sense, although it later emerged that there may have been an element of self-preservation underlining his argument – by weakening us it made it easier for him to control us.

But in truth the old faces were growing away from us too. They'd grown up, and the ones who weren't in prison were getting involved in their own businesses, chasing a pound note. Within a few years, Swallow had got into the new acid house sounds. He ended up pretty much running the rave scene in Essex and around the M25. Wellsy just disappeared; he went back to Grays and I didn't see him until years later when he turned up working the doors on nightclubs in Southend. Dickle and Butler went their own ways. Carlton Leach slipped away into a life of skulduggery; Skully did twenty years for Skully-duggery: ten years for springing Kendall from Gartree prison in a helicopter and ten more on top of that for the Archway security job. H moved away. Hodges and Hoxton Tom had the 4-Skins on the road until Garry Hodges quit. He ended up doing time for armed robbery. Tom carried on with a guy called Panther on vocals, but the band had petered out by 1985. So the Rejects and the firm kind of lost touch, for a few years at least.

At Easter 1983 we decided it was time to do a new demo. Pete Way was going to produce it again. We booked Wave Studios in Hoxton, East London. We booked it overnight because night rates were all we could afford. I'd catch a bus down to the

Greenwich foot tunnel, walk through the tunnel and hop on a bus to Old Street.

The first night I arrived a bit late. Wilf Wright was in the studio alone, the rest of them had gone to the pub. 'I'll take you for a beer,' he said.

I didn't know my way around the area so I just followed him. He took me to this boozer which had every single window boarded up. I just assumed someone had put the windows in. The pub was called the London Apprentice, which meant nothing to me. Wilf opened the door and stood back, ushering me in. I couldn't believe what I was seeing. The bar was wall to wall gays, all these geezers kissing each other and cruising. As soon as we walked in everyone started eyeing us up. Wilf Wright, the bastard, just stood there with a big smug grin on his face. I said 'Get out of this fucking pub now.' I kicked the door open and walked. I had never been so unsettled in me life. If I'd been in the middle of the Shed with just thirty West Ham battling 300 Chelsea, I wouldn't have given a fuck, but to stand there in a pub full of shirt-lifters worried the fuck out of me. I can honestly say I was frightened. I pushed him against the wall and said, 'What the fuck are you doing?' But Wilf just kept on grinning. It was a mistake, he said. I don't know whether it was one of his mind-games or whether there was some other motivation, some sick fantasy of his. But, when we got back to the studio, he was full of it. He told everyone that I'd taken him to a gay pub. He thought it was hysterical. I said to Mick, 'That's it, he's gotta go. I don't care what kind of hold he's got and what promises he's making, he's out. I don't want nothing more to do with the bloke.' And Mick agreed.

We went ahead and recorded two new tracks, 'Wish You Were Here' and 'Shot Down'. They were pretty strong so we decided to try and go it alone. We set up a showcase with Bronze Records without Wilf knowing about it. The A&R geezer loved us. He wanted to sign us there and then. I was ecstatic. I got on the phone to Debbie, jamming a lolly stick in the machine to make the call 'cos I didn't have any money. I told her that we'd got a deal at last, the good times were going to roll again. I was over the moon. We thought we'd cracked it.

Then the weeks start to pass by and we heard nothing back from them. The silence was becoming ominous. I made a few fruitless phone calls and, when I finally got through to this fella, all he said was, 'Sorry I can't sign you.' The deal had been blocked from above he said. We were back to square one.

Our next move was to ring up Chris Briggs, the man who'd originally signed us to EMI. He'd now moved on to Phonogram and he agreed to see us. We decided we needed a makeover, so me and Mick went to the meeting wearing suits and carrying briefcases. We weren't going to look like yobs any more, now we were businessmen. What a pair of twats! We played Briggs the new songs and had a good chat with him. We were still young. I was eighteen, almost nineteen; Mick was only twenty-two. We still had age on our side. Briggs liked what he heard and agreed to work with us again on one condition: under no circumstances would he have any dealings with Wilf Wright. We immediately bullshitted him that we'd got shot of Wilf and were managing ourselves. So we were game on. Then for some inexplicable reason, probably related to having too many beers that night, Mick took it on himself to tell Wilf we were in negotiations with Chris Briggs at Phonogram. I begged him not to but Mick was adamant. We don't do things behind people's backs, he said. We're straight. And he rang Wilf and told him.

Two days later we tried to call Briggs and found that he'd

become permanently unavailable. He was in a meeting, washing his hair, walking his cat, de-scaling the fridge. We couldn't get him on the phone for days. But, when he finally did take our call, Chris was steaming. Wilf Wright had been on to him, insisting he was still our manager, and Briggs refused to give us a deal because of it. There was nothing I could say that would make any difference. Mick's ten-pint honesty session had blown us out of the water.

Now I really was at my wit's end. I didn't know where else to turn. I was losing the plot, smoking more pot, getting into a state. And that was when we got the killer blow. Rock band Twisted Sister were coming over from the States to gig and it turned out that Wilf Wright had an interest in them. He asked us if the band could borrow our back-line, our amps and the drum kit. Because we knew them, and knew they were mates of Garry Bushell's and Ross Halfin's, we agreed.

We never got the request from the band themselves, just from Wilf. But we believed what he told us. We thought it would make people see us in a new light, as the nice easy-going Rejects and that, if we did Twisted Sister a favour, they'd do us one, maybe even give us a nice support slot on a US tour. To be honest, I think our heads were up our arseholes with the periscopes closed.

A week later we got a phone call from Wilf Wright. 'Bad news,' he said. 'The back-line's gone.' He said it had been stolen out the back of a truck. All the Marshall amps, the Peavey bass gear, the drum kit – everything. It was our livelihood; it was worth thousands. And it was gone. None of it was insured either, because we didn't do things that way.

Wilf told us that the tailgate of the lorry had come open on Tower Bridge and that our entire back-line had just fallen off the back of it. He reckoned the driver hadn't realised and that he had driven off without it, apparently oblivious to the chaos he'd left in his wake.

If that much gear had fallen off a lorry on Tower Bridge it would have held up traffic for ages and caused a tailback all through the City and East London. Anyone who'd nicked it would have needed a truck to get it all away. It was absolute bollocks from start to finish. I said, 'Well, where's Dee Snider and the rest of Twisted Sister?' Oh, he said, they've gone back to New York, the fucking lying weasel.

If I'd thought it was anything to do with them, I would have hunted them down and stabbed every last one of them, but I don't believe they ever had any of it. We'd been twisted all right, but by a mister not a sister. He'd played us like fairground rubes.

The next we knew, Wilf seemed to have vanished off the face of the earth and we never saw him again. It was the last straw for us. Vince called us up and arranged a meeting at his mother's house. The big man was gutted. He said, 'That's it, I've gotta say goodbye. I can't go on like this any more. We're boracic, and without the back-line we're fucked. We can't start up again from scratch.'

I was choked because Vince was always a real strong geezer. I looked up to him. Whenever there had been a crisis before he would turn round and say, 'Don't worry about it, we'll get through it.' When he said he'd had enough, I was devastated.

That should have been it then. We should have all said enough's enough and gone out and got ourselves jobs. But I couldn't handle giving up.

There was more bad news. The publishing company we'd signed to for *The Wild Ones* turned out to have no money.

Someone else might have gone to the Old Bill to see if they could work out what had happened. But that wasn't something we did. From our background you didn't have anything to do with the police, they were the Filth, the enemy. That was the mentality.

So now we were truly alone. Me old man was too ill to do anything. He was a pensioner but he'd paid his own money to get these cheque copies for us. We didn't have a manager or a record company. We'd burned more bridges than the Viet Cong.

It all had a bad impact on me. I was just smoking me head off, becoming even more solitary. I'd sit in that little flat in Charlton, all me money was going on puff, and I'd look out of the window feeling paranoid, worrying every time anyone drew up outside. I didn't even want to go into pubs or anything because I'd got banned from my new local and I couldn't face drinking anywhere else.

I'd made The Swan in Charlton Village my regular haunt because Debbie's dad Georgie Townsley drank in there. But, even though I'd become this dope-smoking pacifist, I managed to get myself barred. No one who had known me at fifteen would have recognised me four years later. I'd grown my hair much longer and now when trouble reared up I'd usually walk away from it. My body was in South London but my head was in Haight-Ashbury. And yet, even in that hippie frame of mind, trouble found me. I got in there one night and there were all these geezers playing pool. I kept putting me money down on the table for a game and they kept taking it off. I was smoking a cigar and one of them, quite a big geezer in his thirties, looked up when he was taking his shot and said, 'Who are you looking at, Clint Eastwood, puffing on your fuckin' cigar in the corner?'

All his drinking buddies had a good laugh at my expense. I tried to keep cool, but inside I was fuming. I went into the khazi and it was playing on my mind. It was too much even for Hippy Turner to put up with. I looked at myself in the mirror and thought, I'll teach him to try and mug me off. I came out of the gents, went straight up to the geezer and hit him with a combination. I just flattened him. He was down on the floor and he wasn't getting back up. 'You fucking South London cunt,' I said. 'I may look a twat with me long hair, but I'm from Custom House.' And I kicked him in the guts. My only regret is not asking him, 'Do you feel lucky, drunk?' Fucking Clint Eastwood. I hit him every which way but loose. I'd showed him but that was it; that got me barred. And I never went drinking locally again. It's a pity because there were a lot of decent people in Charlton. If I hadn't got so doped out and depressed I could have had a good time there 'cos there were a lot of headbangers: Colin Smith from The Blood, Bobby Nelson, Johnny Matthews. We all used to play football together. Charlton was like a home from home in that respect but I just like cut myself off from everyone.

I didn't like going over to Custom House, but one evening I was visiting me mum and I badly wanted a puff. So like a fool I headed for Hackney. There was a black place down there that masqueraded as a pool hall but was really a front to score drugs. I went in there, the only white boy in the place, jean jacket on, jeans, a ZZ Top T-shirt, armed with £15. I scored three £5 packets of dope. Debbie's aunt lived around the corner on top of a bakery so, while I was in the area, I popped round for a couple of joints, washed down with vodka and cider mixed together. I got absolutely rat-arsed.

It was too late to get back to Charlton, so I decided to crash at me mum's. I got the train to Plaistow and I could hardly walk. The 262 bus used to run down to Prince Regent's Lane from there. It was a twenty-pence fare but as I went to get on the bus I realised I only had eighteen pence left, and the poxy driver wouldn't let me off the two pence. He looked like Blakey from *On The Buses*. He shut the doors on me, the officious bastard. So I had to walk home, mangled. And the inevitable happened. It was twenty-past midnight, staggering down Plaistow Broadway, and I got pulled by two Old Bill. They searched me, found the two remaining wraps of puff, and called for assistance.

An Old Bill car pulled up and the driver was Denton, the cop who was after us at the Forrest trial and who Mick had slapped and told he looked like Gary Dickle. Luckily, because of the state I was in with me long hair and me jean jacket, he didn't recognise me, which was just as well. They got me to the station, the other two charged me, and they gave me a date to go back after they'd had the gear analysed. I gave them me old woman's address, thinking nothing of it. Of course, I didn't breathe a word of it to her; Mum hated drugs.

The night before I was supposed to go back, I got a phone call from me mum. She was going absolutely berserk. The Old Bill had gone round, knocked on her door asking for me and told her that they'd had to put the date back. She wanted to know what it was all about, and when they said possession of a controlled Class B drug, that was it. The shit hit the fan. She was going to sort out whoever had sold it to me, she didn't want me back in the house... it was a nightmare.

I got charged for it. I had to go to court and plead guilty. I got a £25 fine. It could have been worse. But as far as I was concerned I'd reached rock bottom. I was in the gutter. From EMI to being in the dock, pleading with some uppity magistrate to be lenient on me. I had to pay it off at £1.50 a week. I felt so low. I was on £18 a week from the social, there were no more royalty cheques, I was banned from me local. I was too proud to work on a building site. I tried but I couldn't handle it, I walked off site after one day. That was where I'd come from and I didn't want to go back to it. I was dazed and confused, a pathetic teenage hippy.

All that I was grateful for was that my court appearance hadn't made the *Newham Recorder*. No one on the manor would know how far the local neighbourhood rock star had fallen.

It's funny how you start thinking when you're cut off from the outside world. We were living in our own little bubble, Mick and me, and we found ourselves listening to a lot of head music: the Grateful Dead, Wishbone Ash, Barclay James Harvest, Golden Earring, early Zeppelin, a bit of Free. Slowly, the idea began to crystallise that we should re-emerge as a hippy band based on just the two of us. We started writing songs with banjos and mandolins and singing about paper planes. Looking back, it was just madness but that's what we wanted to do. The funny thing is I'd always hated hippies, couldn't stand 'em, and now I was turning into one... although I was never 100 per cent hippy, I still managed to bathe every night.

We did all the demos on a four-track in my brother Steve's house. By a process of elimination we ended up making a connection with some joker called Paul Birch, who signed us to his indie label, Heavy Metal Records, up in Wolverhampton. We had to get the coach up there from Victoria for the meetings, but even scraping the money together for the fare was a problem, we were so broke. We'd sit on that coach on the way back watching all the other passengers munching into the mini-bar, drinking coffee and scoffing cheese rolls while me and Mick just had to sit there starving with nothing in our pockets. But we went through it to get an album deal. The worst part of the ordeal was listening to their bullshit. There was Paul Birch and another geezer called Dave Roberts. They signed the great Manchester band The Stone

Roses a bit later and that ended up in a court case between them. The band ended up dousing their offices with paint...

But we signed to do the album. We got Gary Edwards back at the helm as producer and booked back into Redan to record all our new hippy songs with keyboards and saxophones. Gary brought in some top-class session men. We had a blinding Scottish bassist called Ian Campbell, and he could really slap that bass. There was Mark Feltham from Nine Below Zero, who played harmonica. We had Wizzard's sax-player, Nick Pentelow, whose dad played Henry Wilks in *Emmerdale Farm*, as it was called back then. We should have got Joe Sugden in on cow-bells. Mick played the drums. We really got a good sound. And for us the recording was virtually trouble-free. The only bit of agg came from another band who were in there. This bloke called Simon Laffy, who used to be in Girl with Phil Collen, was in the next studio with a few junkies. We were in the middle of listening to a play-back when their mouthy sidekick came bowling in to our studio demanding a lighter at the top of his voice. We told him quite politely that we didn't have any lighters and he went into one. 'Well that's not fucking good enough,' he said. 'I come in here for a fucking lighter and no one's got one. What are you going to do about that?'

I showed him all right. We might have been a bit long in the tooth but we never let another band take a liberty with us. I jumped off the stool, grabbed him by the throat and smashed him round the face. I said, 'Don't you ever, ever come in our studio shouting and complaining while we're working, because I will take you outside and kick the fuck out of you.'

He went, 'Hey, sorry, man.'

I said, 'You think you're fucking tough 'cos you're doing a bit of smack, you're nothing, the shit on my shoes.' And I gave him another slap and bundled him out, but even as I kicked his arse out the door I started to get paranoid. Had I blown it? Would it get back to the record company that we were still a bunch of thugs?

No need to worry. As I turned around, Gary Edwards actually applauded me. He said it was the best thing he'd ever seen in a recording studio and how dare this lowlife burst it on us like that.

That was the only bit of trouble we had with the album. We called it *Quiet Storm*. We took it back to Heavy Metal Records who wanted to put it out with pictures of us wearing leathers and bullets belts, waving swords with salamis and socks stuffed down our strides. But we were always more Manor Park than Man O' War and there was no way that was going to happen.

So we ended up giving them an album of stuff that a heavy-rock label could do fuck-all with. There were two or three tracks that were in the Bad Company vein but the rest of it was hippy stuff that was never going to go anywhere. I think the album went Teflon. It went wood on the Isle Of Wight. You can't even buy it on CD anywhere now.

But at the time we loved it. Somehow we thought we could go to America with this brave new sound and conquer the world. They'd be limos, girls, stadiums. We'd be playing Madison Square Gardens...

Well, we did pull off some of that. We did get to America...

CHAPTER THIRTY-ONE

California Dreaming

The phone call came out of the blue. Leona Faber, a New York promoter, rang up in February 1985 offering us a big American tour: thirty dates across the States, starting in Los Angeles. This was huge. But there were a couple of major problems. First, she was a punk promoter; she thought she'd be getting The Cockney Rejects of the vintage 'Ready To Ruck' era, and she didn't realise all we wanted to do these days was belt out some twelve-bar blues and sit on the stage strumming acoustic guitars. Second, the last two years had knocked all the confidence out of me. I was as paranoid as a drug-smuggling speed-freak in a compound full of police dogs. It was hard enough for me to walk out of the flat, let alone contemplate getting on a plane and giving it the big one on a West Coast stage. I really didn't want to go, but Mick managed to talk me into it. He said it was do or die, and he was probably right – except it was very nearly us who got done. We ended up being kidnapped by potty Yank punks and held prisoner at gun-point in our own hotel rooms.

Blood was going to spill and it could well have been our own.

The band was still only three-handed; we hadn't got around to replacing Vince so we had to persuade Ian Campbell to join up and play bass. He was twenty-four and he'd just married a woman with four kids a week before, but he said he'd come along for the crack. Leona was providing all the back-line, so all we took with us were our guitars, bass and lead. Me dad dipped into his savings once again to put up the money for our flights. Good old Dad, he never let us down.

We flew in to Newark, New Jersey. Leona met us; she was an oldish bird with a face like a corduroy cap and spikey black hair. Her face when she saw us was an absolute picture. She was expecting street-fighting punks. She got Mick with Captain Birdseye whiskers, me with hair down me back, a bass player who looked like Robert Plant's delinquent love-child, and Sticks who could have passed for a fucking Red Indian. If this scene had been in a cartoon, Leona's jaw would have hit the floor.

Finally she recovered the power of speech. 'You look different,' she said.

I thought, She hasn't heard us play yet.

That was her next question, of course. 'You are going to play the old stuff aren't you?'

Mick said, 'We're not sure.'

Leona got the hump. 'That's what we want,' she said. 'That's what you've been booked to play. There will be trouble if you don't.'

There was going to be trouble anyway 'cos we'd rehearsed something completely different. Ian didn't know any of the old gear, he hadn't heard one song, and we were due on stage in a little over thirty hours.

We got a connecting flight to Los Angeles where we were met by two geezers who claimed to be from a band called The Circle Jerks, Roger Rogerson and his side-kick. The side-kick was a big fucker, built like a brick shit-house, but Rogerson was the bigger jerk. They were whooping it up from the off. They took us in a van, driving at a hundred miles-an-hour, and it was: 'Where do you want to go and party, where do you want to go and get some blow, where do you want to do this and that, what you gonna do, who do you wanna screw…?'

All we wanted to do was sleep. We asked him to take us to the hotel so we could get some kip, but that wasn't good enough for Rogerson. He started arguing with us saying that we were 'fucking boring bastards', and that he was going to round up some girls and some Charlie for a party. I remember thinking, Why the fuck have I got back into this?

As we talked, it turned out that our opening-night venue, the Olympic Auditorium, was a massive hall which held about 10,000 people. These two jokers were telling us it was going to be full of rival gangs, punks and skins and bikers who all hated each other's guts and they'd be fighting and stabbing each other. Rogerson said, 'It's not just your music we love, dude, it's your aggression…' Maybe this sounds naïve, but I was shocked. We'd left all that far behind.

I said to Mick, 'I wanna go home, I don't wanna be here.' I wanted to turn around and go back to the safety of me little Charlton flat. Mickey felt exactly the same way. But by now we were pulling up outside our hotel in Santa Monica. And these Circle Jerks, who were wired to the nines, were still talking about getting birds and drugs brought over. Roger Rogerson was taking huge slugs out of a bottle of JD, trying to live up to some rock'n'roll wildman image.

We had a quick band conflab and decided we were pulling out. We asked them to drop us back at LAX. Rogerson didn't say a word. He went over to the van, and when he came back he had a .38 in his hand. 'You're going nowhere,' he said. The mood had changed now, the big lump was glaring. What could we do? We were knackered and unarmed. Rogerson went on, 'You are gonna stay here the night and tomorrow you're going to play the gig,' he said. 'We are gonna make sure of that.'

The worst night of our lives was about to begin. Rogerson stayed in our hotel room drinking bourbon and smoking spliffs while me and Mick were huddled on a bed together. Sticks and Ian were in another room, with the other Septic standing 'guard'. We had a muttered conversation in back-slang. The plan was to stay awake and make a move as soon as the chance arose.

Rogerson was getting drunker, more stoned and cockier by the minute. He was sitting there playing with the gun, saying, 'You fuckers, you can't mess with me, we're Americans.'

We didn't even answer him. We just sat there, watching and waiting. I kept thinking, What am I doing here? And are we ever gonna get out? The irony was my big dream had always been to get to the States, especially with Pete Way and Wilf Wrong filling our heads with tales of Led Zeppelin's rock'n'roll misdemeanours in the Marriott. But the dream had gone sour within twenty-four hours of landing and we'd fallen into the clutches of this crazy cunt with a gun.

Hours passed. It was 5.17 am when Rogerson finally crashed out. His right hand fell open and the gun dropped on the floor. We crept out of the room and woke up the other two. The big lump was nowhere to be seen. We got our cases and bolted. But where the fuck could we go?

Our first thought was the British Embassy. We got a cab up to

Wiltshire Boulevard and told this chinless wonder what had happened but he didn't want to know. To be honest, I don't think he believed me. He said they couldn't do anything to help and that we'd have to wait in the States until it was time for our scheduled flights home. The only thing he did do for us was contact Leona. We had a conversation with her and she was very insistent that we go ahead with the tour. The tickets were non-transferable, she said.

So we were stranded 8,000 miles from home, but we weren't entirely friendless. By luck we'd met a fella on the plane called Bo Harwood who wrote film scores for Hollywood movies. He lived nearby, in West Hollywood, and he'd given me his number to ring if we were in any trouble. We belled him from the Embassy and he immediately offered to come and pick us up. Top man. He was a fucking sight more helpful than the British civil service.

As we waited outside for Bo, all these locals started turning up, skinheads and heavy-looking geezers on motorbikes who had been alerted by Leona. Rogerson didn't show, but about a dozen others did and they gave us the message loud and clear: play the gig or we wouldn't get out of Los Angeles alive.

What the fuck could we do? Me and Mick couldn't fight them all. We had next to no cash and no way of changing our tickets. Our only option was to go through with the gigs. It was the only way to survive.

We agreed to play but they still trailed us back to Bo Harwood's place, just so they knew where we were. Bo looked after us well, he fed us and watered us and let us rest. But, after a few hours, Leona's lot were back, ringing the doorbell wanting to take us to a big Hollywood record store to sign autographs. This was a real eye-opener. I hadn't thought The Cockney Rejects meant a light in the US, but hundreds of punks turned up clutching our records for us to sign. It was mad. They were queueing out the door and around the block. I'd expected to be unknown and it turned out that we were bigger in the USA than we'd ever been in England. These kids knew all the early stuff, which was a damn sight more than Ian did. I was thinking, Shit, we've gotta go on stage tonight and we ain't rehearsed one of the songs this lot want to hear. The bass player hadn't even heard them and we had to play the Olympic Auditorium... The gig was a disaster waiting to happen.

On the plus side we met Paul Rossi at the record store, the guy who ended up having a kid with Patricia Arquette, and he turned out to be a big Rejects fan. He volunteered to stand with us and roadie for us. He was a good man and we've remained mates to this day. At last we had a friendly face on the firm. I did a line of coke to wake me up a bit. I was in a real state, even more paranoid than usual and worried out of my skull.

When we got to the Olympic Auditorium, I really started shitting myself. The place was huge. There were already hundred of Billies – Billy Bunters, punters – milling about outside. The Dickies were supporting us, and they were fans too. They told us to expect at least 8,000 in that night. Unfortunately, we weren't the Rejects they'd come to see. We looked like a pile of shit, with our long hair and cut-down jeans. If we'd been more clued up we might have taken a razor to each other there and then and had number-one crops all round, but at the time we just weren't thinking straight.

We got backstage and started tuning the guitars and, out of the blue, as cocky as you like, in walks Roger Rogerson, the Circle Jerk, only this time he's not packing a piece. He started mouthing off immediately. 'What the fuck is the matter with you, you fucking pussies?' he said, and on he went.

Mick just put down his guitar, walked over and said, 'You

fucking bastard, I've had enough of you.' And he smashed the fuck out of him. He knocked his teeth out, broke his nose and two ribs, and his mouth was smashed up. The security men had to pull Mick off him. The geezer was just a mess of blood.

Rogerson got up. He wasn't looking so cocky now. 'If you guys get on stage tonight, you're fucking dead,' he said. And he ran out of the room – and the auditorium – screaming.

I was pleased he'd had a pasting but now there was a new worry. We'd be on stage knowing there could be a nutter with a gun in the audience. How much worse was this going to get?

We did the sound check and went back to Bo's in a panic. We sat in his bedroom teaching Ian three of the old songs: 'Police Car', 'Bad Man' and 'The Greatest Cockney Rip Off'. That's all he had time to learn – we were due on stage in two hours' time. The rest of the set would have to be hard-rock numbers like 'City Of Lights' and 'The Way Of The Rocker' from *The Wild Ones* album.

When we got back to the venue, the Old Bill were already there, there'd been a big skinhead gang fight and the first thing we saw was a geezer on a stretcher in an oxygen mask. He'd been stabbed. It wasn't anything new to me but in my state of mind it was a portent of doom.

I didn't want to go in. Mick said we had to. There was no turning back. He almost had to push me through the door.

They put us backstage with Leona's people there to make sure we stayed put. Some geezer came in and made us sign a new contract. She'd cancelled the rest of the tour. The deal now was do the gig, get paid and fuck off.

I was still absolutely petrified about the show and my mood didn't improve as they marched us through the crowd. On the way to the stage, all these punks and skins were saying things like

'Hey, don't play none of that *Wild Ones* shit.' The place was jam packed. There were 10,000 in, we had to play for an hour but we only had three songs they wanted to hear.

We got up there and opened with the old Kinks number 'Till The End Of The Day'. The missiles started coming almost immediately. At one stage, a big metal padlock came whizzing by. It missed my head by inches and went crashing into the amps. We went down like Billy Connolly at a Bigley family reunion. We had the three old favourites, which were the only songs that were well received, but we had to disperse them through the set. The rest of the songs were either rocky or twelve-bar blues. We had no choice, we hadn't rehearsed anything else. They hated it. They were booing, trying to can us off.

How we got off that stage alive I'll never know.

Afterwards, the security wouldn't let anyone in to see us backstage because they all wanted to kill us. The local promoter was the only one who came in and that was just to say we were shit. The geezer who was selling our T-shirts for us fucked off with all the takings. And that was it, part one of the America Dream had turned to crap.

We played one more gig to an Oi crowd. Leona's lot told us not to do it but a local promoter got in touch and it was a sweet deal: $2,000 dollars to play to a thousand people in Azusa. That went just as badly. The crowd were all mad for the old stuff, and we still hadn't rehearsed any more of it. But even then we didn't learn our lesson. Being pig-headed bastards, we decided to stay in LA. Bo Harwood knew someone who had an apartment we could rent on Marshall Avenue off Melrose Strip. The plan was we'd become a hippy band and play our own gigs with none of the punk baggage. None of us had a green card, we were undesirables. It was nuts, career suicide.

Bo was tremendous, though. He was putting bits of money and work our way, taking us round the big film studios. He even got us work as extras – blink and you'll miss me as a toilet cleaner in *Top Gun*. That's the way it was out there: your next-door neighbour could suddenly become an actor and within a week they'd have their own shrink.

We started getting our own gigs. We blagged our way on to a Ban The Bomb night in a café, even though it went against everything I believed in. It paid $80 and we were the last band on. The place was full of old hippies who were stuck in the sixties. There were pictures of Hiroshima all over the walls. It was only a little place with about sixty or so in. The other bands had played acoustic sets, we came on and blasted into real heavy-rock stuff from *The Wild Ones*. The whole place was shaking, but after three numbers the Old Bill came in and pulled the plug.

The next night we got ourselves on the bill at a club called Madame Wong's, supporting a bunch of wong 'uns who played Sweet covers and wore make-up. They were probably milkmen during the day. It was a bit of a comedown from playing to 10,000 people at the Olympic Auditorium.

The irony was we could have made a go of it out there as a punk band, but no, we'd decided we wanted to be Led Zeppelin and we were playing gigs to eighty people instead, going nowhere fast. We must have been nuts.

We started taking tapes round to local record companies, having fruitless meetings with 'hey dude' A&R men and all that. Then one afternoon we were on the Strip and who came walking along the road? I kid you not, it was Boy George and Tony Gordon, our former manager. He couldn't believe it. We were the last people in the world he wanted to see. He shit a brick when he saw us. We told him we were based out there, that we'd got ourselves a record deal and were cracking away. We were lying through our teeth but we wanted to bullshit him into believing we were doing OK without him on our backs. Boy George didn't know where to look. He was a real state, his make-up running with sweat. He said, 'Oh, hi guys,' like he knew us but we just blanked him. He was out there doing *The A-Team*, I think, but that didn't impress us at all.

We weren't getting anywhere but we were having a real blast. There was plenty of coke and blow about and we were shagging lots of birds. Of course, the good times had to stop. I was getting grief from Debbie, too; she was phoning the apartment threatening to come over if I didn't come home soon. I should have done, but no, I stayed out there for eight weeks playing nondescript gigs in obscure places and living hand-to-mouth.

Ian was getting more earache than me, though. He'd only just got married. He didn't want to go back, but he was the first to crack under the pressure. So then we had to try and find an American bass player. Our mate Paul Rossi, who had a band called Wasted Youth – nothing to do with the East End band of the same name – said he'd help us, but after Ian went I finally realised that it was all futile. One night I turned round to Mick and said, 'I gotta go.'

He tried to persuade me to stay on but I knew that we were finished and that I had to get back to Charlton. I couldn't take any more of it.

I flew home alone. Mick said he'd stay on for another week. I felt terrible because I thought I was abandoning him, but I had to get away for my own sanity. My plan was to forget about the band and work on a building site, but when Mick came back he talked me into going back into the studio to have one last try with a new demo tape.

We recorded it at Easy Studios next to Pentonville Prison in North London. It was run by a fella called Bill Caley, a lovely geezer who used to road manage Thin Lizzy. We'd met him when he worked for UFO and Mick managed to blag into him. Bill agreed to give us free studio time overnight. He must have liked what he heard 'cos, when we were in there, he said, why not do an album? Another fella called Graham, who owned the studios, offered to manage us. It was now November 1985 and we'd moved away from *Quiet Storm*, we were rocking it up again. We recorded songs like 'I'll Take The Weight' and 'Rough Diamond'. Mick and Ian Campbell were working well together; they were really starting to gel. Phil Lynott kept his bass there and Ian used it on a few tracks. Phil died while we were in there. I was gutted about that. He was a real rock hero.

Unfortunately, the album took four months to finish. The word got out that we were getting free studio time; so other people who worked there and had bands of their own were getting jealous. They would come in during the day and sabotage what we'd done the night before. We were sniffing loads of gear to get us through the nights, which makes you paranoid anyway, but there was definitely a lot of snidey behaviour behind our backs. The studio gave us a fella called Mo Mulligan as engineer. By the end we wanted to kill the bloke but we kept holding back because we knew this was our last chance saloon. Not that trouble was ever far way.

We used to drink at a pub just around the corner from the studio and we soon found out that there was a big family in the area called the Stones who everyone was terrified of.

You had to walk through a car park to get to the studios. There always used to be some geezer hanging about in the evening trying to chat up the girl who worked on the reception, and every time you walked past him he'd be screwing you out. One night I had enough of him. We walked up the stairs to the studio and this geezer was there glaring at everyone. So when I got to the top I stuck my face into his and said, 'What do you keep fucking screwing us out for, you fucking mug? Every time I'm up here you're in my face. If you're trying to impress the bird we'll go in the courtyard now and I'll kick you all round the fucking place.'

All his bravado went then. I told him to fuck off and he did.

Later that night Bill Caley came to find us in the pub and he was in a right state. Apparently the geezer I'd had words with was one of the Stones family and I'd upset him. We couldn't give a shit, but Bill was convinced the whole tribe would come looking for us firm-handed. The poor sod started having sleepless nights because of it.

We were more worried about the practical side of making the album. The longer it was taking the more the Easy Studios people were losing interest. But we had one last trick up our sleeve: we decided to get Steve Marriott of The Small Faces to produce the album. Marriott was from our manor and he was a proper rock legend, but he'd fallen on hard times. We managed to track him down through the rock grapevine and he came and met us in this pub. But how had the mighty fallen. Stevie Marriott was just a wreck. He was in a terrible state, really loud, shouting his mouth off and talking at a hundred miles and hour. God knows what he was on. It was like someone had cut his speed with essence of nuisance. And he was dressed like a fucking tramp. He had his old woollen hat on; he looked like he'd been sleeping rough in Itchycoo Park. But he loved the idea of working with us – probably because he was as down and out as we were – and he agreed to come back the next night to hear the tracks.

He turned up with this old git who Stevie said was the world's best harp player. He must have been about seventy. The whole experience turned out to be a nightmare. Steve wanted to sing a track with me, a song called 'Keep Clear', but, after we'd recorded it, he said we shouldn't be using a twenty-four-track studio. He wanted to go back to the sixties. 'Don't mic up the drums or guitars,' he said. 'We'll take the lot in one go using one mic between us.'

He was in a bit of a mess and that saddened us all. Like us, the great Steve Marriott was at the end of his road, and now we had to put up with his ideas. It was a disaster. Mick was having more to drink, and him and Marriott were really clashing badly. They were arguing about everything, the vocals, the guitar lines, who should play the harmonica. Marriott had absolutely lost the plot. In the end Mick stood up and said, 'I'm telling you now, you scruffy cunt, I don't care what the fuck you've done in the past, the stairs are out there, and I'm gonna kick you down 'em if you don't fuck off.'

Marriott was flabbergasted, he pleaded with me but I said, 'Walk away with your reputation intact 'cos otherwise you're gonna get hurt.'

It was gutting for me to see one of my idols in such a state. He was a legend but now he was a washed-up junkie, a scruffy old bastard. He was a rock god with feet of clay and a cauliflower brain.

To save him from Mick I had to get hold of Marriott by his cravat, swing him round and kick him out of the studios. We weren't in a much better state than he was to be honest, but Stevie had fallen a lot further than we had.

I wanted to stop work on the album after that. I was sick of the studio, sick of the time it was taking. I was getting so much grief indoors. But yet again Mick convinced me to stay.

One Friday night at about 11.45 pm Mick had popped round

the pub for afters leaving me and Sticks in the studio. There was a knock at the door. Sticks went to answer it and came back saying there was trouble.

I shot over and there was a geezer with curly hair, about my age, out of his head on something. 'We're going to come in and rob you,' he said.

I said, 'Not while I'm here you won't, go on fuck off. You ain't gonna get in here.'

He backed off, but when I looked down the stairwell there was another fella with him. We didn't know them but the word was they had something to do with the Stones family. So now we had a stand-off. By luck Mick rang from the pub. I left Sticks holding the fort and told Mick to come straight round. While we waited, these two morons started verballing me. I noticed the geezer at the bottom had his hand inside his jacket as if he was holding a tool. But I figured if they were armed with anything they'd have come at us already. Knowing Mick was due to burst through the downstairs door at any time I started taunting them to distract them. 'Come and try and rob us then if you're that brave,' I said. 'There's only me and me mate here.' And that's when I saw Mick come round the gate and smack him one. The geezer went down and as I suspected he had nothing in his coat at all. He started begging for mercy but Mick just steamed into him while I went for the curly-haired tosser. He tried to get down the stairs but I got him straight in the teeth with my first punch and smashed the fuck out of him. He lost three teeth and ran crying out of the gate. Then me and Mick were fighting each other over who should finish off the one on the floor. The Beatles at Abbey Road it wasn't...

The next day Graham and this other geezer who we called Deputy Dawg pulled us and accused of us assaulting the two geezers. They'd found teeth on the floor. I was livid. 'Assault?' I said. 'We saved your fucking studio from being robbed. They were high on drugs and they were breaking in. You could have lost thousands. You should be giving us rewards, you cunt.' They were speechless. They didn't know what to say and that was it with them, but for me all I could hear was the back of a very large camel breaking.

We only had two more days of recording left but I said to Mick, 'That's it, after we're done here, we've got to call it a day. Admit it, bruv, can you really take any more of this?' Mick shook his head. I was in tears. 'We've got to admit that it's over,' I said. 'We're both having a breakdown, it's going nowhere, it's just agg after agg. It's finished.'

We decided to do one more night in the studio, finish the final mix, walk away with the reel-to-reels and never come back.

And that's what we did. We waited for the engineer to go to the pub for afters, then we hugged each other, loaded everything into the car and fucked off. That was it. We decided there and then that The Cockney Rejects story had come to an end.

The studio weren't happy. They kept ringing me mum asking where the tapes were but me old woman just changed the number. The tapes were never released. We didn't even bother to try and get a deal. The irony was that it was quite a good album. It was a cross between *The Wild Ones* and *Quiet Storm*. It started off like *The Wild Ones* and got bogged down with drugs, drink, local hoodlums, Steve Marriott and all-night working from five o'clock in the evening till six the following morning to get in there and get it finished... and all for nothing.

A couple of days after the Great Tapes Robbery I said to Mick, 'You do realise that there can be no more, you do whatever you've got to do, but for me the band is finished.' He knew it.

We shook hands, and rang up Sticks to tell him. No one else was notified. Campbell had already gone. He was in too much of a state to know about anything anyway. There was no more Wilf Wright, or Tony Gordon, no firm, no press interest. There was no more anybody.

Mick went back to his flat. I'd moved while we were doing the recording and so I went home to our new place in Plumstead, South London, only nobody was there. Debbie had packed her bags and done a moonlight flit. She'd had enough. I hadn't been back there for about a fortnight. I hadn't even rung her. I was just devoting myself to the album. So that was two chapters in my life over at the same time. She was gone and the band was kaput. I was absolutely beaten.

Epilogue

1986 was the worst year of my life. I was only twenty-one years old but compared to how I was when it all started I was a different person, a burned-out shell. I was as thin as a rake with long hair, virtually a hermit. I had no more fight to put up. It took me years to fully get over it and get back on my feet. I was scarred emotionally and psychologically by the whole experience. I wasn't the only one. Mick's hair was falling out from the shock of it all and he'd hit the booze big time. I looked at him and I looked at myself in the mirror and all I could hear was my mum's voice pleading with us not to ever get into the music business. And if you'd asked me back then I would have said that she was right.

We met some good people – Pete Way, Garry Bushell, Joe Strummer and Bill Caley, who we sadly let down. But they were outweighed by the scum, the crooks and the liars, the bent cops, the shysters and the stitch-up merchants.

1986 was very difficult. The first months were awful, diabolical.

I was living alone in Plumstead without Debbie. The loneliness and emptiness were gnawing away inside. I don't blame her for leaving me, though; she had a hell of a life. I hated Plumstead, too. It was nothing like Charlton. It never felt like home the way Charlton Village had. By the beginning of 1987 I'd had enough of it all and I plucked up the courage to go back to Custom House. I was expecting people to laugh at me and take the piss but it wasn't like that at all. I started bumping into me old mates and they were genuinely pleased to see me. No one ever said, 'You fucked it up,' which is what in my paranoia I had been so afraid of. Even a year or two before, if I'd seen any old faces I would always lie and say I had bundles in the bank. It was down to pride, I suppose. But they really didn't give two shits. I started working again, training, getting in the pub. I was running, playing football and cricket on a Sunday. I started going to West Ham again – I hadn't gone since 1982. My life came back together and, bang, I was reborn. I remember thinking, Fuck me, what have I been missing?

If I'd known how it was going to be, I would have packed up the band and moved back home in 1983.

My only real regret about the Rejects is that we hung on too long. We should have quit at the top instead of dragging it out from one humiliation to another. I'm still proud of what we achieved, though. For me, our stand-out songs were 'I'm Not A Fool', which is up there with 'Pretty Vacant' and Bad Man'. But some of the rock stuff, like 'City Of Lights' and 'Rock 'N' Roll Dream', stand the test of time, too. To be making music like that just two years after 'Flares 'N' Slippers' was a bold move.

Pretty much everyone in the music business and the student end of the rock press ended up hating us – which is OK because we detested them as well. They thought that we were beyond the pale. Ironic when you think that a few years later those same white liberals were wetting themselves over rappers and hip-hop acts who shot each other and sang anti-Semitic songs. Biggie Smalls was gunned down; Tupac too. Snoop Dogg, who was on stage at the Brits this year, is a self-confessed crack dealer and has been cleared of murder, and he's a respectable pop icon of today along with Pete Doherty, who has serious drug problems - a great role model for your kids! We never had guns. Well, maybe we had the odd air rifle, but we weren't driving around with semi-automatics like that geezer from So Solid Crew. Funny how things change.

Guns N Roses came along in the late 1980s boasting about having fist fights in bars and on planes and everyone said they were wonderful. They were surrounded by minders and getting million-dollar contracts. All the papers were calling them dangerous and outrageous... they should have locked them in a room with us and seen how dangerous they really were.

Kurt Cobain shot himself and the *NME* said he was a hero. Well, he ain't to me. He had a baby who had to be weaned off heroin; he committed suicide and left his child fatherless. He's not a hero; he's the scum of the earth.

These days the 'Bizarre' column in the *Sun* thinks it's fantastic if a chart star has a punch-up. That Liam Gallagher gets me, walking around in a Parka coat with a bunch of minders from an agency, picking on a little photographer. The only time Oasis were on their own, they took on a bunch of computer businessmen who absolutely whacked them. What a bunch of phonies.

I would never have been in somewhere like Brown's having a row with paparazzi. I'd have been in the Paul's Head dragging someone over the pool table arguing over who had their money down first.

The problem with us was we were too real. We were the

genuine article, plus we were white, English and working class – the only group it's permissible to sneer at these days.

I don't know how my life would have gone if it wasn't for The Cockney Rejects. I could have ended up in prison, although there was more chance of that happening being in the band. I would probably have been the same as most people round my way; get in a bit of bother, grow up, leave it behind, work on a building site, have your kids, have your divorce... and just get on with it.

I never got back together with Debbie. After her, I met and married a Plaistow girl, whose name I won't mention. We married in 1991 and divorced eleven years later. But I have got three great kids now, a daughter and two sons. I'm living in a place called Battle (appropriately enough) on the South Coast with my girlfriend Karon. I've turned into a yokel. I'll have a straw in me mouth on the next album.

Inevitably, I finally caught up again with Vince Riordan. I bumped into him in the Army & Navy. He was as good as gold. He'd been working the doors, although he never lost the taste for coke.

I was painting and decorating for a living, over on the new Docklands development. Mick did the same; he got his own flat in Canning Town.

Then, in the late 1980s, we were approached by a guy called Stuart Black, a fan of the band who ended up working for us. Stuart asked us if we'd re-form and do a few gigs in France and Germany, playing the old songs: 'Bad Man', 'East End' and that. They paid well so we thought, Why not? We re-formed with Vince on bass and Sticks drumming, but we looked at it differently – almost as a sideline, a hobby. Something to do because we enjoyed it but not ever believing it was our route back to the charts or anything. Just for the crack. If someone wanted to pay for us to have a weekend in Paris, and play a few songs, why not?

Play a gig, go on the piss, spunk the money, enjoy ourselves. Fuck all the pretentious stuff. And we really enjoyed those gigs. They were absolutely brilliant, so we started doing a few more, three or four a year. They weren't all as great as those first ones but we didn't have any agg with it.

Then the serious side started to creep back in. In 1989, we recorded a new rock album above a hairdresser's in Hastings. It was called *Lethal*, and it came out on Neat Records, another piss-poor indie label. But then I had second thoughts about it all. I really didn't want the band to get serious again and for me to get dragged back into it all. I had me life, me job, a new girl and I didn't want to take a chance on losing that again, so I knocked it all on the head. That was 1990. I got married the next year and we didn't do a thing as a band for ten years.

Then one morning in 1999 the phone started ringing at half past three in the morning. I was living in a farmhouse in Kent and had to get up for work at 5.00 am. When the phone rings that early, you expect to hear there's been a tragedy. It was Mick. 'You won't believe this...' he said. He'd been watching TV and he'd just seen a Levi's ad which featured 'I'm Not A Fool'.

'Fuck work,' he said. 'We're on an advert. The Clash got seventy grand.'

Of course, we didn't get anything like that much. My share was a cheque for £1,300 from an ad shown all over Europe. I used it to take the kids to Butlin's at Minehead – and that was a disaster because I very nearly ended up bashing a clown. I might as well have got that money and just stuck it on the favourite in the 3.30 at Doncaster. But that didn't matter. It got us thinking about the band. I got the bug to get up there and do it again. And what made it easier was that married life had turned sour. To be honest, my domestic situation was torture. I was working, then coming home to a row.

After the ad came out, we were offered a deal with another indie label to record a new album in Newcastle for £10,000. We went up there, much against my wife's wishes, and knocked out an album in three days. Sixteen tracks! It was madness. Sticks and Vince were no longer involved. We got a drummer and bass player from a local band called Red Alert, Andy Laing and Tony Van Frater; and just went for it. It was awful, you can't do a decent album in that time, but the label seemed happy. That was *Greatest Hits Vol 4*. When the word got out that we'd done it, we started getting offers from all over the world to come and play for decent money. In 2000, we got £3,500 for one gig in Spain in front of 1,700 people; in 2001, we got £7,500 to play Morecambe; we did five nights in Germany for £10,000, then we got gigs in Switzerland, Japan and the USA. This was through people approaching us, not us touting for work and it's carried on ever since. There are Oi fans and Oi scenes all over the world, from Canada to Indonesia, Argentina to Red China. We're playing more gigs now to bigger audiences than we ever did in the seventies. We played to 5,000 people in San Bernardino, 12,000 at a gig in the Basque country in Northern Spain last year, another 12,000 at a skateboard festival in Leipzig. They go crazy and there's never any trouble. We did a kind of comeback album in 2001, *Out Of The Gutter*, largely because the fans asked us to.

In early 2004 we played West Ham Working Men's Club. We had 550 in – the capacity was 250. Tickets were changing hands on ebay for over £100. One bloke payed £180 for a ticket! It was great to see all the old faces again, Bunter, Hodges, Cass Pennant, Skully who I hadn't seen for over twenty years; well, he'd been inside for fifteen of them. It was incredible, even though the PA was shit. Cass booked it – he was the promoter. He had cameras there, too. He said he was just filming it for us to have a look at, but within a week he was selling it as a video on his stall! He's the black Del-Boy, a proper entrepreneur. The atmosphere was fantastic, though. There wasn't a sniff of trouble. People brought their kids along.

A couple of months later we got a call asking us to play Morrissey's Meltdown. Turned out Morrissey is a big fan. He's been known to go on stage to 'East End' in a Rejects T-shirt and introduce himself as Stinky Turner! He's even got himself a West Ham Boys' Club boxing shirt – the exact one I wore on *Greatest Hits Vol 1*. We ended up on the same bill as Alan Bennett and Nancy Sinatra at the Royal Festival Hall. Then the unthinkable happened – we had a nice write-up in *The Times*.

Not bad for a gang of rogues who crashed our way into the music scene.

When we started we were like Fagin's gang but with back-up. I'd never glorify what we got up to. I think some of the things we did were appalling, especially wrecking studios. What we needed was a Frank Warren or a Frank Maloney to say don't muck about, and to smack us round the ear-hole, but you can't change the past. We're working on a new album now, but we've got our feet on the ground. I still hope that something will come along, but I'd never lose sleep over it. If we get a decent deal, terrific. If not, so be it. You'll still find us in the pub, playing football or watching the boxing. We never made out we were anything other than what we are. We never compromised. We've never changed.

We never will.

S o that was The Cockney Rejects story in all its gory detail; the fighting, the nicking, the court appearances…

But there's one important element I haven't touched on nearly enough: the music! And I should do because I'm as proud as a peacock of most of the band's musical achievements. We started as a no-nonsense, snot-nosed, brick-wall punk band but within the space of just a few years we recorded songs in many different styles. We were versatile and keen to grow. We took risks and got better. Don't take my word for it. The proof is all there for the listening. Mick and I were good songwriters (we still are) and we were always game to have a go at anything. To our minds, there were no barriers. If someone said, 'You can't do that,' our answer was: 'You try and stop us.' Barriers to us were only there to be driven through.

We recorded our first EP, 'Flares 'N' Slippers', before we had even played a gig. Although it was raw, it had the ingredients that were to become our trademarks: hooks, riffs and choruses as catchy as an STD in Bangkok. By the time we recorded our debut album, our sound had developed significantly. The new songs were harder and tougher. We aimed for a Pistols style because Steve Jones's guitar sound was the best any punk band has ever had; you always have to aim to be up there with the best. I still remember the thrill I got when we were recording 'I'm Not A Fool' at Polydor. Mick set up his Marshall, and hearing that riff come through the monitors blew me away. It was an awesome arse-kicking force and it set the tone for what I believe to be one of the best punk albums ever made. 'Bad Man' was another great cut, a blinding, bounce-along brash pop-punk tune. It's got balls and its got a terrific sing-along hook. That first album is full of classics. I still love 'Join The Rejects'. It started with an acoustic intro with some Hank Marvin-style lead over it, then kicked in as a band anthem. The chorus has got real clout.

We let ourselves down a bit with the second album, *Greatest Hits Vol 2*, probably because of the utter turmoil that surrounded the band at the time. There are still two classic Rejects songs on it, though: 'War On The Terraces' and 'The Rocker' – our first foray into a heavy metal sound. Mick's guitar solos on 'The Rocker' were pure metal madness that more than made up for the shabby vocal performance.

We were brought up on the cream of rock music: Zeppelin, Queen, Aerosmith, the Stones and Van Halen, amongst others, and after the second album we felt it was time to broaden our horizons. We used EMI's recording studios as our workshop. We were always in there demoing new ideas. We experimented with metal, reggae, dub, funk, ballads, the lot. One unreleased gem is an acoustic masterpiece called 'England'. It sounded like something from a film score, very atmospheric. Paul Weller came and did some vocals on it and killed it stone dead – his delivery was as flat as a pancake; it was better as an instrumental. Another demo we recorded was a song called '1984', which had a funky bass line with some cool vocals and a jangly guitar running through. We played it to some sap at EMI and he thought it was the Rolling Stones. Honestly!

Our next album, *The Power & The Glory*, was our first real departure from a basic punk sound. We brought in a keyboard player, Neil Carter, who played with UFO and guitar great Gary Moore. Steve Churchyard, our producer, had also worked with UFO and The Stranglers. It was a buzz working with these people. The album has been likened to the sound Paul Cook and Steve Jones achieved with The Professionals, although I think we were more versatile. Some of our greatest songs came from this album. The title track is an anthem, powerful but melodic with heartfelt lyrics. Then there was 'On The Run' and 'The Greatest Story Ever Told', which powered along. 'Lumon' was very different. It was beautiful, multi-layered; an acoustic instrumental which sounded like John Williams meets Jimmy Page on Bryn-Y-Aur. I still like the single from the album, 'On The Streets', which we recorded at Abbey Road (if it was good enough for the Beatles…). *The Power & The Glory* was not the hit it should have been for reasons detailed elsewhere, but it showed we were growing in confidence and musical and songwriting ability.

Our next change of direction was the biggest. We decided it was time to aim for our real musical roots and go for an AC/DC, Aerosmith type of sound. We always did love a challenge…

During the sessions for *The Power & The Glory*, we recorded a bonus instrumental featured on later compilations called 'Van Bollocks'. It was Mick's answer to the great Eddie Van Halen's

'Eruption' – just over a minute of top-notch rock guitar which I think gives 'Eruption' a good run for its money. It's pukka. Listening to that you knew that Mick was without doubt punk rock's premier guitarist, and we knew that if the rest of the band didn't rise to his standard he could have walked away and left us pissing in the wind. And who would have blamed him? So, *The Wild Ones* was our attempt to be as good as Mick and as good as our heroes. We got Pete Way, the legendary bass-player from UFO, to produce it. John Fiddler, an ex-Yardbird and a brilliant blues man, assisted him with Garry Edwards (who had worked with Rainbow and The Scorpions) as engineer. Heavy rock was to be the next challenge, and we relished it. Bring it on!

We worked on *The Wild Ones* meticulously. It was planned like a military campaign. Me and Mick did all the arrangements. We aimed for the stars and we reached them. To me, the album is a great achievement and we were still very young. I was only seventeen when we completed it, and Mick was twenty. It kicked off with 'The Way Of The Rocker' (unintentionally similar to Black Sabbath's 'Symptom Of The Universe'). 'City Of Lights' was a foot-stomping, head-shaking anthem with a kick on it like a mule. It still gets played on rock radio stations to this day. We even covered a Kinks classic, 'Till The End Of The Day'. I'm not really into doing covers, but I believe we did it justice. For once the album received widespread critical acclaim, and Mick's guitar-playing was getting taken seriously.

When Randy Rhoads died in a tragic flying accident in 1982, Mick got a call asking him to audition for Ozzy Osbourne. I thought, Fuck! Ozzy wants my brother to play with him! In all honesty, I was dead chuffed. I urged Mick to do it, but he refused to even audition. Mick's response was: 'The only person I wanna be in a band with is you, bruv.' To Mick, auditioning for Ozzy would have been like turning his back on me, and he would never have done that.

So in 1991, after Freddie Mercury died, and Brian May sounded me out to be his replacement, I kindly returned the compliment. Just kidding.

Our next album was an even more radical departure from our brick-wall Bridge House sound. *Quiet Storm* developed out of an introspective, experimental period for me and Mick. He played drums and bass as well as guitar on most of the songs and Garry Edwards took over production. We mixed up heavy blues-based rock, some funk, and acoustic folk. Nick Pentelow, who worked with Roy Wood, played sax on it. The banjo came out on a hillbilly ditty called 'Fourth Summer'. We even went for our first big ballad, 'Back To The Start'. It was heartfelt and emotional. We even brought in a female session singer to complement the vocals. The heaviest song on the album was 'I Saw The Light', which was a kind of cross between Bad Company and Bachman Turner Overdrive. We were delighted with the final mix. Hearing it back over the speakers was better to me than having sex. Garry Edwards swung round in his chair and said it was as good a song as any he'd ever worked on. Seeing as he'd worked with Rainbow and Deep Purple that was some compliment. His words will live with me till the day I die.

Commercially, *Quiet Storm* was suicidal, but I'm very proud of it. It was another notch on the versatility belt.

Our next album, *Get Involved*, was never released. It was rockier and featured a fair amount of synth, as well as Mark Feltham, once of Nine Below Zero, on harmonica. The best track is probably 'I'll See You Later', which had a George Thorogood feel. With the harp and Mick's slide guide mixed in with a crushingly heavy riff, we pretty nearly blew the studio walls down. Another lost track featured my duet with Steve Marriott, as well as 'Rough

Diamond', which sounds like early Dire Straits. It's a good album and one that deserves to see the light of day still.

Vince and Sticks were back in the fold for the next album, *Lethal*. This was more in *The Wild Ones* vein (but not nearly as good). Mick's guitar playing was leagues ahead of the rest of the band and the songs we were playing.

Roll forward to 2001. We had a new band, with Tony Van Frater on bass and Les 'Nobby' Cobb on drums – the rhythm section we'd always been looking for. We announced our return with a good come-back album, *Out Of The Gutter*. This had a bit of everything the Rejects had done over the years thrown in to the pot. There's power-pop punk, metal, great riffs, melodies, heavyweight hook-lines and more traditional terrace-style choruses. I'm proud of this album. Unfortunately, it came out on a small label that couldn't do it justice, but no matter. It shows what our new line-up is capable of and if you ever loved the Rejects you should give it a listen. You won't be disappointed. Try and see us live again, too, because we now play ten times better than we ever did before.

By the time you read this, our next album will be in the can, if not on the shelves to buy, and from the early demos it will be the dog's bollocks.

I don't think the Rejects will ever be as diverse and experimental as we once were. We've got all that out of our system. We've had a twenty-year apprenticeship and we don't have anything left to prove to anybody. We only ever wanted to prove to ourselves what we could and can do.

The band as it is now is the way it should be. The way it will always be. And I tell you now, we're still here. We're still going. Stronger than ever.

Discography

SINGLES

'Flares 'N' Slippers', 1979

'I'm Not A Fool', 1979

'Bad Man', 1980

'The Greatest Cockney Rip Off', 1980

'I'm Forever Blowing Bubbles', 1980

'We Can Do Anything', 1980

'We Are The Firm', 1980

'Easy Life', 1981

'On The Streets Again', 1981

'Till The End Of The Day', 1982

ALBUMS AND COMPILATIONS

Greatest Hits Vol 1, 1980

Greatest Hits Vol 2, 1980

Greatest Hits Vol 3, 1981

The Power & The Glory, 1981

The Wild Ones, 1982

Quiet Storm, 1984

Unheard Rejects, 1985

Lethal, 1990

Punk Singles Collection, 1997

Greatest Hits Vol 4, 1997

Back On The Street, 2000

Out Of The Gutter, 2003